COMPUTER GRAPHICS
WITH PASCAL

Detail of cover photograph

COMPUTER GRAPHICS
WITH PASCAL

MARC BERGER

University of Colorado, Colorado Springs

The Benjamin/Cummings Publishing Company, Inc.

Menlo Park, California •
Reading, Massachusetts •
Don Mills, Ontario • Wokingham, U.K. •
Amsterdam • Sydney • Singapore • Tokyo •
Mexico City • Bogota • Santiago • San Juan

Sponsoring Editor: Alan Apt
Production Editor: Cici Oremland
Book and Cover Designer: Design Office • Bruce Kortebein
Copy Editor: Carol Dondrea
Photography Research: Monica Suder
Technical Artist: Linda Harris-Sweezy
Composition: Vera Allen Composition

Cover photograph courtesy of Los Alamos National Laboratory

Library of Congress
Cataloging-in-Publication Data

Berger, Marc.
  Computer graphics with Pascal.

  Includes index.
  1. PASCAL (Computer program language)
2. Computer graphics. I. Title.
QA76.73.P2B47   1985   001.64'43   85-11184
ISBN 0-8053-0790-7
BCDEFGHIJ-HA-89876

The Benjamin/Cummings Publishing Company, Inc.
2727 Sand Hill Road
Menlo Park, California 94025

The Benjamin/Cummings Series in Computing and Information Sciences

K. Buckner et al.
Using the UCSD System (1984)

G. Booch
Software Engineering with Ada[1] (1983)

J. G. Brookshear
Computer Science: An Overview (1985)

D. M. Etter
Structured FORTRAN 77 for Engineers and Scientists (1983)

D. M. Etter
Problem Solving with Structured FORTRAN 77 (1984)

D. M. Etter
WATFIV: Structured Programming and Problem Solving (1985)

A. Kelley, I. Pohl
A Book on C (1984)

C. Negoita
Expert Systems and Fuzzy Systems (1985)

J. Price
How to Write a Computer Manual (1984)

W. Savitch
Pascal Programming: An Introduction to the Art and Science of Programming (1984)

R. Sebesta
VAX 11:[2] Structured Assembly Language Programming (1984)

R. Sebesta
PDP-11: Structured Assembly Language Programming (1985)

M. G. Sobell
A Practical Guide to the UNIX[3] System (1984)

M. G. Sobell
A Practical Guide to UNIX[3] System V (1985)

For more information, call toll-free: (800) 227-1936 (USA),
(800) 982-6140 (Calif.), or write to the publisher.

---

[1]Ada is a registered trademark of the Department of Defense.
[2]VAX 11 is a registered trademark of Digital Equipment Corporation.
[3]UNIX is a registered trademark of Bell Laboratories.

PREFACE

Computer graphics dates from the early days of computers when computer systems were able to produce primitive line drawings on line printers. Scientists early recognized the advantages of converting large volumes of numeric data into meaningful and readily interpreted images. But widespread use of computer graphics did not come about until the late 1970s when the low cost of microprocessors and memory made graphics display hardware affordable. Since that time computer graphics has become an integral part of science, business, engineering, medicine, and the arts.

PURPOSE

The purpose of this introductory text is to provide the reader with a clear understanding of the fundamental principles of computer graphics. To achieve this goal, I have introduced all topics with a detailed explanation of their underlying concepts and applications. Since many important ideas cannot be fully understood without implementation, I have included many complete graphics programs and subroutines. I chose Pascal as the programming language because it is the preferred choice of most computer science departments. Pascal is both simple and powerful, while its modular structure lends itself to the design and readability of complex programs. Though the programs are written in Pascal, the student could easily rewrite them in C or FORTRAN.

This text is the outgrowth of a one-semester course for computer science majors I taught for three years at the University of Colorado, Colorado Springs. Except for the two chapters that cover three-dimensional viewing and hidden-surface removal, all material was presented in 15 weeks, with each student completing at least six programming projects.

LEVEL

I have kept the mathematical level low so that a student with only a precalculus background can understand all the concepts introduced. Experience has shown, however, that in order to understand three-dimensional graphics, a knowledge of calculus and vectors is helpful. The text is intended mainly for undergraduate college students. The reader should know Pascal or a suitable high-level programming language such as C or structured FORTRAN. A knowledge of data structures would be beneficial, but is not necessary.

GRAPHICS SOFTWARE

Selecting a graphics subroutine package is difficult at best. No accepted set of graphics commands currently applies to all display systems. In this book I have taken the relatively safe course of following many of the specifications of the CORE system. These graphics commands are similar to those available on many microcomputers and inexpensive graphics display systems.

ORGANIZATION AND COVERAGE

The text begins with a description of the history and applications of computer graphics, which is followed by an introduction to the hardware and software components of a graphics system. Included are hardcopy output and input devices, CRT technology, raster-scan and random-vector systems, the display processor, and scan conversion. In Chapter 2 the student begins to draw images using the screen coordinates. The difficulties in drawing basic figures such as lines and circles are explored. The next chapter introduces the reader to the world coordinate system and the viewing transformation. Chapter 4 uses the concepts presented in the previous chapter to create shaded business and artistic graphics.

Chapter 5 describes the fundamentals of two-dimensional geometric transformations. Chapter 6 implements the concept of display file segmentation.

Chapter 7 examines the requirements of a user-friendly graphics program. After an initial discussion of the problems inherent in running graphics programs on a microcomputer, the reader is led through a detailed description of error-handling and menu-generating routines.

Chapter 8 treats interactive techniques, while Chapter 9 extends these concepts to animation.

Chapter 10 provides frame buffer and scan conversion algorithms for polygon and area filling. Chapter 11 introduces the coordinate systems and transformations needed for three-dimensional viewing. Chapter 12 describes the generation of realistic images using curves and surfaces, and Chapter 13 extends this realism by implementing hidden-surface removal.

The appendix describes the fundamental features of the two-dimensional graphics standard GKS.

ACKNOWLEDGEMENTS

This book would not have been possible without the assistance of many individuals. The following people contributed comments on the manuscript at various stages of its development: Chris Pappas, Broome Community College; Paul Ross, Millersville State College; Sharon C. Daniel, Orange Coast College; Rita Bordano, San Antonio Junior College; Terry Wagner, University of Texas, Austin; Michael Moshell, University of Tennessee; Patrick Fitzhorn, Colorado State University; James Burnette, Michigan State University; Charles Williams, Georgia State University; B. Mittman, Northwestern University; Richard Cooper, Diablo Valley College; John Staudhammer, University of Florida; and Richard L. Phillips, University of Michigan.

I am especially indebted to the students in my graphics courses who tested most of the programs and helped correct preliminary versions of the book. As partial payment, I have included several of their assignments in the illustrations. A special thanks to James Bankston who produced most of the code in Chapter 7. I also wish to thank Eileen Entin, Wentworth Institute of Technology, and Michael Rider, Ohio Northwestern University, who reviewed several drafts of the book and made many valuable suggestions and corrections. A final thanks to Alan Apt and Mary Ann Telatnik of the Benjamin/Cummings Publishing Company for their assistance throughout the writing of this book.

BRIEF TABLE OF CONTENTS

CONTENTS

CHAPTER 6   Display File Segmentation   145

CHAPTER 7   Graphics Program Design   163

COMPUTER GRAPHICS
WITH PASCAL

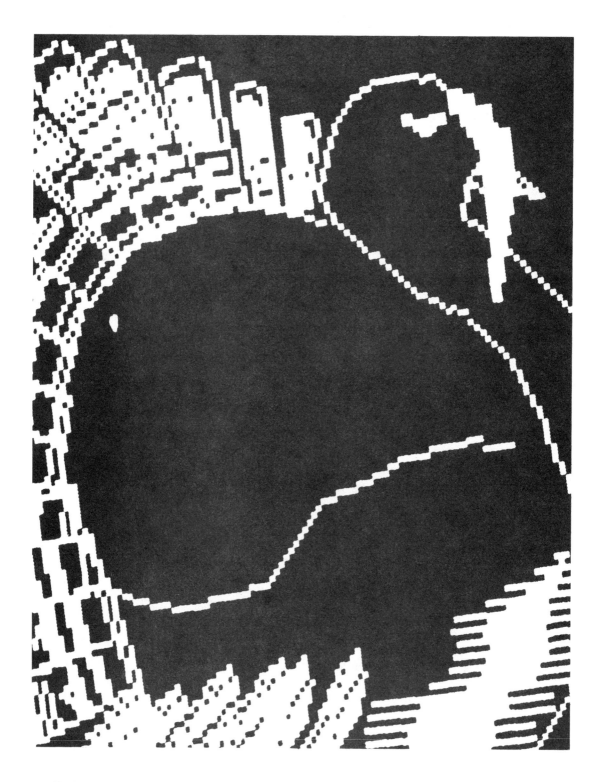

Detail of Figure 1–1

1
INTRODUCTION TO COMPUTER GRAPHICS

1–1 OVERVIEW

Computer graphics can be defined as the creation and manipulation of graphic images by means of a computer. This short definition does not, however, describe the diversity of applications and the impact of this rapidly developing field of computer science. Certainly, computer graphics started as a technique to enhance the display of information generated by a computer. This ability to interpret and represent numerical data in pictures has significantly increased the computer's ability to present information to the user in a clear and understandable form. Large amounts of data are rapidly converted into bar charts, pie charts, and graphs. Graphics displays have also improved our understanding of complex systems such as molecular biology, reaffirming the saying that one picture is worth a thousand words.

While not many users and managers of computer systems would argue over the advantages of pictorial displays, most pre-1980 computer installations had few if any graphics capabilities. Information was conveyed to and from the computer primarily in numeric and textual formats. There were two reasons why graphics display was not used. First, the time-sharing environment of the 1970s was not suitable for graphics. The processing requirements of several simultaneous graphics users would have had catastrophic effects on the response time of the other users of the system. A second reason for the lack of graphics was the exorbitant cost of these display systems. For the most part, they were too expensive to justify their purchase.

In the 1980s, however, with the introduction of microcomputer workstations, the overall complexion of computer installations has changed. These stand-alone computers take advantage of the low cost of both microprocessors ("computer-on-a-chip") and memory. No longer must several users share the same computer. In fact, a single graphics workstation often consists of several microprocessors, each with its own memory, and each designed to perform a specific alphanumeric or graphic function.

It may *appear* that all is rosy in the world of computer graphics. One need only buy a graphics display system and create pictures. Unfortunately, this is not the case. While graphics displays are inexpensive for General Motors, sophisticated workstations sell from $15,000 to over $100,000. In addition, graphics systems at the low end of this price range have limited hardware and software capabilities, requiring an application programmer to write graphics programs that enhance existing software.

In this text, we assume the availability of very little graphics hardware or software. Low-cost microcomputers (under $5000) with minimal graphics features include the Apple II, IBM PC, DEC Rainbow, Atari,

FIGURE 1–1
Examples of computer graphics

and Tandy 1000. It is our purpose to describe how realistic graphic images can be produced on these inexpensive systems. Figure 1-1 illustrates several examples of computer graphics generated on a low-resolution Apple II computer. The techniques used to produce these images are described throughout the text.

More expensive graphics display systems, such as the Silicon graphics IRIS workstation (Figure 1-2), have implemented within this software and hardware many graphics capabilities that facilitate the production of high-quality images, as seen in the color plates inserted in this chapter. However, the serious user of these sophisticated systems should still possess a thorough understanding of the underlying principles of graphics hardware and software. Before examining these features, let's look at how computer graphics began.

FIGURE 1–2
An IRIS 1400 display system (courtesy of Silicon Graphics)

Introduction to Computer Graphics

1–2 BRIEF HISTORY OF COMPUTER GRAPHICS

The computers of the 1940s used primitive hard-copy devices requiring users to sift through reams of alphanumeric printout. The Whirlwind computer built in 1950 at MIT to investigate aircraft stability and control was probably the first computer to use a cathode ray tube (CRT), or television-type, display (see Section 1-4). Prior to this, computer designers had not thought of connecting this common display device to a computer. What prompted the marriage was the desire to speed up the interaction between user input and computer output.

The SAGE air-defense system of the 1950s converted radar blips into crude computer-generated images. This system was the first to use a light pen (see Section 1-4) to select symbols on a display screen.

In the late 1950s and early 1960s, the computing community at MIT was actively involved in both research and construction of their own computer systems. Out of this environment emerged the most profound influence on modern computer graphics: the 1963 Ph.D. thesis of Ivan Sutherland. Sutherland developed the Sketchpad line-drawing system, which enabled the user to sketch by pointing, with a light pen, to points on the screen. Between points, the graphics system could draw lines and construct polygons. Complex diagrams were generated by replicating simple objects. This remarkable interactive graphics system was the precursor of modern computer-drafting systems. Several years after leaving MIT, Sutherland and Dave Evans cofounded Evans and Sutherland, a firm dedicated to the design and manufacture of high-performance, special-purpose graphics display systems.

The early CRTs had the ability to draw a straight line between any two points on the display screen. However, since, a line faded very quickly on the screen, it had to be redrawn many times a second. In the early 1960s, this required expensive memory in which to store the line endpoints and expensive hardware with which to rapidly redraw the line. In 1965, IBM introduced the first mass-produced CRT of this type. A price tag of over $100,000 just for the CRT deterred many computer installations from entering the field of graphics.

In 1968, Tektronix introduced the storage-tube CRT, which permanently retains a drawing until the user erases it (see Section 1-4). These displays eliminated the need for costly memory and a hardware redrawer. A $15,000 selling price made them the preferred display screen for about 5 years.

The mid-1970s marked the beginning of a period of dramatic reduction in the cost of both memory and hardware logic units. This reduction led to the current proliferation of memory-intensive raster-scan displays on which realistic-looking shaded and colored images can be produced in an interactive environment (see Section 1-4).

So far we have been examining the role of hardware in the development of computer graphics. We should not forget, however, that software also played a crucial part in its development. Ivan Sutherland is the early leader in this field, having designed some of the major algorithms and data structures on which computer graphics is based. The pioneering works of Steven Coons (1966) and Pierre Bezier (1972) with curved surfaces led the way to interactive computer generation of realistic three-dimensional images (see Chapter 12). Over the last 10 years, many people have developed important algorithms used in computer graphics. Not surprisingly, many of them studied at the University of Utah where Ivan Sutherland was a professor. (Sutherland is currently a visiting scientist at Carnegie–Mellon University.)

During the 1980s many universities and industries have been undertaking computer graphics research projects. The fruits of their labor promise even more exciting developments in this rapidly changing and growing field.

1–3 APPLICATIONS OF COMPUTER GRAPHICS

The number of uses for computer graphics continues to grow with our imaginations. **Computer-aided design (CAD)** is a generic term that encompasses any activity where a computer aids in the design of a product. CAD systems help design engineers create new, and modify existing, aircraft and automobiles. Drawings produced with the aid of these systems usually go through several stages in their creation. Early sketches have the appearance of wire-frame or line drawings (Figure 1-3). Further on in the design process, more detail and realism is added. And the final drawing can be colored and shaded, giving it the look of the actual object (Figure 1-4).

CAD systems are also finding their way into the studios of artists. Animated movies, television commercials, and even portions of major movies are produced using these video display systems. In one particularly simple technique used in program title sequences, the computer draws the outline of objects. This so-called wire-frame animation is relatively easy to program and requires a small amount of processing time. The final image can be hand colored to give it a realistic appearance. Using the computer to produce a realistic animated sequence involves three-dimensional modeling techniques. The rendering algorithms must include such things as shadows, textures, reflections, and hidden line removal. The film *The Last Starfighter* has 25 min of computer imagery (color plate). Each frame of this futuristic outer space imagery required dozens of algorithms and hundreds of thousands of polygons. It is estimated that by producing these frames on the computer, the

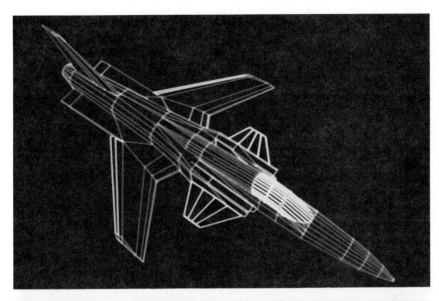

FIGURE 1–4
A PS 340 raster-screen rendering of the X-29 experimental aircraft (courtesy of Grumman Aerospace Corporation and Evans & Sutherland)

producer saved 50% in both cost and time over more traditional methods.

Art students and professional artists use this new medium to create realistic and abstract drawings. **Graphic design** and **paint-programming systems** provide graphic tablets that closely approximate the drawing/painting surface, and a stylus (see Section 1-4). The tablet is sensitive to hand pressure, giving the user a more natural feel while painting. The painter's palette and brush selection is emulated by allowing the user to mix colors and create user-definable brushes. Some of the more sophisticated graphic design systems provide electronic rulers, scissors, glue, and different type faces. When recorded on video film or slides, these computer-generated images are often mistaken for the more traditional art forms (color plate).

Airplane pilots and spaceship astronauts are trained on computer-generated graphic **flight simulator systems** (Figure 1-5). Realistic simulators are expensive to develop, and their design requires complex mathematics and physics. Real-time flight simulators use multiple special-purpose processors and often use multiple screens, giving the trainee a 180-degree view. The best simulators accurately model airport scenes and various weather conditions. A user of these systems can experience engine failure, emergency takeoffs and landings, air and ground collisions, and a host of other situations, all without danger to the flight crew or aircraft simulator. Although a realistic simulator may take several years to build and cost hundreds of thousands of dollars, the cost of using one to train a pilot is only a fraction of the cost of using a real aircraft.

Students from elementary school through college are learning on computer graphics systems. This form of **computer-aided instruction (CAI)** often uses animated sequences to illustrate educational concepts. While still not in widespread use, graphics will eventually find its way into many course curricula.

One of the more exciting uses of graphics is its ability to make personal computers friendlier to the user. Until 1983, a typewriter key-

FIGURE 1–5
A mid-air refueling program (courtesy of Evans & Sutherland)

board and knowledge of command languages was the only way a user could communicate with a computer—despite the fact that many people did not feel comfortable with this means of input. In 1983 Apple Computer introduced the Macintosh personal computer, which enables the user to point to graphics symbols or icons (a clock, calculator, file folder, and so on) displayed on the screen (Figure 1-6). Many computer tasks that previously required the user to memorize cryptic commands can now be performed simply by choosing a readily identifiable graphic representation of the operation. This efficient and user-friendly graphics interface successfully shows that graphics will be an integral part of future computer systems.

FIGURE 1–6
Apple Computer's Macintosh with mouse pointing device (courtesy of Apple Computer, Inc.)

1–4 INTERACTIVE GRAPHICS SYSTEM

When a computer generates a multicolored graph on a hard-copy device, we usually do not mind waiting several minutes for it to appear. Such graphics are known as **passive** or **static graphics**. However, when we are playing a video game, a response time of more than one-tenth of a second after a joystick is moved will probably be unacceptable. An immediate response to the user's action is required. Such graphics, in which the display is changed and regenerated fast enough to give the appearance of a user-controlled picture, are called **interactive** or **dynamic computer graphics**. The requirements of interaction place strenuous demands on the graphics system. High-performance systems have special hardware devices whose sole task is to monitor and react to user actions. It is important to realize that the more complex and realistic an image is, the greater the difficulty in changing that image quickly.

A typical interactive computer graphics system has four components: computer, video display screen generation, user input devices, and hard-copy output devices (Figure 1-7 on page 12). The computer

FIGURE 1–7
The Macintosh
graphics display sys-
tem (courtesy of
Apple Computer,
Inc.)

plays a central role in any graphics system. Each of the other components must, at some time, communicate with each other or the computer
via a data channel (bus). We shall ignore the data communication requirements and the main computer and concentrate on the different
hardware technologies of the three subsystems.

VIDEO DISPLAY GENERATION

Most video display screens are the same type of **cathode ray tubes
(CRTs)** that are used in home television sets (Figure 1-8). The electron
gun contains a cathode that, when heated, emits a beam of negatively
charged electrons toward a positively charged phosphor-coated screen.
Along the way, the electron beam passes through the focusing and deflection system, which consists of an electrostatic or magnetic field.

The focusing system concentrates the beam so that by the time the
electrons reach the screen, they have converged to a small dot. The
deflection system, which consists of two pairs of deflection plates (horizontal and vertical), directs the electron beam to any point on the screen.
Both pairs of plates have equal voltages but with opposite signs; that is,
one has a positive charge, the other a negative charge. When a negatively
charged electron passes through the plates, it is attracted to the positively charged plate, resulting in a deflection of the electron. The
amount of deflection depends on the magnitude of the voltage on the

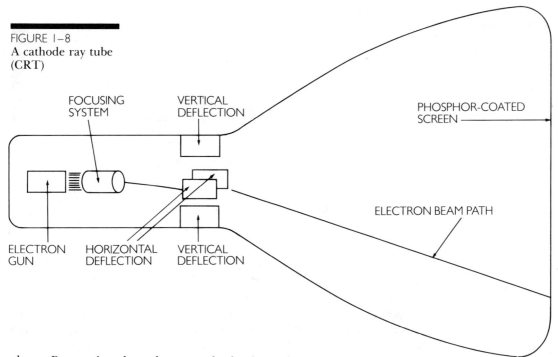

FIGURE 1–8
A cathode ray tube
(CRT)

FOCUSING
SYSTEM

VERTICAL
DEFLECTION

PHOSPHOR-COATED
SCREEN

ELECTRON BEAM PATH

ELECTRON
GUN

HORIZONTAL
DEFLECTION

VERTICAL
DEFLECTION

plates. By varying the voltage on the horizontal and vertical plates, the electron beam can strike any point on the screen.

When this focused electron beam strikes the screen, the phosphor emits a spot of visible light whose intensity depends on the number of electrons in the beam. A blank spot on the screen corresponds to no (or very few) electrons being sent to that location. The light on the display screen starts to fade as soon as the beam moves to another location. The duration of this light, called persistence, depends on the type of phosphor that coats the screen. Normally, visible light lasts for only a fraction of a second. In order to give the viewer the appearance of a continuous flicker-free image, each illuminated dot on the screen must be intensified many times per second. This type of video display is called a **refresh CRT.** Two types of refresh CRTs are available: raster scan and random vector. Although both are currently in use, the raster-scan system is preferred for most microcomputers and for applications that require color or shade.

A color CRT has three electron guns, one for each of the three primary colors: red, green, and blue. A delta-gun system arranges the three guns in a triangular pattern with a perforated metal grid or shadow mask placed between the guns and the face of the display screen (Figure 1-9 on page 14). Each pixel is composed of a triangular pattern of a red, green, and blue phosphor dot. The holes in the shadow mask are aligned so that each electron gun excites its corresponding phosphor dot.

FIGURE 1–9
Color CRT electron
guns and a shadow
mask

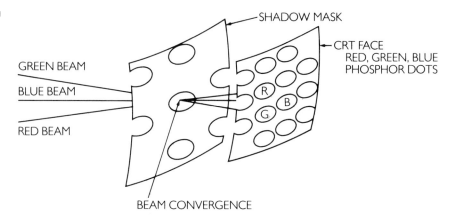

RASTER-SCAN DISPLAY

The video display screen used by most microcomputers is divided into very small rectangles or dots. These dots are referred to as picture elements or **pixels**. We can consider the CRT screen to consist of a grid of vertical and horizontal lines, where each horizontal line is made up of pixels (Figure 1-10). These horizontal lines are called **raster-scan lines** and the video display is referred to as a **raster-scan display**. The quality of a raster display is often described in terms of its resolution. This is a two-dimensional term that measures the number of scan lines and the number of pixels on a line, or dots per unit area. The greater the resolution, the greater the detail of an image can be. Low-resolution

FIGURE 1–10
A raster display
screen

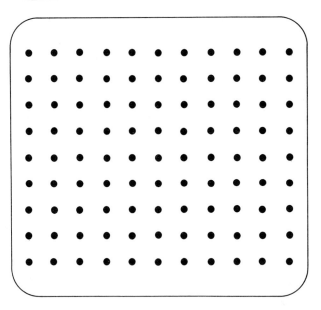

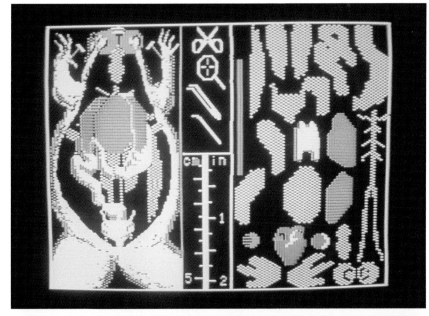

This computer simulation of a frog dissection makes use of a software program designed to work with Apple II and Commodore computers. Students can use simulated laboratory instruments to dissect the frog, examine the organs and body systems, and put the frog back together. *(courtesy of Scholastic, Inc.)*

This "Gunstar" graphic is part of 25 min of computer imagery from the movie, *The Last Starfighter*. The film's computer graphics were produced using Ramtek display generators and Digital Productions game simulations.
(© 1984, all rights reserved, courtesy of Ramtek Corporation and Digital Productions)

A bar chart is typical of most business graphics systems and is easily produced with microcomputer software. *(courtesy of Matrix Instruments, Inc.)*

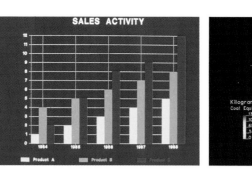

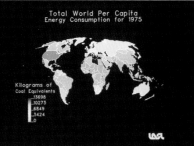

A three-dimensional surface map represents radiometric data gathered from one flight path of an aerial reconnaissance survey for the National Uranium Resource Evaluation Project. *(courtesy of Los Alamos National Laboratory)*

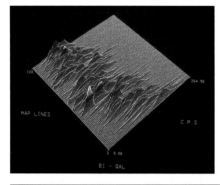

A world map shows per capita energy consumption by country. Color helps quickly identify patterns of energy consumption. *(courtesy of Los Alamos National Laboratory)*

This Van der Waals molecular surface of ATP (adenosine triphosphate) illustrates molecular modeling with interactive color computer graphics in real time. The surface dots are color coded by atom type: carbon (green), nitrogen (blue), oxygen (red), and hydrogen (white). *(courtesy of Computer Graphics Laboratory, University of California, San Francisco)*

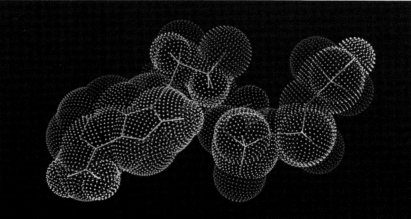

Computer-aided design and computer-aided manufacturing (CAD/CAM) enable engineers, computer scientists, and designers to design a product starting from its component parts and taking it to its completion. This

smooth-shaded, solid cut-away reveals assembly complexity using Ramtek 2020 technology. *(courtesy of Ramtek Corporation)*

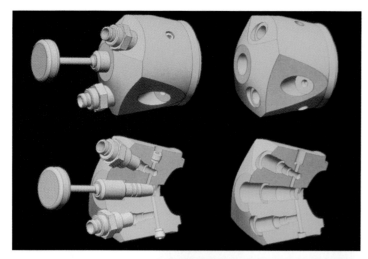

With computer-aid design and computer-aided manufacturing (CAD/CAM), the computer can keep track of all details, maintain the designs of all the parts in memory, and combine the parts electronically as required. *(courtesy of Ramtek Corporation)*

This computer-drawn B DNA simulates the type of colored, plastic, space-filling molecular models used by chemists. The colors represent the different atoms: hydrogen (white), nitrogen (blue), oxygen (red), phosphorus (yellow), and carbon (dark blue). The outlines of the visible part of each atom are computed on a CDC-7600 and are colored in with shading and highlights on a Dicomed D-48 color film recorder controlled by a Sperry Univac V-75 minicomputer. *(by Nelson Max, courtesy of Lawrence Livermore National Laboratory)*

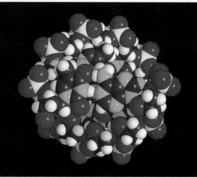

Daimler Benz uses a special Evans & Sutherland 180-degree projection system and CT5 visual system in its driving simulator. A driver sees a full 180-degree simulation of city and highway traffic as well as varying weather conditions including rain, snow, and fog. *(courtesy of Evans & Sutherland and Daimler Benz)*

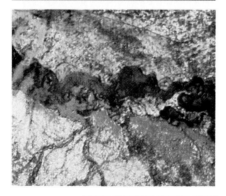

Satellite data is here processed by Control Data/Image Processing software on a Cyber computer. *(courtesy of Control Data Corporation)*

Thermography (infrared thermal imaging) converts temperature distribution patterns into visual images. Computer programs can determine differences in temperature, mass, and density, and can visually display changes, registering temperature variations to fractions of a degree, within microseconds. *(courtesy of Richard Lowenberg)*

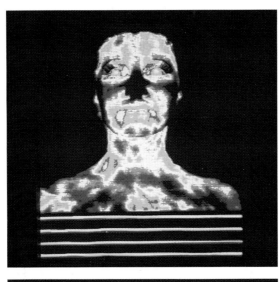

Fine detail, subtle shading, and metallic effects are illustrated in this computer graphic of King Tutankhamen produced on the Artronics/3M eight-plane studio computer (Artron) system. *(by Scott Lewczak, courtesy of Artronics, Inc.)*

This color-enhanced medical image data of a thorax uses a Ramtek display generator in a nuclear magnetic resonance system. *(courtesy of Ramtek Corporation)*

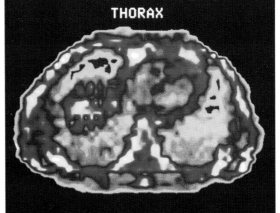

Computer graphics were used to create the image for this official Olympic poster, 1984 Summer Olympics. *(by Joni Carter, courtesy of Matrix Instruments, Inc.)*

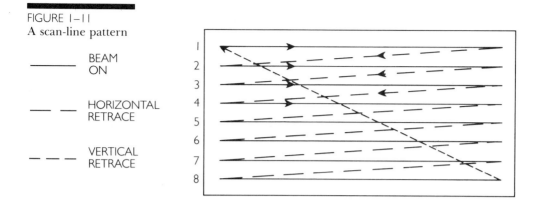

FIGURE 1–11
A scan-line pattern

——————— BEAM ON

— — HORIZONTAL RETRACE

— — — VERTICAL RETRACE

displays have about 300 scan lines, each containing about 400 pixels. High-resolution displays have at least 1000 scan lines with over 1000 pixels per line.

A raster-scan system displays the image on the CRT in a certain fixed sequence (Figure 1-11). Initially, the vertical and horizontal deflection plates are set to display a pixel at the upper-left corner of the screen. The voltage of the horizontal plates is then continuously changed, steering the electron beam across the scan line. When the beam is at the end of the scan line, the electron gun is turned off (no visible beam) and both pairs of deflection plates are set to send the beam to the left-most pixel on the second raster-scan line. The blanking of the video signal is called horizontal retrace. This left-to-right scanning pattern continues until the electron beam reaches the bottom-right corner of the screen. At that time, the beam is turned off and is steered to the top-left corner of the screen, a process called vertical retrace.

Since an illuminated phosphor dot emits light for only a fraction of a second, this left-to-right, top-to-bottom scanning pattern must be repeated many times per second. The **refresh rate** is the number of complete images, or frames, drawn on the screen in 1 second. The reciprocal of the refresh rate is the time between each complete scan and is called the **frame time.** Although a pixel is actually off for a longer time than it is on, a fast enough refresh rate gives the eye the impression of a continuous illuminated image.

Most inexpensive display systems have a refresh rate of 30 times/sec. The scanning process is usually divided into two phases, with each phase lasting 1/60 of a second. In the first phase, the odd-numbered raster lines are displayed; the even-numbered raster lines are displayed in the second phase (Figure 1-12 on page 16). The result of this interlaced refresh cycle is a reduction of the flickering effect that accompanies a noninterlaced frame time of 1/30 of a second. Observe that interlaced

FIGURE 1–12
An interlaced scan-
line pattern

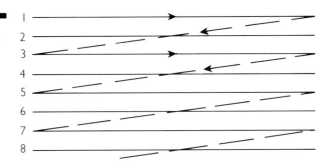

displays require two vertical retraces per frame time. Higher quality raster-scan systems have a noninterlaced refresh rate of 60 times/sec.

Whenever an image is displayed on the screen, it is necessary to illuminate the appropriate pixels. How does the display screen hardware know which pixels should be turned on, and how is this information sent to the display screen? The task of illuminating the appropriate pixels requires a display unit composed of three components: frame buffer, display controller, and scan conversion algorithms (Figure 1-13).

FRAME BUFFER

Each screen pixel corresponds to a particular entry in a two-dimensional array residing in memory. This memory is called a **frame buffer** or a **bit map**. Some graphics systems have a frame buffer memory distinct from main memory. The current trend is to have the frame buffer accessible to the central processing unit (CPU) of the main computer, thus allowing rapid update of the stored image. The number of rows in the frame buffer array equals the number of raster lines on the display screen. The number of columns in this array equals the number of pixels on each raster line. The term *pixel* is also used to describe the row and column location in the frame buffer array that corresponds to the screen location. A 512 × 512 display screen requires 262,144 pixel memory locations. Whenever we wish to display a pixel on the screen, a specific value is placed into the corresponding memory location in the frame buffer array. In Figure 1-14, a value of 1 placed in a location in the

FIGURE 1–13
A raster-scan dis-
play unit

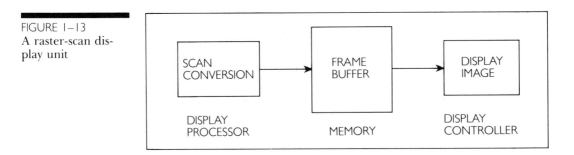

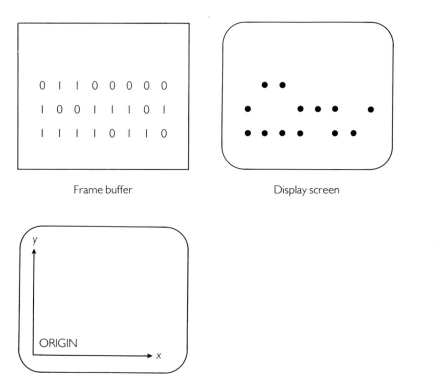

FIGURE 1–14
A number one (1)
in a frame buffer
corresponds to an
illuminated pixel on
a display screen

Frame buffer   Display screen

FIGURE 1–15
A display coordi-
nate system

y

ORIGIN ────────▶ x

frame buffer results in the corresponding (black) pixel being displayed
on the screen.

Each screen location pixel and corresponding memory location in
the frame buffer is accessed by an (x, y) integer coordinate pair. The x
value refers to the column, the y value to the row position. The origin
of this coordinate system is usually positioned at the bottom-left corner
of the screen (Figure 1-15), although the image is still displayed in scan-
line order from top to bottom. This screen coordinate system is described in Chapter 2.

Each pixel in the frame buffer array is composed of a number of
bits. A black-and-white image that has only two intensity levels, on/off,
has a single-bit–plane frame buffer. In order to display a color or a black-
and-white-quality image with shades of gray, additional bit planes are
needed. Figure 1-16 on page 18 illustrates a 3-bit–plane frame buffer.
The eight distinct values from the 3-bit planes are interpreted as intensity levels between 0 and $2^3 - 1 = 7$. A black-and-white-television-
quality image requires 8-bit planes, giving 2^8 or 256 intensity levels.
High-quality color display systems have frame buffers with up to 24 bit
planes. Each of the three primary colors—red, green, and blue—uses 8-
bit planes to drive its color electron gun, producing a total of $2^{24} =$
16,777,216 colors. A full-color frame buffer with 512 × 512 resolution

FIGURE 1-16
A three-bit–plane
frame buffer

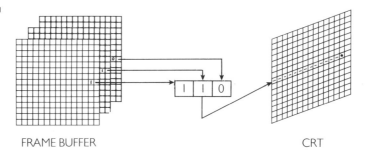

FRAME BUFFER   CRT

requires $512 \times 512 \times 24 = 6{,}291{,}456$ bits of memory. Low-cost microcomputer graphics systems have limited memory, providing between one and four bits per pixel.

DISPLAY CONTROLLER

The second component of the display unit is the **display controller**. This hardware device reads the contents of the frame buffer into a video buffer, which then converts the digital representation of a string of pixel values into analog voltage signals that are sent serially to the video display screen. Whenever the display controller encounters a value of 1 in a single-bit–plane frame buffer, a high-voltage signal is sent to the CRT, which turns on the corresponding screen pixel. The display controller sequentially cycles through the frame buffer, satisfying the refresh rate. The frame time, 1/refresh rate, is the sum of the vertical retrace time (two retraces if interlaced), the total horizontal retrace time (one per scan line), and the time to display all pixels. As an example, suppose that the display screen has resolution 512×512 and has an interlaced refresh rate of 30 frames/sec. For this size display, horizontal retrace time is 11 μsec (10^{-6} sec), vertical retrace time is 1200 μsec, and frame time of 33,333 μsec. A pixel in the frame buffer will be accessed by the display controller in 0.096 μsec. The formula relating these video times is

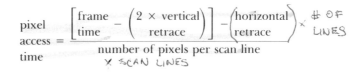

$$\frac{\text{pixel access time} = \dfrac{\left[\dfrac{\text{frame}}{\text{time}} - \left(\dfrac{2 \times \text{vertical}}{\text{retrace}}\right)\right] - \left(\dfrac{\text{horizontal}}{\text{retrace}}\right) \times \text{\# OF LINES}}{\begin{array}{c}\text{number of pixels per scan line}\\ \times \text{ SCAN LINES}\end{array}}}{}$$

A noninterlaced refresh rate of 60 frames/sec has only one vertical retrace, and the pixel access time is reduced to 0.0375 μsec. These systems require a very fast and expensive frame buffer memory and display controller.

SCAN CONVERSION

Only rarely is an image described in terms of the two-dimensional array of pixels comprising the frame buffer. Images are usually defined in terms of equations—for example, $x + y = 5$—or graphic descriptions such as "draw a line from point A to point B." **Scan conversion** is the process of converting this abstract representation of an image into the appropriate pixel values in the frame buffer. Sophisticated raster graphics systems have a separate display processor that performs scan conversion and other screen update functions. Inexpensive microcomputer graphics systems use the CPU and a library of software routines to perform scan conversion. These software-based graphics systems are slower and consequently have difficulty in creating a real-time environment for the user. It is important to realize that each time an image is modified, hundreds of scan conversion calculations may be required. In Chapter 2 we examine some of these scan conversion routines.

RANDOM-VECTOR DISPLAY

We've seen how a raster-scan system uses a frame buffer to display an image in scan-line order: from top to bottom, left to right. This is not the only way to create an image using a refresh CRT. Indeed, if we wish to draw only lines, a line-drawing graphics system is preferred. Line-drawing systems are also called **random-vector** or **calligraphic systems**. The principle behind this type of graphics display is simple. There is a memory region, called a display file, consisting of line-drawing commands such as "draw a line from A to B." Either a special display processor or the CPU inserts the correct line-drawing command into the display file. A special vector-generating hardware processor interprets these commands and sends the correct voltages to the deflection system of the CRT, moving the electron beam in a straight line from the initial to the final point (Figure 1-17). Unlike with a raster-scan system, it is not necessary to direct the electron beam over the entire screen during each refresh cycle. The beam is moved only over those parts of the screen where there is a straight line, or vector. Random-vector systems usually have a (noninterlaced) refresh rate of 60 times/sec.

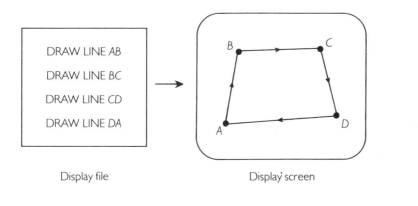

Display file   Display screen

FIGURE 1–17
A display file

FIGURE 1–18
A "line" from *A* to
B—The staircase
effect

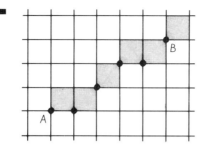

COMPARISON OF RASTER-SCAN AND RANDOM-VECTOR DISPLAYS

A random-vector display's major advantage over a raster-scan display is its ability to draw straight lines accurately. Raster-scan systems can illuminate only those pixels at grid points, thus producing jagged lines with gaps (Figure 1-18). In addition, a random-vector display does not require complex scan conversion routines. By storing only the endpoints of a line, a random-vector display requires much less display memory than a frame buffer in a raster-scan system. A random-vector display can modify portions of the screen faster, since erasing or changing an object simply requires removing it from or changing its coordinates in the display list.

The major disadvantage of a random-vector display is its inability to fill in areas and create realistic color or shaded images. The complexity of an image is limited in random-vector systems since only a certain number of lines can be drawn during the time allocated for the refresh cycle. (This is becoming less of a problem with new, faster vector generators that draw 10,000 1-in. lines in 1/60 of a second.) In raster-scan systems, image refresh is independent of the image's complexity. Whatever resides in the frame buffer is displayed in one refresh cycle. The low cost of memory and the proliferation of television-type raster-scan CRTs, as well as enhanced color and shading capabilities, have made raster-scan displays the overwhelming choice for most graphics display systems.

STORAGE-TUBE DISPLAY

A **direct-view storage tube (DVST)** is a CRT display that does not need to be refreshed from memory. A storage surface area or grid is situated behind a long persistence phosphor display screen (Figure 1-19). As the electron beam strikes the storage grid, a positively charged pattern is created. A second electron gun, called a flood gun, continually emits low-energy electrons that uniformly cover the entire screen, causing the positively charged stored image to be transferred to the phosphor screen and remain visible for up to 1 hour. The stored image is erased by giving the entire storage grid a positive charge. This results in the characteristic flash of white light before the screen becomes dark.

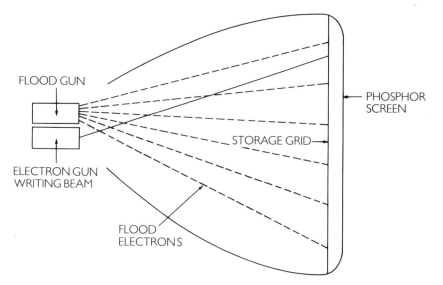

FIGURE 1–19
A direct-view storage tube

FLOOD GUN

ELECTRON GUN
WRITING BEAM

FLOOD
ELECTRONS

PHOSPHOR
SCREEN

STORAGE GRID

The advantages of a DVST include high-resolution, nonstaircase-like lines combined with a flicker-free image. Its major disadvantages include the lack of selective erase and dynamic update. Each change of the image requires that the entire image be erased and redrawn.

LIQUID-CRYSTAL DISPLAY

A **liquid-crystal display (LCD)** is one type of flat-panel display technology that eliminates the long neck tube in the CRT. Two glass plates are separated by an organic conductive liquid crystal. Electrical charges convert the liquid back and forth from a visible to an invisible state. Medium-resolution displays have a single display that is divided electrically into a number of smaller displays that are displayed simultaneously (Figure 1-20).

FIGURE 1–20
The Hewlett-Packard 16-line by 80-column portable liquid crystal display (courtesy of Hewlett-Packard)

The major advantages of LCD screens are their portability and low power requirements. Their disadvantages include the lack of gray scale and color. In addition, the high reflective property of the liquid crystals and the glass panel arrangement causes an annoying reflection of the surrounding environment.

INPUT DEVICES

The user of an interactive graphics system communicates with the graphics program by means of input devices. These devices provide a natural dialogue between the user and the program. In this section we examine some of the more common input devices.

The most familiar input device is the **keyboard**. It is primarily used to enter programs and data into the computer. Whenever a key is pressed, a unique character code is transmitted to the computer. There are either 128 (ASCII) or 256 (EBCDIC) codes, each of which can be used to signal a different response from the graphics program.

A **paddle** is a positioning device that has a knob connected to a potentiometer, a device that changes voltage levels. Whenever the knob is turned, the potentiometer sends a voltage to an analog-to-digital converter, which transforms the voltage into an integer value that is then used as an input value to the computer (Figure 1-21). Most paddles also have a button that, when pressed, transmits a signal that changes a logical bit from 0 to 1. The knob is often used to move an object across the display screen; the direction the knob is turned indicates the direction of movement. The button is pressed when we wish to fix the object onto a position on the screen.

A **joystick** is a rod connected to two potentiometers (Figure 1-22). This rod can be moved in any rotational direction. One potentiometer senses movement about the horizontal axis; the other senses movement about the vertical axis. Together they give values that can be converted into coordinates of a point on the display screen. One joystick with buttons can perform the same tasks as two game paddles.

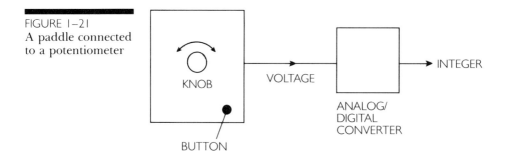

FIGURE 1–21
A paddle connected to a potentiometer

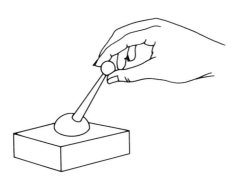

FIGURE 1–22
A joystick

A **light pen** is a penlike device with a photocell that, when activated by depressing the tip against the screen, sends back to the computer the location of the illuminated pixel in its field of view (Figure 1-23). What is actually sent to the computer is the time during the display controller's scan refresh cycle when that pixel is displayed. From this information the computer is able to determine the screen location of the pixel. The pixel must be lit in order to find it using a light pen.

A **mouse** is a hand-held device that takes advantage of the user's natural eye–hand coordination to enable the user to locate and choose an object on the display screen accurately and comfortably. The mouse has two perpendicular rollers on its bottom that are connected to potentiometers. As the mouse moves across a surface, its relative movement can be determined. This movement is used to input screen coordinate values. Pressing the buttons on top of the mouse inputs the binary values 0 or 1 (Figure 1-24 on page 24).

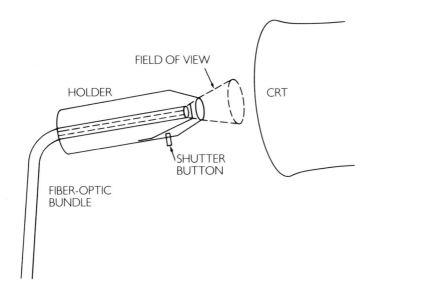

FIGURE 1–23
A light pen

FIGURE 1–24
The Summa mouse
pointing device
(courtesy of
Summagraphics
Corporation)

A **graphics tablet**, or **digitizer**, is a flat surface that has a hand cursor or stylus (pen) connected to it (Figure 1-25). The pen is moved over the surface in the same way we sketch on a pad. The tablet's surface has a coordinate system similar to that of the display screen. A coordinate location is transmitted to the computer when the user pushes down on the stylus or presses a button on the cursor. Some tablets determine coordinate locations by employing a grid of electrically charged wires in the tablet's surface. When the stylus or cursor is activated, the voltage at the nearest grid intersection point is recorded and converted into screen coordinates by a sophisticated control unit.

FIGURE 1–25
A graphics digitizer
(courtesy of ALTEK
Corporation)

Introduction to Computer Graphics

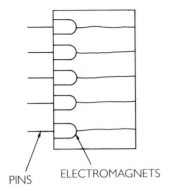

FIGURE 1–26
A dot-matrix print
head

PINS   ELECTROMAGNETS

HARD-COPY OUTPUT DEVICES

A **dot-matrix printer** is an inexpensive device that produces low-
to medium-quality graphic output. The movable print head has a column of pins that can be pressed against the paper by small electromagnets (Figure 1-26). Each pin selected produces a dot on the paper
corresponding to a lighted screen pixel. A print head with five pins
moves across the screen plotting up to five rows of pixels simultaneously.
The resolution of dot-matrix printers ranges from 10 to 120 dots/in.

Ink-jet printers use electrical impulses to project drops of ink onto
the paper. As the print head moves across the page, up to 12 jets eject
ink drops at each specified point. Ink jets produce high-quality shaded
and color images with resolution of up to 200 dots/in. (Figure 1-27).

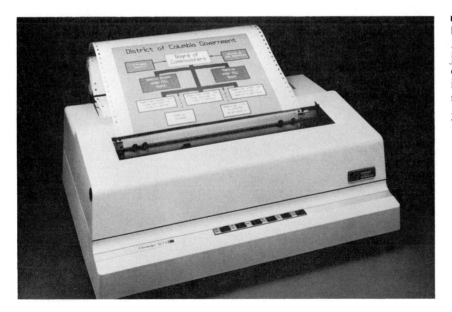

FIGURE 1–27
An Act-II Chroma-
jet™ ink-jet printer
capable of display-
ing 125 color
shades (courtesy of
Advanced Color
Technology)

Point plotters produce images by moving the pen between any two points on the paper (Figure 1-28). If the paper does not move, the pen must move in two orthogonal directions. If the paper moves, the pen will move only in one direction: perpendicular to the direction of the moving paper. Pens of different colors and thickness can be used to produce high-quality images.

Electrostatic plotters are raster plotters that can produce high-quality color images with resolution as high as 200 dots/in. Electrostatic dots are placed on the paper as the paper moves over the fixed writing head. The paper is then exposed to liquid toners, which produce a colored or shaded image. The paper must pass over the writing head one time for each of the three or four toner colors, if color is wanted (Figure 1-29).

FIGURE 1–28
A 1040 Series 8-pen point plotter (courtesy of CalComp)

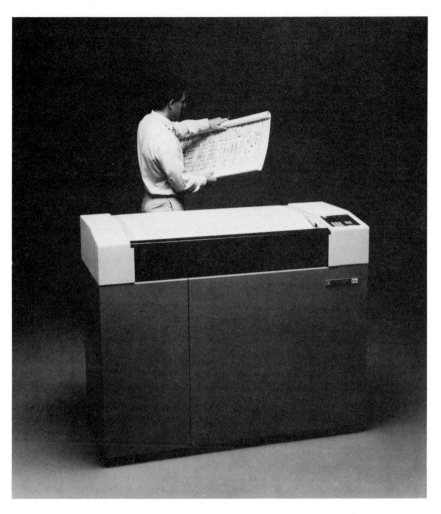

1–5 **GRAPHICS SYSTEM SOFTWARE**

Graphics software is a fundamental component of any graphics display system. Systems with the most sophisticated and expensive hardware devices would be useless for most people if they didn't also have high-performance, user-friendly software. The capabilities of software graphics packages are increasing while their costs are decreasing. This happy occurrence will bring more graphics to more users.

In 1979 the Graphics Standard Planning Committee (GSPC), in an attempt to standardize graphics software in the United States, designed a **Core Graphics System (CORE)**. Its intent was to provide the capabilities needed to support high-performance, interactive three-dimensional graphics display systems. Currently there are over 200,000 users of CORE-type systems. Unfortunately, each of these systems differs from the others, making program portability difficult at best.

At about the same time, the West German National Standards body, DIN, developed its own graphics standard called the **Graphical Kernel System (GKS)**. GKS has excellent two-dimensional features but lacks three-dimensional capabilities. In 1982 GKS became an international standard. At present, the international graphics community is trying to merge the strengths of CORE and GKS into one unified graphics standard. Of course, a lot of politics are involved in this ongoing activity.

Most pre-1982 graphics software packages developed in the United States have implemented only a small subset of the CORE system. Except in the more expensive display systems, many interactive and three-dimensional features have been omitted. However, even the least expensive ones provide the fundamental line drawing and geometric transformations necessary to perform the simplest type of graphics.

This text is written independently of any software graphics package. For the most part, we follow the specifications of the CORE system. For those interested in GKS, the appendix has an introduction to some of its fundamental features. All graphics commands in the text are explained as needed and only those commands available in most low-cost graphics systems will be assumed. Graphics commands are actually procedures or functions. An application programmer includes them in a Pascal program in much the same way that the function sin(x) or the procedure Read(A,B) are invoked.

Finally, it is important to recognize that there are two types of users of graphics display systems. One is the application programmer, who writes graphics programs using the programming features of the software package. This is the user we primarily refer to in this text. The second user is a person such as an artist or pilot who uses graphics but does not need to know anything about programming. It is for this person that the application programmer writes graphics programs.

1–6 **CONCLUSION**

In this chapter, we presented an overview of computer graphics. We included a brief history, several graphics applications, and a discussion of graphics hardware and software. As computer graphics continues to develop, the diversity of hardware and software innovations will lead to many more applications, as well as reductions in cost and size. Our discussion in the remaining chapters examines the fundamental algorithms and features of a raster-scan display system.

EXERCISES

1. Compute the pixel access time for a display screen having resolution 1024×1024 and a noninterlaced refresh rate of 60 frames/sec.

2. A typical frame buffer may require 400 ns between consecutive memory (pixel) accesses (referred to as a cycle time). The example in the text has a pixel access time of 96.5 ns. Using a memory chip size of $16K \times 1$, explain how the display controller can supply data fast enough to the display screen, which has access time requirements four times faster than the speed of memory.

3. Describe several applications where random-vector and direct-view storage-tube displays are more effective than raster-scan displays.

4. A random-vector display with resolution 512×512 has drawing instructions containing the coordinates of a point. How many data bits must each of these instructions have?

5. A DVST has a write-through mode that illuminates the phosphor screen without storing the image. Describe some advantages and disadvantages of this feature.

Detail of Figure 2−1a

2
DRAWING ELEMENTARY FIGURES

2–1 **INTRODUCTION**

Computer-generated images are produced using primitive graphic objects such as points, straight lines, and circles, and graphics screen operations such as "erase the screen" or "place the image on part of the screen." Most pre-1980 computers have hardware and software graphics capabilities that help the application programmer write graphics programs. These application programs access the software graphics package, which is a collection of efficient subroutines. In this chapter we present algorithms for some fundamental drawing primitives. After reading this chapter, you will be aware of some of the more important techniques in computer graphics. Figure 2-1 illustrates moire patterns generated by a combination of circles and lines.

2–2 **PLOTTING POINTS**

In order to draw a picture on a raster display, we must determine the corresponding points in the frame buffer that make up the picture. To perform this task we must write scan conversion **point-plotting algorithms**.

FIGURE 2–1
Moire patterns

Both the frame buffer and the display screen are given a two-dimensional coordinate system with the origin at the lower-left corner.

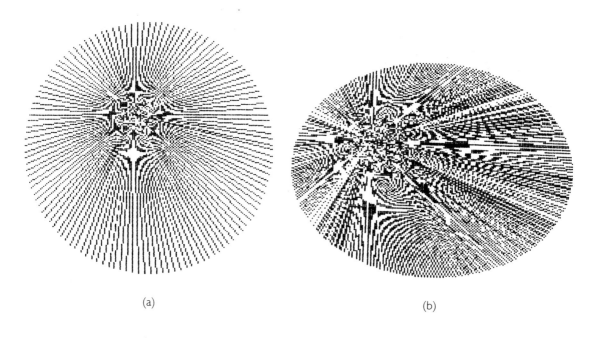

(a)

(b)

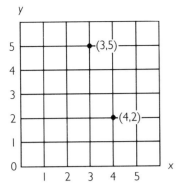

FIGURE 2–2
A display screen co-
ordinate system

Each pixel is accessed by a nonnegative integer (x, y) coordinate pair. The x values start at the origin, 0, and increase from left to right; the y values start at 0 and increase from bottom to top (Figure 2-2). (There is no standard, however, for the location of the origin. In fact, hardware engineers prefer to place the origin at the upper-left corner since this corresponds to the scanning operation of the CRT display controller.)

None of the x or y coordinate values should be beyond the boundaries of the display device. Any attempt to plot such values can produce a wraparound effect: The point "wraps around" and appears on the other side of the screen. An attempt to draw line AB, for example, results in the two lines AC and DE, as shown in Figure 2-3. To prevent this undesirable effect, graphics programs should test each value to determine if the point it represents lies within the screen boundaries. If x is negative or greater than the largest x value, or y is negative or greater than the largest y value, an appropiate action should be taken. One particularly simple solution is to assign zero to a coordinate having a negative value and assign the maximum screen value to a large, out-of-range coordinate. This problem is discussed in detail in Chapter 3 when clipping is examined. Assume for now that all points are within the screen boundaries.

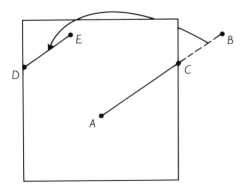

FIGURE 2–3
A wraparound
effect

FIGURE 2–4
An aspect ratio of
1.33

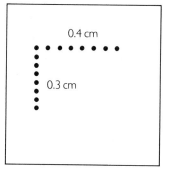

0.4 cm

0.3 cm

To draw a point on the display screen, a point-plotting procedure is required. We assume the availability of the command

plotpoint(x,y)

a graphics system-supplied procedure that turns on the pixel at screen (frame buffer) location (x, y). The parameters x and y must be nonnegative integer constants or expressions.

2–3 **ASPECT RATIO**

If we use the point-plotting procedure to plot eight pixels horizontally on the display screen and then measure the line, we find that it is 0.4 cm wide. If we plot eight pixels vertically, we find that the line is 0.3 cm high (Figure 2-4). Thus the horizontal and vertical plots of an equal number of pixels have different lengths. The ratio of the horizontal width to the vertical height, namely $0.4/0.3$ or 1.33 in this example, is called the **aspect ratio**. This ratio is a consequence of non-square pixels and rectangular display screens. In the early days of television, the TV industry designed its CRT with an aspect ration of 4/3 to correspond with the size of a frame of movie film. Today, (non-TV) displays are available with a wide range of aspect ratios. The current trend is toward a square screen (and square pixels), with an aspect ratio of 1.

The ratio affects the accuracy of pictures drawn on the display. As an example, let's draw a square box 80 pixels wide. For this display, with an aspect ratio of 4/3, the width is 4 cm. If 80 pixels are also plotted vertically, however, the height of the display will be only 3 cm, 1 cm less than its width. The result is a nonsquare box. In order to adjust for this difference, the number of vertical pixels (80) must be multiplied by the aspect ratio (1.33). Thus a 4 cm × 4 cm square has 80 pixels horizontally and $80 \times 1.33 = 107$ pixels vertically.

The same problem arises with a circle—an equal number of pixels horizontally and vertically will result in a display that looks like an egg (an ellipse). To avoid this distortion, whenever a picture is drawn using the screen coordinates, the vertical height must be multiplied, as with a

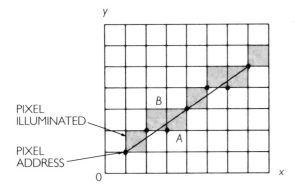

FIGURE 2–5
Pixels representing
a straight line

PIXEL
ILLUMINATED

PIXEL
ADDRESS

square, by the aspect ratio. It is important to observe that a picture that looks square on a TV monitor may not be square when displayed on a printer or on a display device with a different aspect ratio. When obtaining a hard copy, be certain to use the aspect ratio of the display device.

2–4 LINE DRAWING

Many computer-generated pictures are composed of straight-line segments. A line segment is displayed by turning on a string of adjacent pixels. In order to draw a line, it is necessary to determine which pixels lie nearest the line and provide the best approximation to the desired line. Figure 2-5 illustrates a line drawn on a raster display. Observe that a pixel is addressed by its lower-left-hand coordinates. The accuracy and quality of the displayed line depends on the resolution of the display device. High-resolution displays (1024 × 1024) draw lines that look straight and continuous, and that start and end accurately. Lower-resolution displays may draw lines with gaps and annoying jumps (Figure 2-6). Line-drawing routines in high-performance graphics systems are

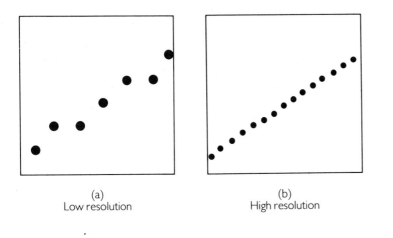

(a)
Low resolution

(b)
High resolution

FIGURE 2–6
A display screen
resolution

FIGURE 2–7
A horizontal line

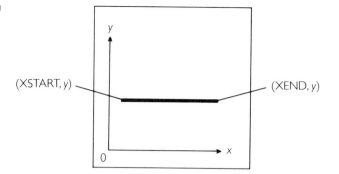

implemented in hardware that rapidly generates the pixels comprising the line when it is given the two endpoints. Most low-cost display systems still rely on slower software routines to accomplish line drawing. In either case, the line-drawing routine should be accurate, fast, and easy to implement. In the following sections we examine algorithms for lines that start and end at (integer) pixel coordinates. For noninteger endpoints, we must first determine the nearest integer coordinate.

HORIZONTAL AND VERTICAL LINES

The simplest lines to draw are horizontal and vertical lines. The screen coordinates of the points on a horizontal line are obtained by keeping the value of y constant and repeatedly incrementing the x value by one unit. The following Pascal code draws a horizontal line from (xstart, y) to (xend, y), xstart $<=$ xend (Figure 2-7).

```
{draw horizontal line}
for x := xstart to xend do
    plotpoint(x,y);
```

If xstart $>$ xend, the **to** in the **for** loop must be replaced by **downto**. Observe that the screen display of horizontal lines has no gaps since the electron beam is kept on at the same intensity for the entire span of the line.

To draw a vertical line, the x value is fixed and the y value varies. A vertical line may have noticeable gaps when drawn on a low-resolution raster display, a result of the scanning pattern of the display.

DIAGONAL LINES

To draw a diagonal line with a slope equal to $+1$, we need only repeatedly increment by one unit both the x and y values from the starting to the ending pixels (assuming the aspect ratio equals 1). Recall that slope is defined as the change in y values divided by the change in *x* values. The following program segment produces such a diagonal line.

```
{draw diagonal line}
{initial point}
x := xstart;
y := ystart;
i := 0;
{to final point}
while (x + i) <= xend do
    begin {while}
        plotpoint(x + i, y + i);
        i := i + 1
end; {while}
```

To draw a line with a slope equal to -1, replace y + i by y $-$ i in the code.

ARBITRARY LINES

Drawing lines with arbitrary slope creates several problems. First, because the display screen can be illuminated only at pixel locations, a raster-scan display has a staircase effect that only approximates the actual line (Figure 2-5). Although it may not be possible to choose pixels that lie on the actual line, we want to turn on the pixels lying closest to it. For example, in Figure 2-5, the pixel at location A is a better choice than the one at location B. Second, determining the closest (best) pixels is not easy. Different algorithms calculate different pixels to make up the approximating line. The choice of algorithm depends on the speed of line generation as well as on the appearance of the line. To understand these criteria better let's look at several different line-generating algorithms.

DIRECT METHOD

Perhaps the most natural method of generating a straight line is to use its equation:

$$y = (m \times x) + b$$

where *m* is the slope and *b* is the *y*-intercept. Recall that the *y*-intercept is the line's *y* value when *x* equals zero. Using this equation, we first calculate the slope and *y*-intercept. We then draw the line by incrementing the *x* value one unit from (xstart, ystart) to (xend, yend) and at each step solve for the corresponding *y* value. For each computed (*x*, *y*) coordinate value, the corresponding pixel is illuminated by invoking **plotpoint**(x, **round**(y)), where the Pascal **round** function is used to obtain an integer coordinate value.

There are two fundamental problems with this method. The first is the computational time required to draw the line. On many computer systems the operations of multiplication and division can take from 50 to 200 times longer to perform than an addition. Yet the one-time calculation of both the slope and y-intercept may require division, and m and x are multiplied together for each pixel on the line.

The second problem concerns lines with a slope whose absolute value is greater than 1. These lines will be near the vertical. Using the direct method, the displayed lines will have gaps between plotted points. Figure 2-8 is an exaggerated situation illustrating a line with slope $\frac{5}{2}$ that has only one pixel plotted between the starting and ending pixels.

There are several methods of correcting both problems. Repeated multiplication can be eliminated by performing incremental calculations at each step based on the previous step. The second problem can be resolved by incrementing y by one unit and solving the straight-line equation for x when **abs**(m) > 1. Unfortunately, though, we are still faced with a one-time divide operation. Let's see how we can implement these improvements.

SIMPLE DDA

Simple digital differential analyzer (simple DDA) is a line-drawing procedure that is easy to program and produces reasonably good lines.

To illustrate, we still want to draw the line segment with endpoints (xstart, ystart) and (xend, yend) having slope

$$m = \frac{(\text{yend} - \text{ystart})}{(\text{xend} - \text{xstart}).}$$

Any two consecutive points $(x1, y1)$, $(x2, y2)$ lying on this line satisfies the equation:

$$(2\text{--}1) \quad \frac{(y2 - y1)}{(x2 - x1)} = m.$$

FIGURE 2–8
A line having a
slope greater than 1

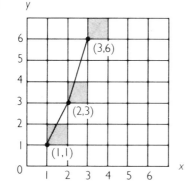

Drawing Elementary Figures

For **abs**(m) < 1 and xstart < xend, we generate the line by incrementing the previous x value one unit until xend is reached and then solve for y. (If xstart > xend, swap the two endpoints.) Thus for these consecutive points

$$x2 = x1 + 1 \quad \text{or} \quad x2 - x1 = 1.$$

Substituting this difference into equation 2-1 yields

$$(2\text{--}2) \quad \frac{(y2 - y1)}{1} = m \quad \text{or} \quad y2 = y1 + m.$$

Equation 2-2 enables us to calculate successive values of y from the previous value by replacing the repeated multiplication with floating-point addition. This method of obtaining the current value by adding a constant to the previous value is an example of **incremental calculation.** Using knowledge of one point to compute the next point is a great time-saving technique we use throughout the book.

If **abs**(m) > 1 and ystart < yend, we generate the line by reversing this procedure. Namely, we increment the y value one unit until yend is reached and solve for x. (If ystart > yend, swap the two endpoints.) For two consecutive points

$$y2 = y1 + 1 \quad \text{or} \quad y2 - y1 = 1.$$

Substituting this difference into equation 2-1,

$$(2\text{--}3) \quad \frac{1}{(x2 - x1)} = m \quad \text{or} \quad x2 = x1 + \frac{1}{m}.$$

Equation 2-3 is the desired incremental line equation.

It is important to notice that in the preceding two cases the computed incremental values for $y2$ and $x2$ may not be integers. Therefore, once again, each time a point is plotted, the Pascal function **round** is used to convert to integer screen coordinates. The following procedure, Draw_Line, draws a nonvertical or nonhorizontal line, based on the previous discussion. Prior to calling this procedure, we should test if $x1 = x2$ to ensure that the line is nonvertical (a vertical line would cause a division by zero in the slope) and test if $y1 = y2$ to ensure a nonhorizontal line (a horizontal line would use an unnecessarily long routine). If neither condition is met, Procedure Draw_Line is invoked.

```
Procedure Draw_Line (
          xstart, ystart,                    {starting point}
          xend,yend:integer);                {ending point}

var
          xi,yi,                             {incremental values}
          xr,yr,                            {computed values}
          m,                                {slope}
          minverse:real;                    {inverse slope}
```

```
begin
    m   := (yend − ystart)/(xend − xstart);
    {now test if starting values are before ending values}
    if (abs(m)<1) and (xstart>xend) or (abs(m)>1) and (ystart>yend)
        then
            {swap endpoints}
            swap(xstart,ystart,xend,yend);
    {plot first point}
    plotpoint(xstart,ystart);
    if abs(m)<1 then
            {increment x values by 1}
            begin {if}
                yr:= ystart;
                for xi  := (xstart + 1) to (xend − 1) do
                    {calculate y and plot points}
                    begin {for}
                        yr  := yr + m;
                        plotpoint(xi,round(yr))
                    end {for}
            end {if}
    else {slope > 1}
            begin {else}
                minverse  := 1/m;
                xr  := xstart;
                for yi  := (ystart + 1) to (yend − 1) do
                    {calculate x and plot points}
                    begin {for}
                        xr  := xr + minverse;
                        plotpoint(round(xr),yi)
                    end {for}
            end; {else}
    {plot last point}
    plotpoint{xend,yend}
end; (Draw_Line)
```

Procedure Swap interchanges the starting and ending points of the line. It is implemented as follows:

```
Procedure Swap (
    x1,y1,                          {first point}
    x2,y2  :  integer);             {second point}

var
    temp  :  integer;                          {for swapping}

begin {Swap}
        temp  := x2;
        x2  := x1;
        x1  := temp;
```

```
        temp  := y2;
        y2    := y1;
        y1    := temp
```

end; {*Swap*}

Figure 2-9 illustrates the use of the simple DDA to plot the line from (2, 2) to (6, 7).

INTEGER DDA

The simple DDA has the disadvantages of using two operations that are expensive in computational time: floating-point addition and the Pascal **round** function. Several good line-drawing algorithms avoid these problems by using only integer arithmetic. We present one of them.

The basic idea of **integer digital differential analyzer** (integer DDA) is to replace the real valued slope by its integer components. That is, the integer values of delta_y = yend − ystart and delta_x = xend − xstart are used in a clever way that avoids floating-point arithmetic.

The algorithm is divided into four cases that depend on the slope of the line. Each case has its own set of rules. We list the rules first and then explain how each works. The error indicates the distance a plotted

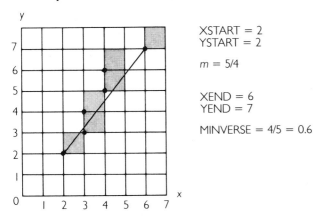

XSTART = 2
YSTART = 2

$m = 5/4$

XEND = 6
YEND = 7

MINVERSE = 4/5 = 0.6

FIGURE 2–9
Simple DDA

ITERATION

1. yr = 3
   xr = 2 + 0.6 = 2.6
   PLOTPOINT (3,3)
2. yr = 4
   xr = 2.6 + 0.6 = 3.2
   PLOTPOINT (3,4)
3. yr = 5
   xr = 3.2 + 0.6 = 3.8
   PLOTPOINT (4,5)
4. yr = 6
   xr = 3.8 + 0.6 = 4.4
   PLOTPOINT (4,6)

point is from the actual line. The endpoints must be ordered as indicated in each case.

CASE 1.
Slope between 0 and 1 with delta_x and delta_y nonnegative:

If the error is negative, plot the point one unit to the right of the previous point and add delta_y to the error; otherwise plot the point located one unit up and one unit to the right of the previous point and add delta_y − delta_x to the error.

CASE 2.
Slope greater than 1 with delta_x and delta_y nonnegative:

If the error is negative, plot the point located one unit up and one unit to the right of the previous point and add delta_y − delta_x to the error; otherwise plot the point one unit up from the previous point and subtract delta_x from the error.

CASE 3.
Slope between − 1 and 0 with delta_y nonnegative and delta_x negative:

If the error is negative, plot the point one unit to the left of the previous point and add delta_y to the error; otherwise plot the point located one unit up and one unit to the left of the previous point and add delta_x + delta_y to the error.

CASE 4.
Slope less than − 1 with delta_y nonnegative and delta_x negative:

If the error is negative, plot the point located one unit up and one unit to the left of the previous point and add delta_x + delta_y to the error; otherwise plot the point one unit up from the previous point and add delta_x to the error.

The error is initialized to 0 and becomes 0 again at the end of the line and whenever a calculated point lies on the actual line. Each case uses the sign of the error differently, and an example for Case 2 should give the reader some insight into the operation of the algorithm.

Figure 2-10 illustrates the actual line and the plotted line (using this algorithm) between the points (2, 2) and (6, 7). Any line satisfying Case 2 goes up (y direction) more than it goes to the right (x direction). The rule says, depending on the error: Plot a point up or diagonally from the previous point. Thus at no time is there more x movement than y movement, which corresponds to a line having slope greater than 1.

The number of points plotted is delta_x + 1 for Cases 1 and 3, and delta_y + 1 for Cases 2 and 4. Procedure Integer_DDA draws a straight line according to this algorithm. It is not necessary to compute

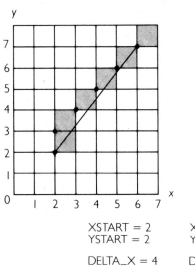

FIGURE 2–10
Integer DDA

XSTART = 2   XEND = 6
YSTART = 2   YEND = 7

DELTA_X = 4   DELTA_Y = 5   DELTA_Y − DELTA_X = 1

ITERATION

1. ERROR = 0
   x = 2
   y = 2 + 1 = 3
   ERROR = 0 − 4 = −4
2. ERROR = −4
   x = 2 + 1 = 3
   y = 3 + 1 = 4
   ERROR = −4 + 1 = −3
3. ERROR = −3
   x = 3 + 1 = 4
   y = 4 + 1 = 5
   ERROR = −3 + 1 = −2
4. ERROR = −2
   x = 4 + 1 = 5
   y = 5 + 1 = 6
   ERROR = −2 + 1 = −1

the slope (a division operation) to decide which case is appropriate. Since delta_y is nonnegative for all cases, we first test this and swap endpoints if delta_y is negative. The starting and ending points of the line are plotted separately since these values are known from the input data.

```
Procedure Integer_DDA (
          xstart,ystart,                {starting point}
          xend,yend : integer);         {ending point}

    var
          delta_x, delta_y,             {rates of change}
          count,                        {number of points}
          error,                        {amount off line}
          x,y : integer;                {plotted points}
```

```
begin
    {initialization}
    error   := 0;
    delta_x  := xend − xstart;
    delta_y  := yend − ystart;
    {is delta_y nonnegative?}
    if delta_y < 0 then
    {swap endpoints}
    begin {if}
        swap(xstart,ystart,xend,yend);
        {change delta values accordingly}
        delta_y  := − delta_y;
        delta_x  := − delta_x
    end; {if}
    plotpoint(xstart,ystart); {first point}
    {initialize x and y values}
    x  := xstart;
    y  := ystart;
    if delta_x >= 0 then
    {Case 1 or Case 2}
        if delta_x >= delta_y then
        {Case 1}
            for count := 1 to delta_x − 1 do
            {plot up to next to last point}
            if error < 0 then
                begin {if}
                    x := x + 1;
                    plotpoint (x,y);
                    error := error + delta_y
                end {if}
            else {error >= 0}
                begin {else}
                    x := x + 1;
                    y := y + 1;
                    plotpoint(x,y);
                    error  := error + delta_y − delta_x
                end {else and for}
        else {Case 2}
            for count  := 1 to delta_y − 1 do
            {plot points}
            if error < 0 then
                begin {if}
                    x   := x + 1;
                    y   := y + 1;
                    plotpoint(x,y);
                    error  := error + delta_y − delta_x
                end {if}
```

```
            else {error >= 0}
                begin {else}
                    y   := y + 1;
                    plotpoint(x,y);
                    error   := error − delta_x
                end {else and for}
    else {Case 3 or Case 4}
        if delta_x >= delta_y then
        {Case 3}
        for count := 1 to delta_x − 1 do
{plot points}
            if error < 0 then
                begin {if}
                    x   := x − 1;
                    plotpoint(x,y);
                    error   := error + delta_y
                end {if}
            else {error > = 0}
                begin {else}
                    x   := x − 1;
                    y   := y + 1;
                    plotpoint(x,y);
                    error   := error + delta_x + delta_y
                end {else and for}
    else {Case 4}
    for count   := 1 to delta_y − 1 do
    {plot points}
    if error < 0 then
        begin {if}
            x   := x − 1;
            y   := y + 1;
            plotpoint(x,y);
            error   := error + delta_x + delta_y
        end {if}
    else {error >= 0}
        begin {else}
            y   := y + 1;
            plotpoint(x,y);
            error   := error + delta_x
        end; {else and for}
        {plot last point}
    plotpoint(xend,yend)
end; {Integer_DDA}
```

LINE-DRAWING PROCEDURES

All graphics display systems have procedures that allow the user to draw a line between two points. Procedures of this type that perform a graphic action are often called "graphic commands" or just "commands." The command

draws(x,y)

draws a straight line, where *x* and *y* are nonnegative integer values representing screen coordinates of the terminal point of the line.

If the **draws**(x,y) command uses only one endpoint of the line, how does the line-drawing procedure know where to start the line? To understand this problem, it is helpful to think of a hypothetical pen that moves around the display screen. Before drawing a line, we must move the pen to the starting position. The command

moves(x,y)

moves this pen to screen location (x, y); *x* and *y* are nonnegative integer values.

As an example, to draw a line from (2, 6) to (15, 120), execute this sequence of commands:

moves(2,6);
draws(15,120).

Before leaving line drawing, we should recall that most lines drawn on a raster display have a jagged or stair-stepped appearance. This is because the points that are plotted must be pixel grid points, and many of these may not lie on the actual line.

2–5 **CIRCLE DRAWING**

Circles are probably the most used curves in elementary graphics. They often serve as building blocks to generate artistic images (Figure 2-11). This section describes several circle-drawing algorithms.

IMPLICIT REPRESENTATION

A circle is specified by the coordinates of its center (xc, yc) and its radius r (Figure 2-12). The most familiar equation of a circle is

(2–4) $\quad (x - xc)^2 + (y - yc)^2 = r^2.$

If the center of the circle is at the origin (0, 0), equation 2-4 reduces to

(2–5) $\quad x^2 + y^2 = r^2.$

Drawing Elementary Figures

FIGURE 2–11
Computer art with
circles

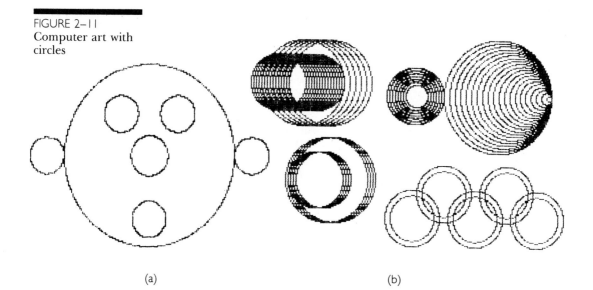

(a)   (b)

Solving equation 2-4 for y,

(2–6) $y = yc \pm \sqrt{r^2 - (x - xc)^2}$.

To draw a circle, increment the x values by one unit from $-r$ to $+r$ and use equation 2-4 to solve for the two y values at each step. It is, of course, necessary to convert to integer values before plotting.

This method of drawing a circle is inefficient for several reasons. First, we are not taking advantage of the symmetry of the circle. Namely, if we have calculated one point to be on a circle, we shall see that seven other points are immediately known to lie on the circle. A second problem is the amount of processing time required to perform the squaring and square root operations repeatedly.

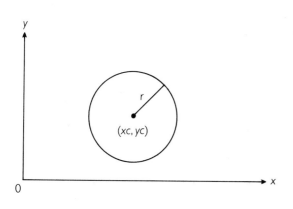

FIGURE 2–12
A representation of
a circle

The third problem is not nearly as obvious. If we plot a quadrant of a circle centered at the origin, we obtain Figure 2-13. From this figure we see that, although the x values are equally spaced (they differ by one unit), the y values are not. The circle is dense and flat near the y-axis, and has large gaps and is steep near the x-axis. An explanation of this requires a knowledge of calculus and is included for those having this background.

For clarity, assume that the center of the circle is at the origin. The change in y value can be related to the change in x value by the (differential) equation $dy = (-x/y)dx$. The change in x, or dx, is fixed at one unit. As x gets closer to zero, the right-hand side of this equation becomes very small, and therefore the change in the y value, or dy, becomes very small. Thus consecutive values of y near the y-axis will be approximately equal. When these y values are rounded off to the nearest integer coordinate, the integer value is the same. This results in the groups of equal y values in Figure 2-13. However, as x gets closer to the radius r, the y values approach zero (since $x^2 + y^2 = r^2$), and dy becomes very large. This accounts for the large gaps between successive y values near $x = r$.

PARAMETRIC POLAR REPRESENTATION

One method of eliminating the problem of plotting points not evenly spaced around the circle is to use the polar representation of a circle:

$$x = xc + r \cos(\theta)$$

$$y = yc + r \sin(\theta)$$

where θ is measured in radians from 0 to 2π. Since the arc length equals $r \times \theta$ and r, the radius, is constant, equal increments of θ, $d\theta$, result in equal spacing (arc length) between successively plotted points (Figure 2-14).

INCREMENTAL DRAWING

One problem of using this polar representation to draw a circle is that, on most microcomputers, the repeated calculation of values for $\cos(\theta)$ and $\sin(\theta)$ consumes a significant amount of processing time. (The new breed of faster processors is eliminating this problem.) We can speed up the computation by using an incremental method that calculates the points on a circle from the coordinates of the previously calculated points, which is what we did in the line-drawing algorithm. This

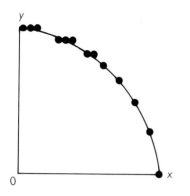

FIGURE 2–13
An unequally
spaced circle with
units × steps

technique requires only an initial calculation of the sine and cosine. Again for clarity of explanation, the center of the circle is placed at the origin.

Two consecutive points $(x1, y1)$ and $(x2, y2)$ on a circle are related by

(2–7)
$$x1 = r \cos(\theta)$$
$$y1 = r \sin(\theta)$$
$$x2 = r \cos(\theta + d\theta)$$
$$y2 = r \sin(\theta + d\theta)$$

where $d\theta$ is a fixed angular step size (Figure 2-12).

Using trigonometry, we get

$$x2 = r \cos(\theta)\cos(d\theta) - r \sin(\theta)\sin(d\theta)$$
$$y2 = r \sin(\theta)\cos(d\theta) + r \cos(\theta)\sin(d\theta).$$

Substituting $x1$ and $y1$ from equations 2-7 we have

(2–8)
$$x2 = x1 \cos(d\theta) - y1 \sin(d\theta)$$
$$y2 = y1 \cos(d\theta) + x1 \sin(d\theta).$$

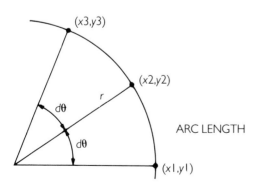

ARC LENGTH

FIGURE 2–14
Equal spacing be-
tween successive
points

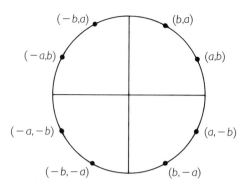

FIGURE 2–15
An eight-way sym-
metry of a circle

These are the incremental equations we want to generate a circle. Starting the circle at $x1 = 0$, $y1 = r$, and fixed-angle increment $d\theta$, we can compute all points on the circle by calculating $\cos d\theta$ only once.

Before using these equations to draw a circle, let's discuss symmetry. If a point (a, b) lies on the circle $x^2 + y^2 = r^2$ centered at the origin, then so do seven other points: $(-a, b)$, $(a, -b)$, $(-a, -b)$, (b, a), $(-b, a)$, $(b, -a)$, $(-b, -a)$, as illustrated in Figure 2-15. (To verify this, substitute all eight points into the circle equation.) We take advantage of this symmetry by calculating values only for one-eighth of a circle, namely an angular interval of 45 degrees. If the first point is at $(0, r)$, the calculations are terminated when $y = x$.

To find the symmetric points on a circle centered at (xc, yc), add xc to the first coordinate and yc to the second coordinate for each of the eight points.

The following procedure, Circle, calculates points on the circle centered about the origin and then adds xc to x values and yc to y values, moving the center to (xc, yc). To make the circle look circular, the y values are multiplied by the aspect ratio before plotting. Since integer screen coordinates are used, the radius is an integer distance from the center of the circle (otherwise use the **round** function). It is desirable to obtain spacing of approximately one unit between adjacent points. This implies that the arc length, $r \times d\theta$; should be one unit; therefore $d\theta$ should be 1/radius. Before we invoke this procedure, we should test that the circle lies within the screen boundaries by using the calling procedure. This is accomplished by comparing $xc \pm r$ and $yc \pm r$ with the maximum and minimum horizontal and vertical screen coordinates, respectively.

```
Procedure Circle(
     xc,yc                              {center of circle}
     radius : integer);                 {radius of circle}

const
     ar = 1.33;                         {aspect ratio}
```

```
var
    dtheta,                                    {angle increment}
    ct,st,                                     {sine and cosine dθ}
    x,y,                                       {computed points}
    xtemp : real;                              {stores old x value}

begin
        {initialization}
        dtheta := 1/radius;
        ct := cos(dtheta);
        st := sin(dtheta);
        {initial coordinates}
        x := 0
        y := radius;
        while y >= x do
        {plot symmetric points}
            begin {while}
                plotpoint(round(xc + x),round(yc + y*ar));
                plotpoint(round(xc − x),round(yc + y*ar));
                plotpoint(round(xc + x),round(yc − y*ar));
                plotpoint(round(xc − x),round(yc − y*ar));
                plotpoint(round(xc + y),round(yc + x*ar));
                plotpoint(round(xc − y),round(yc + x*ar));
                plotpoint(round(xc + y),round(yc − x*ar));
                plotpoint(round(xc − y),round(yc − x*ar));
                {compute new x and y}
                xtemp := x;
                x := (x*ct − y*st);
                y := (y*ct + xtemp*st)
            end {while}
end; {Circle}
```

A circle can also be drawn by using many small line segments. By setting the number of line segments equal to a constant times the radius, larger circles will look as smooth as smaller ones. In general, the greater the value of the constant multiplier, the smoother the circle (more and smaller line segments). Figure 2-16a on page 52 illustrates a circle with 10 line segments. Figure 2-16b is the same circle produced by procedure Circ_Draw, which has a constant multiplier of 16, resulting in 16 × radius number of line segments.

```
Procedure Circ_Draw (xc,yc,radius:integer);

    const
        two_Pi = 6.28318;

    var
        dtheta,ct,st: real;
        count,x,y,xtemp : integer;
```

FIGURE 2–16
Circles composed of
different numbers
of line segments

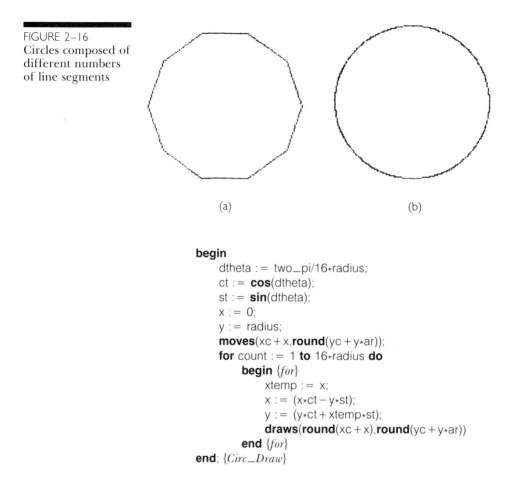

(a)   (b)

```
begin
    dtheta := two_pi/16*radius;
    ct := cos(dtheta);
    st := sin(dtheta);
    x := 0;
    y := radius;
    moves(xc + x,round(yc + y*ar));
    for count := 1 to 16*radius do
        begin {for}
            xtemp := x;
            x := (x*ct − y*st);
            y := (y*ct + xtemp*st);
            draws(round(xc + x),round(yc + y*ar))
        end {for}
end; {Circ_Draw}
```

BRESENHAM'S CIRCLE ALGORITHM

A particularly efficient circle-generating algorithm was developed by J. Bresenham. Values of a circle centered at the origin are computed in the 45-degree sector from $x = 0$ to $x = $ radius$/\sqrt{2}$. The remaining seven sectors are obtained from the eight-point symmetry of the circle.

By examining Figure 2-17 we notice that the y values are decreasing as x increases from $x = 0$ to $x = r/\sqrt{2}$. Therefore, if $(0, r)$ is the starting point of the algorithm, then, as x increases by one unit (pixel), the corresponding y value either remains the same or is decreased by one unit. In particular, if (x_i, y_i) is a pixel on the circle, the next pixel describing the circle is either A or B:

A: $(x_i + 1, y_i)$; to the right of the previous point
B: $(x_i + 1, y_i - 1)$; down and to the right of the previous point.

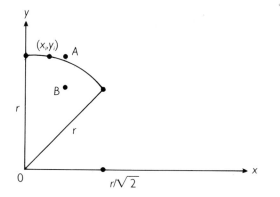

FIGURE 2–17
Pixel choices for
Bresenham's
algorithm

The algorithm now proceeds to choose pixel A or B by finding and comparing the distances from each pixel to the point on the circle that has x value of $x_i + 1$. Since these distances measure how far from the circle each pixel is, the pixel with the smallest distance is the best approximation to the circle.

The square of the distance of pixel A from the center of the circle (the origin in this case) is

$$(x_i + 1)^2 + y_i^2.$$

From this we are able to conclude that the difference between this squared distance and the squared distance to the closest point on the circle is

$$d(A) = (x_i + 1)^2 + y_i^2 - r^2.$$

Similarly, for pixel B we obtain the equation

$$d(B) = (x_i + 1)^2 + (y_i - 1)^2 - r^2.$$

A point lies on the circle if its d value equals 0. According to the previous discussion, we want to choose whichever pixel, A or B, has the smallest d value. To do this we actually examine the sum

$$s = d(A) + d(B).$$

There are three cases to consider. Refer to Figure 2-17.

1. If the circle goes between A and B, then $d(A) > 0$ and $d(B) < 0$. If **abs**$(d(A)) >$ **abs**$(d(B))$, then B should be chosen since it lies closer to the circle. In this case $s > 0$. If, however, **abs**$(d(A)) <=$ **abs**$(d(B))$, then A should be chosen and $s <= 0$.
2. If the circle goes through or above A, then $d(A) <= 0$ and $d(B) < 0$. Here, A is obviously the better choice and $s < 0$.
3. If the circle goes through B or below B, then $d(A) > 0$ and $d(B) >= 0$. Here B is the better choice and $s > 0$.

From these cases we arrive at the following rule: If $s > 0$ choose pixel B; otherwise choose pixel A. The implementation of Bresenham's algorithm is left as an exercise for the reader.

2–6 ELLIPSES

An ellipse is a variation of a circle. Stretching a circle in one direction produces an ellipse. We shall examine only ellipses that are stretched in the x or y direction. The polar equations for this type of ellipse centered at (xc, yc) are

$$(2\text{–}9) \quad \begin{aligned} x &= xc + a \times \cos(\theta) \\ y &= yc + b \times \sin(\theta) \end{aligned}$$

where the angle θ assumes values between 0 and 2π radians (Figure 2-18).

The values of a and b affect the shape of the ellipse. If $b > a$, the ellipse is longer in the y direction. If $b < a$, the ellipse is longer in the x direction. The ellipse can be drawn using four-point symmetry: If (c, d) lies on the ellipse, so do the points $(-c, d)$, $(c, -d)$, and $(-c, -d)$.

The following incremental equations for an ellipse are derived from equations 2-9:

$$(2\text{–}10) \quad \begin{aligned} x2 &= x1 \cos(d\theta) - (a/b)y1 \sin(d\theta) \\ y2 &= y1 \cos(d\theta) - (b/a)x1 \sin(d\theta). \end{aligned}$$

Procedure Circ_Draw can be modified to plot an ellipse by initializing x to 0 and y to b and replacing the circle equations by equations 2-10. In fact, procedure Circ_Draw can draw an ellipse simply by changing the aspect ratio. This is left as an exercise for the reader.

FIGURE 2–18
An ellipse with major axis a and minor axis b

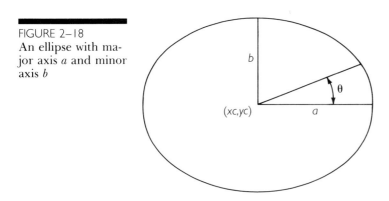

Drawing Elementary Figures

2-7 **APPLICATIONS**

SPIRALS

A spiral is another variation of a circle. Spirals can be plotted by gradually increasing the radius when plotting a circle. Procedure Spiral produces the spiral in Figure 2-19 using the parametric equations of the circle. It does this by incrementing the radius while incrementing the polar angle. The initial and final values of the radius, 10 and 50, respectively, are arbitrary and affect the size and number of loops in the spiral. Figure 2-20 illustrates another spiral—one with constant radial increment of two units and an angle increment of 1.5 radians.

```
Procedure Spiral;
var
      theta,                          {angle}
      xinit,yinit,                    {initial points}
      x,y : real;                     {subsequent points}
      xc,yc,                          {center}
      radius : integer;               {changing radius}

begin
      radius := 10;                   {initial value}
      theta := 0;                     {initial value}
      {compute initial points}
      xinit := radius*cos(theta);
      yinit := radius*sin(theta);
```

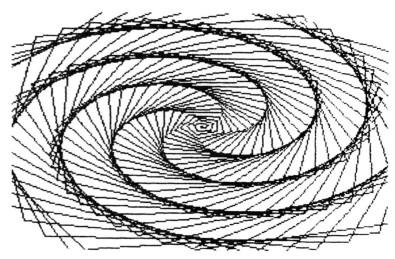

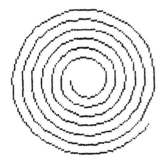

FIGURE 2–19
A spiral

FIGURE 2–20
A spiral with radius incremented two units and an angle changing by 1.5 radians

```
{move to initial point}
moves(round(xc + xinit),round(yc + yinit));
{compute remaining points}
while radius < 50 do
  begin {while}
    theta := theta + 0.1;          {increment theta}
    radius := radius + 0.1;        {increment radius}
    {subsequent points}
    x := radius*cos(theta);
    y := radius*sin(theta);
    {draw from previous point}
    draws(round(xc + x),round(yc + y))
  end {while}
end; {Spiral}
```

MOIRE PATTERN

Moire patterns are wavy patterns that occur naturally as interference waves. They are caused by viewing similar patterns at slightly different distances or angles. Moire patterns can be strikingly beautiful while retaining their characteristic mirrored image look (Figures 2-1 and 2-21).

These patterns can be computer-generated by taking advantage of the jagged lines that are produced with a raster display. Lines that differ from each other by a small shift produce these wavy patterns. In fact, almost any geometric shape that is repeatedly drawn and then displaced by a small distance or angle can generate a Moire effect. Many fascinating Moire patterns can be drawn through trial and error.

The following program Moire uses circles to produce the moire pattern in Figure 2-21. The idea is simple. Draw closely spaced concentric circles, shift the radius to the left, and then redraw the concentric circles.

```
Program Moire;

const
    xcenter = 300;                  {center of}
    ycenter = 200;                  {display screen}
    increment = 2;                  {difference between radii}
    maxradius = 40;                 {largest radius}

var
    x,y : integer;                  {points for lines}
Procedure Concentric (
        xc,yc,      {center}
        radius: integer);
{Draws concentric circles}
```

```
begin     {Concentric}
while radius < maxradius do
    begin     {while}
        circ_draw(xc,yc,radius);
        radius := radius + increment
    end     {while}
end;     {Concentric}

begin     {Moire}
    Concentric(xcenter,ycenter,4)
    {shift circles}
    xcenter := xcenter − 10;
    Concentric(xcenter,ycenter)
end.     {Moire}
```

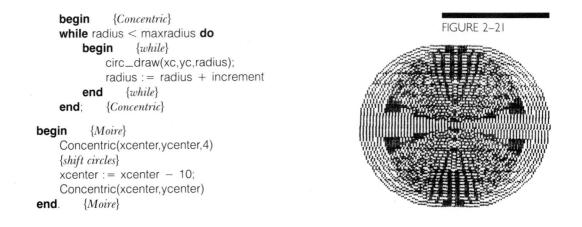

FIGURE 2–21

2–8 CONCLUSION

Many images can be created using point-plotting and line-drawing procedures. The speed at which graphic images are produced is affected by the capability of the computer and the efficiency of the scan conversion–drawing algorithms. Since floating-point multiplication and division can take as much as 200 times longer than integer addition, graphics-drawing procedures should use integer arithmetic whenever possible.

EXERCISES

1. Compute the aspect ratio for your display screen and printer. Use this ratio to draw a circle and a square.
2. Draw your initials on graph paper and write a program to display them using line-drawing commands.
3. Modify procedure Circ_Draw to draw an ellipse.
4. Generate a Moire pattern using lines and ellipses.
5. Construct the Moire patterns in Figure 2-1 by drawing lines from any point inside the cirle to the circumference of the circle. If possible, alternate the color of the line between successive draws.
6. Procedure Integer_DDA initializes the error to zero. This often results in lines that "jump" after plotting the initial point. Smooth out the line by initializing the error to delta_x/2 if **abs**(slope) < 1. What should the error be initialized to if **abs**(slope) > 1?
7. Derive equation 2-10.
8. Implement Bresenham's circle algorithm. Try to find an incremental equation relating successive s values.

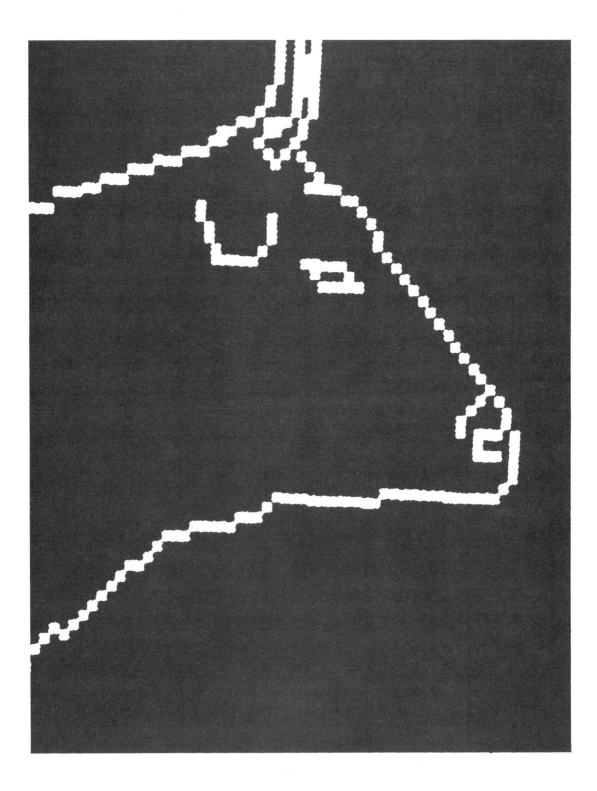

Detail of Figure 3–24b

3
GRAPHICS FUNDAMENTALS

3–1 INTRODUCTION

In the previous chapter we described several graphics algorithms for lines and circles that generated the image using the coordinate system of the display screen; the x and y coordinates are integers with values within the horizontal and vertical screen boundaries.

For many applications this coordinate system is too restrictive. As an example, assume a map designer using a computer-aided design system wants to draw a map of the United States. The best coordinate system might be one with the origin in the middle of the map and coordinate values ranging from -1000 to 1000 in both the horizontal and vertical directions. Furthermore, while drawing the Rocky Mountains, the designer may want to work with an enlarged display of only the Rocky Mountain states.

A graphics display system having these capabilities gives both the application programmer and the end user additional control of the display screen. A user can choose a suitable coordinate system and display the image or portion of a scaled image anywhere on the display screen. Figure 3-1, for example, illustrates partial interior and exterior views of a sports car displayed on different parts of the screen. This chapter discusses the concepts and algorithms needed for this enhanced graphics display system. The last section has several programs illustrating the use of these features.

3–2 DISPLAY SCREEN VIEWING

In the world we live in, different objects have their own units. A clock uses the values 1 to 12 for hours and 1 to 60 for minutes and seconds. A computer measures execution speed in millionths and billionths of seconds. We would like to be able to choose a coordinate system that enables us to describe an object in terms of its natural units. Once we have chosen this coordinate system and·described the image using it, we then use an algorithm to transform this image to a region of the display screen.

WINDOWS AND CLIPPING

A **world coordinate system** is a user-defined coordinate system chosen for a specific application. These screen-independent coordinates can have a large or small numeric range, negative values, and fractions—whatever helps to describe the image in the most natural way. Further-

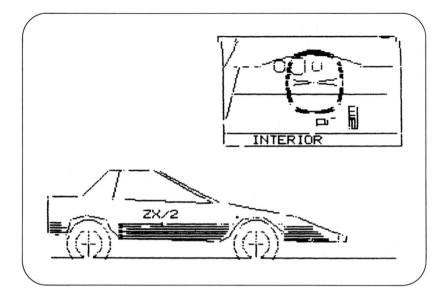

FIGURE 3–1
A display screen of
the interior and ex-
terior of an
automobile

more, sometimes the complete image described in the world coordinate system is too complicated to be viewed clearly on the display screen. The user may want to view (and enlarge) only a portion of the image. This capability of displaying part of the image, enclosed in a rectangular region, is called **windowing**. The rectangular region is called a **window** (Figure 3-2).

Different parts of the image are displayed by placing a window

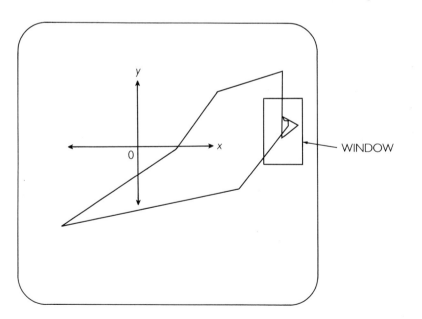

FIGURE 3–2
A window inside an
entire world coordi-
nate space

FIGURE 3–3
A display of the
window in Figure
3–2

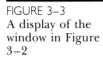

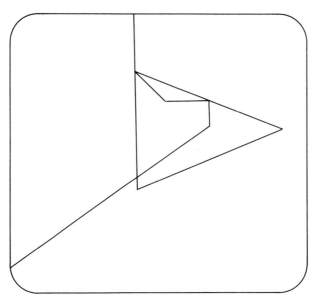

Display screen

around different portions of the world coordinate system. Adjusting the size of the window has the effect of enlarging, shrinking, or even distorting a portion of the image or the entire image. A small window surrounding part of the image enlarges that subimage. Figure 3-3 illustrates the effect of displaying the contents inside the window of Figure 3-2. Choosing a window whose width is greater than its length gives a different appearance to the same subimage. (Compare Figure 3-3 and Figure 3-4.) The entire image is displayed if the window surrounds the image. A window larger than the image reduces the size of the displayed image (Figure 3-5).

The portion of the image lying outside the window is not displayed. The process of cutting away the image at the window's boundaries is

FIGURE 3–4
Changing the di-
mensions of a win-
dow producing a
different image

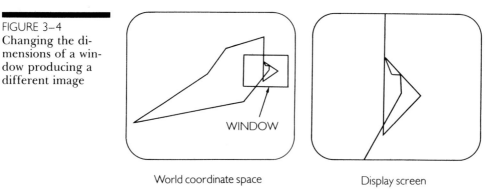

World coordinate space   Display screen

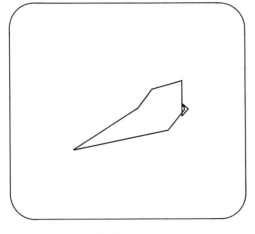

FIGURE 3–5
A large window
around the entire
object

Display screen

called **clipping**. If clipping is not performed correctly, the wraparound
effect can occur.

VIEWPORT

Sometimes we want to display different portions or views of the
image in different regions of the screen. A rectangular region of the
screen where the contents of the window are displayed is called a **viewport** (Figure 3-6). Using the same window and several viewports, the
same object can be placed in different regions (viewports) of the display
screen. Choosing different windows as well as viewports results in a

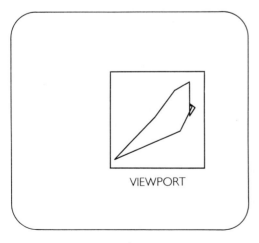

FIGURE 3–6
A viewport near the
center of the screen

VIEWPORT

Display screen

FIGURE 3–7
Three different
viewports on one
screen

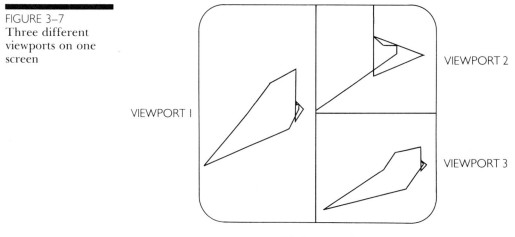

VIEWPORT 1

VIEWPORT 2

VIEWPORT 3

Display screen

screen with multiple images. Many word processors and video games use this technique. In Figure 3-7, viewports 1 and 3 display the entire image using the same window. Viewport 2 displays the contents of the window in Figure 3-2. Observe how the size of the viewport affects the size of the image.

PANNING

Moving a window around the world coodinate image allows the user to view different portions of the image. The location and size of the window can be controlled interactively using a suitable input device such as a joystick. This moving window operation is called **panning**, a process implemented in either hardware or software.

The hardware implementation stores the entire image in a frame buffer memory that is much larger than the dimensions of the display screen. For example, a display screen with dimensions 512×512 can have a corresponding frame buffer with dimensions 1024×1024. As a screen-size window roams about this large memory, it sends to the display controller the present location of the window, and only the window's contents are displayed on the screen. The low cost of memory is making this implementation attractive for many graphics display systems.

With software, panning is achieved by the following sequence: Draw the windowed image, erase it, move the window, draw the new windowed image. All these steps must be performed fast enough so that the panning motion is smooth. Presently, most low-cost display systems do not have this capability; erasing and drawing take too long. It will be interesting to see if the new generation of microcomputer graphics display systems implement panning with more memory (hardware solution), with more powerful processors (software solution), or with a combination of both.

NORMALIZED DEVICE COORDINATES

While it is possible to describe the viewport in terms of the coordinates of the display screen, it is better to use a device-independent coordinate system called **normalized device coordinates (NDC)**. These units vary from system to system. Some use real numbers having both x and y values ranging from 0 to 1, with the origin at the lower-left corner (Figure 3-8a); others have x and y values ranging from -1 to 1, with the origin at the screen center (Figure 3-8b), while others use units that agree with the display screen aspect ratio (Figure 3-8c).

The NDC system allows the application programmer to write graphics programs independent of the resolution of the display screen, thereby increasing the portability of the programs. The display system has a device driver (hardware or software procedure) that converts NDC units to screen (device) units

3–3 DRAWING IN WORLD COORDINATES

An image in the two-dimensional world coordinate system is composed of points and lines. Only those portions of the image that are contained within the window are displayed within the viewport. This section describes some of the graphics commands that support world coordinate drawing.

POINT AND LINE-DRAWING COMMANDS

As with the screen coordinate system, it is convenient to think of a pen being moved about the world coordinate space drawing lines between points. The following graphics commands (Pascal procedures)

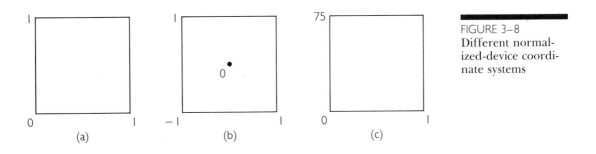

FIGURE 3–8
Different normalized-device coordinate systems

move this pen around. All the operands are in world coordinates.

point2(x,y)

illuminates the point (x, y).

move2(x,y)

moves the pen to position (x, y). No visible drawing is performed.

rmove2(dx,dy)

is a relative move that moves the pen away from the current pen position (x, y) to a new pen position $(x + dx, y + dy)$. No drawing is performed.

draw2(x,y)

draws a line from the current pen position to position (x, y).

rdraw2(dx,dy)

is a relative draw that draws a line from the current pen position (x, y) to a new position $(x + dx, y + dy)$.

rect(x1,y1,x2,y1)

draws a rectangle with sides parallel to the x and y axes. The coordinate pair $(x1, y1)$ is one corner, and the coordinate pair $(x2, y2)$ is the diagonally opposite corner of the rectangle.

EXAMPLE

A square, with lower-left corner at (1, 2) and with sides equal to one unit, can be displayed by invoking the command

rect(1,2,2,3)

The same rectangle is drawn with the sequence:

move2(1,2);	{*lower left corner*}
rdraw2(1,0);	{*bottom*}
rdraw2(0,1);	{*right side*}
rdraw2(− 1,0);	{*top*}
rdraw2(0,− 1);	{*left side*}

VIEWING COMMANDS

window(left,right,bottom,top)

defines the rectangular window having lower-left coordinates (left, bottom) and upper-right coordinates (right, top). The four operands (left, right, bottom, top) are in world coordinate units.

viewport(left,right,bottom,top)

defines the the rectangular viewport having lower-left coordinates (left, bottom) and upper-right coordinates (right, top). The four operands are in normalized-device-coordinate (NDC) units.

The application programmer must invoke both the window and viewport procedures (commands) before using the line-drawing commands. Changing a window or viewport after a picture is drawn has no effect on the displayed picture. Some graphics packages have default window/viewport settings, but it's best to set them according to your specific needs.

In Chapter 2 we saw that in order to draw a box that looked square, it is necessary to multiply the y coordinates by the aspect ratio. The user can have the graphics system do this by choosing a square window with viewport parameters satisfying the condition:

$$\frac{(\text{right} - \text{left})}{(\text{top} - \text{bottom})} = \text{aspect ratio}.$$

Each time a new image is drawn, it is necessary to erase the display screen. The graphics command

fillscreen(black)

erases the current viewport (it is filled with the background color black). To clear the entire screen, set the viewport equal to the screen's NDC units before erasing.

The graphics command

fillscreen(reverse)

reverses the color of the black-and-white pixels of the current viewport.

The graphics command

frame

draws a rectangle just inside the viewport. It is most often used to "frame" an image.

PROGRAMMING EXAMPLE

To illustrate some of these graphics commands, program Illustrate produces the multiple window/viewport image of Figure 3-7. NDC units range from 0 to 1 in both horizontal and vertical directions.

Program Illustrate;

Procedure Saw;
{*describe image in world coordinates*}

```
begin      {Saw}
    move2(0,0);
    draw2(5,7);
    draw2(10,10);
    draw2(10,1);
    rdraw2(1,1);
    rdraw2(-1,1);
    rdraw2(0.2,-0.5);
    rdraw2(0.3,0);
    rdraw2(0,-0.4);
    rdraw2(-4,-7);
    draw2(-10,-10);
    draw2(0,0)
end;       {Saw}

begin      {Illustrate}
    viewport(0,1,0,1);              {set viewport to}
    fillscreen(black);             {erase entire screen}
    window(-15,15,-15,15);         {entire image}
    viewport(0,0.5,0,1.0);         {left half}
    saw;                           {draw image}
    window(9,12,-1,4);             {triangular part}
    viewport(0.5,1,0.5,1.0);       {top right}
    saw;                           {draw image}
    window(-15,15,-15,15);         {entire image}
    viewport(0.5,1,0,0.5);         {bottom right}
    saw                            {draw image}
end.       {Illustrate}
```

3-4 WINDOW-TO-VIEWPORT MAPPING

An image defined in a world coordinate system is viewed through a window and displayed on a portion of the screen, the viewport. The **window-to-viewport mapping** is a transformation function that converts from world coordinates to normalized device coordinates; that is, it transforms a coordinate pair (a, b) in world coordinates to a coordinate pair (a', b') in normalized device coordinates. It produces one specific view of the image. To change this view, we must change the window and/or the viewport and reinvoke this mapping.

The window and the viewport can each be described by the coordinate value of the lower-left vertex of its defining rectangle and the rectangle's height and length. The window's rectangle has lower-left world coordinates

$$x = wx, y = wy.$$

The height is wh and the length wl (Figure 3-9a).

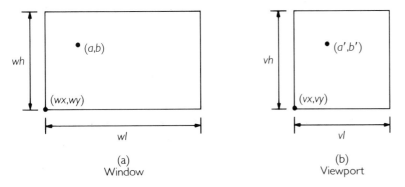

FIGURE 3–9
Window-to-viewport
mapping

(a)
Window

(b)
Viewport

The viewport's rectangle has lower-left NDC

$$x = vx, y = vy.$$

The height is vh and length is vl (Figure 3-9b).

The window-to-viewport mapping sends a point (a, b) lying within the window to normalized device coordinates (a', b') within the viewport, satisfying the following conditions:

1. The distance of a' to the left edge of the viewport rectangle divided by the length of the viewport rectangle equals the distance of a to the left edge of the window rectangle divided by the length of the window rectangle. Namely,

$$\frac{(a' - vx)}{vl} = \frac{(a - wx)}{wl}.$$

Solving for a' we get

$$(3\text{–}1) \quad a' = (vl/wl)(a - wx) + vx.$$

2. The distance of b' to the bottom edge of the viewport rectangle divided by the height of the viewport rectangle equals the distance of b to the bottom edge of the window rectangle divided by the height of the window rectangle. Namely,

$$\frac{(b' - vy)}{vh} = \frac{(b - wy)}{wh}.$$

Solving for b' we get

$$(3\text{–}2) \quad b' = (vh/wh)(b - wy) + vy.$$

Equations 3-1 and 3-2 make up the window-to-viewport mapping.

Since this mapping must be performed often, we should look for ways to reduce the time and frequency of these computations. Examining these equations, we immediately observe that the two ratios

$$vl/wl \quad \text{and} \quad vh/wh$$

are the same for all points. Thus, they need be computed only once, thereby eliminating repeated divisions, a slow process on many computers.

3–5 **CLIPPING**

Placing the rectangular window in the image renders parts of the picture invisible (Figure 3-10). **Clipping** is the process that determines the visible portion of the image lying inside the window. The points (and lines) that survive clipping are sent to the viewport by the window-to-viewport mapping.

POINT CLIPPING

Let's first examine a straightforward method of performing the task of clipping. A point (x, y) is within the rectangular window if the x coordinate lies between the left and right sides of the rectangle and the y coordinate lies between the bottom and top of the rectangle:

xleft $<= x <=$ xright   and   ybottom $<= y <=$ ytop.

It is possible to test these inequalities for each point in the image. However, there are two reasons why we do not want to do this. The first is that an image defined in the world coordinate system may be large and complex, requiring the performance of this test for many points, which is a time-consuming process. The second, and more pressing problem, is that an image is usually not defined by the points making up the image, but rather is defined in terms of lines. That is, an image is defined by giving only the endpoints of lines (Figure 3-11). It is unreasonable to try to determine the (infinite number of) points in world space that lie between the endpoints. It's best to compute the endpoints of the line segments that lie in the window and send these points via the mapping function to normalized device coordinates. We then compute

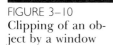

FIGURE 3–10
Clipping of an object by a window

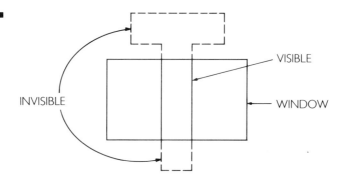

Graphics Fundamentals

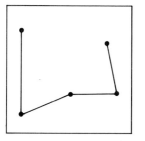

FIGURE 3–11
An image defined
by endpoints

those normalized coordinates that lie between the endpoints. Line-clipping algorithms accomplish this by examining line segments instead of points.

LINE CLIPPING

Figure 3-12 illustrates some of the different possible ways a line segment may or may not intersect the window. Line segment *ab* is entirely within the window and is displayed, lines *ef* and *ij* lie outside the window and are not displayed. Line segment *cd* has one endpoint outside the window and is partially displayed by clipping the line segment at *d′*. Line segment *gh* has both endpoints outside the window, yet the segment *g′h′* is displayed. By convention, any line on a window edge is displayed.

Since complex images can be composed of thousands of line segments, it is necessary to have a line-clipping procedure that efficiently processes line segments. There are two trivial cases. First, line segments that have both endpoints within the window—for example, *ab*—must be

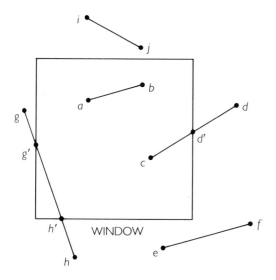

FIGURE 3–12
Different line segments intersecting a window

immediately recognized as being visible. Second, segments that are obviously outside the window should immediately be discarded. Line segments *ef* and *ij* have the property that both endpoints have y value below (above) ybottom (ytop) or have x value to the right (left) of xright (xleft). There are several good line-clipping algorithms available that take advantage of these situations. We shall describe one of them, the Cohen–Sutherland algorithm, which presents a clever method for efficiently recognizing the two trivial cases. Its elegance has led to its widespread implementation in both hardware and software.

3–6 COHEN–SUTHERLAND CLIPPING ALGORITHM

RULES

The algorithm begins by dividing the world coordinate system into nine regions. These regions are obtained by extending the borders of the window (Figure 3-13).

An endpoint of a line segment lies in only one of these nine regions. Any point that lies on an extended border will be considered to lie on the window side of that border. For example, an endpoint on the border between regions 1 and 8 will be considered to lie in region 8, an endpoint lying on the border between 5 and 6 will be counted as being in region 6. Any point on the window border is considered to lie within the window.

FIGURE 3–13
An extended window for intersection calculations

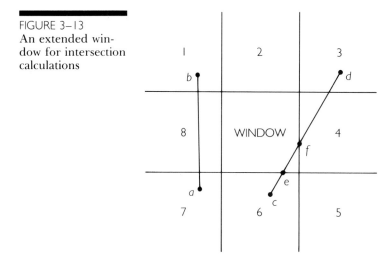

Graphics Fundamentals

Using this scheme, each endpoint can be described in relationship to its direction with respect to the window (Figure 3-13). Points in

region 0 are   inside window
region 1 are   left, top
region 2 are   top
region 3 are   right, top
region 4 are   right
region 5 are   right, bottom
region 6 are   bottom
region 7 are   left, bottom
region 8 are   left

The two trivial cases are:

1. A line segment is visible if both endpoints lie within the window.
2. A line segment is invisible if the endpoints lie in regions that have at least one direction equal. For example, line *ab* is invisible since endpoint *a* lies in region 7 and endpoint *b* lies in region 1 and the direction "left" is common to both regions.

If neither of the two trivial cases is satisfied, the line is subdivided by finding the point of intersection of the line segment with an extended window edge. Each of the four directions is tested in the order: left, right, top, bottom. The part of the line that is clearly outside the window is discarded. The remaining line segment is tested for the trivial cases. This process is repeated until either case 1 or case 2 is satisfied for the remaining line segment. If case 1 is satisfied, part of the line segment is visible, whereas if case 2 is satisfied, the entire line is invisible.

EXAMPLE

To see how this all fits together, let's go through the eight steps necessary to clip line *cd* in Figure 3-13.

1. Clearly neither case 1 nor case 2, the two trivial cases, is satisfied for line segment *cd*.
2. Starting with endpoint *c*, having direction "bottom" in region 6, intersect the line with the bottom edge to obtain the new endpoint *e*.
3. Line segment *ce* is discarded.
4. Line segment *ed* does not satisfy either of the trivial cases.
5. Since endpoint *e* lies within the window, start with endpoint *d*.
6. Since endpoint *d* has directions "right" and "top", and our testing order checks for right before top, intersect *ed* with the right edge

to get the new endpoint f.

7. Line segment fd is discarded.
8. Line segment ef does satisfy case 1 and is therefore displayed.

MATHEMATICS PRELIMINARIES

To calculate the point of intersection of the line segment with the extended window border, the point-slope formula for a line is used. Let's review this equation. If m is the slope of the line segment between points $(x1, y1)$ and $(x2, y2)$, then if $x1 \neq x2$

$$m = \frac{(y2 - y1)}{(x2 - x1)},$$

and for any other point (x, y) on the line

$$\frac{(y - y1)}{(x - x1)} = m.$$

If the line segment crosses a left or right window edge, then $x1 \neq x2$ and the slope m has a nonzero denominator. Similarly, if the line crosses a top or bottom window edge, then $y1 \neq y2$ and the reciprocal of the slope, $1/_m$, has a nonzero denominator.

In the line-clipping algorithm, the slope m is obtained from the two given endpoints. If we are testing against a left or right direction, the x value is known—namely, the left or right edge value. This x value is substituted into the equation for y:

$$y = m \times (x - x1) + y1.$$

Similarly, if we are testing against a top or bottom, the y value is known and is substituted into the equation for x:

$$x = 1/_m \times (y - y1) + x1.$$

IMPLEMENTATION

Several different data structures can be used to implement this algorithm. We shall use the Pascal set construct. Each endpoint has an associated set containing the directions corresponding to the region the point lies in. An endpoint lying in the window is assigned the empty set. The following Pascal environment creates this data structure:

```
type
    direction = set of (left,right,top,bottom);
var
    endpoint : direction;
```

Procedure Region examines an endpoint and assigns to it the correct direction. This is done by comparing the endpoint with the window boundaries, which are denoted by **leftwindow, rightwindow, bottomwindow, topwindow**.

```
Procedure Region (
    xend,yend:real; {endpoint}
    var endpoint : direction);

    begin
        endpoint := []; {initialize to the empty set}
        if xend < leftwindow then {left edge}
            endpoint := [left]
        else
            if xend > rightwindow then {right edge}
                endpoint := [right];
        if yend < bottomwindow then {top edge}
            endpoint := endpoint + [bottom]
        else
            if yend > topwindow then {bottom edge}
                endpoint := endpoint + [top]
    end; {Region}
```

The next four clipping procedures use the appropriate point-slope equation to find the intersection point of the line segment and extended window border. The new endpoint (point of intersection) is designated by (x, y). The slope and inverse slope of the line are defined by:

```
var
    m,                          {slope}
    minverse : real;            {inverse slope = 1/m}

Procedure Clip_Left(var x,y : real);
{left edge}

    begin
        y := m*(leftwindow − x1) + y1;
        x := leftwindow
    end;    {Clip_Left}

Procedure Clip_Right(var x,y : real);
{right edge}

    begin
        y := m*(rightwindow − x1) + y1;
        x := rightwindow
    end;    {Clip_Right}

Procedure Clip_Bottom(var x,y : real);
{bottom edge}
```

```
      begin
            x := minverse*(bottomwindow − y1) + x1;
            y := bottomwindow
      end;    {Clip_Bottom}

   Procedure Clip_Top(var x,y : real);
   {top edge}

      begin
            x := minverse*(topwindow − y1) + x1;
            y := topwindow
      end;    {Clip_Top}
```

The main procedure, Clipping, has the endpoints of the line as its formal parameters. It begins by determining the region for each endpoint. If both regions are the empty set, the line is within the window and is displayed; otherwise, it then checks if both points have a direction in common. If they do, the line is invisible and the procedure is exited. If the line is not invisible, the slope or inverse slope of the line is computed.

In this last case, at least one endpoint of the line segment must have a nonempty direction, and the line is intersected with an extended border whose direction is in this endpoint's region. The point of intersection is obtained by a call to one of the boundary-clipping algorithms. The exterior portion of the line segment is discarded, and the point of intersection is the new endpoint of the remaining line segment. The direction of this new endpoint is determined (procedure Region) and the steps in the boundary-clipping algorithms are repeated until only the visible segment remains.

```
   Procedure Clipping (
         x1,y1,x2,y2 : real    {endpoints});

      var
            x,y        : real;              {point of intersection}
            dir,                            {nonempty direction}
            dir1,dir2 : direction;          {endpoint's direction}

      begin
            {obtain directions}
            Region(x1,y1,dir1);
            Region(x2,y2,dir2);
            {compute once outside loop}
            if x1 <> x2 then
                  m := (y2−y1)/(x2−x1);
            if y2 <> y1 then
                  minverse := (x2−x1)/(y2−y1)
            while (dir1 <> []) or (dir2 <> []) do
                  begin    {while}
                        if dir1*dir2 <> [] then
```

```
                    {direction in common—invisible line}
                    exit(Clipping);
                {dir has direction of discarded endpoint}
                if dir1 = [] then
                    begin     {if}
                        dir := dir2;
                        x := x2;
                        y := y2
                    end     {if}
                else
                    begin     {else}
                        dir := dir1;
                        x := x1;
                        y := y1
                    end;     {else}
                {clip against only one edge at a time}
                if left in dir then Clip_Left(x,y)
                else
                if right in dir then Clip_Right(x,y)
                else
                if bottom in dir then Clip_Bottom(x,y)
                else
                if top in dir then Clip_Top(x,y);
                {update the endpoint and direction}
                if dir = dir1 then
                    begin     {if}
                        x1 := x;
                        y1 := y;
                        Region (x1,y1,dir1)
                    end {if}
                else
                    begin     {else}
                        x2 := x;
                        y2 := y;
                        Region (x2,y2,dir2)
                    end     {else}
            end;     {while}
            {draw visible line segment}
            move2(x1,y1);
            draw2(x2,y2)
    end;     {Clipping}
```

3–7 POLYGON CLIPPING

Line clipping is acceptable when the output can be a set of disconnected line segments. There are, however, situations in which a polygon clipped against a window should result in one or more polygons. For example, a region that is to be shaded must have a closed boundary. Figures 3-14a–3-14d illustrate two polygons and the results of polygon clipping. Observe that those line segments in the clipped polygon that coincide with the window boundary would not appear if line clipping were used.

The Sutherland–Hodgman polygon-clipping algorithm clips a polygon against each edge of the window, one at a time. Specifically, for each window edge it inputs a list of vertices and outputs a new list of vertices, which is submitted to the algorithm for clipping against the next window edge. The input list is a sequence of consecutive vertices of the polygon obtained from the previous edge clipping. The first window edge has as input the original set of vertices. After clipping against the last edge, the output list consists of the vertices describing the clipped polygon.

The algorithm tests a pair of consecutive vertices against a window edge. There are four possible cases, as illustrated in Figure 3-15 where

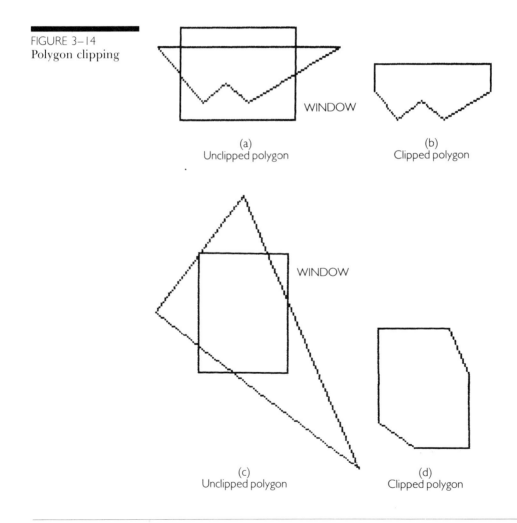

FIGURE 3–14
Polygon clipping

WINDOW

(a)
Unclipped polygon

(b)
Clipped polygon

WINDOW

(c)
Unclipped polygon

(d)
Clipped polygon

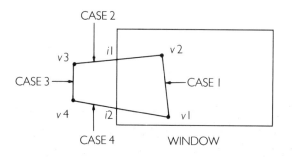

FIGURE 3–15
Clipping against the
left edge of the
window

testing is performed against the left edge. The sample polygon has vertices {$v1$, $v2$, $v3$, $v4$}. Case 1 has the first and second vertices, $v1$ and $v2$, inside the window and the second vertex, $v2$, is sent to the output list. Case 2 has the first vertex, $v2$, inside and the second vertex, $v3$, outside the window. The point of intersection, $i1$, of the side of the polygon joining the vertices and the edge is added to the output list. Case 3 has both vertices, $v3$ and $v4$, outside the window and no point is output. Case 4 has the first vertex, $v4$, outside and the second vertex, $v1$, inside the window. The point of intersection, $i2$, and the second vertex, $v1$, are added to the output list. The result of this left clipping is the transformation of the input list {$v1$, $v2$, $v3$, $v4$} to the output list {$v2$, $i1$, $i2$, $v1$}. Figure 3-16 on page 80 illustrates successive clips against four clip boundaries.

Procedure Suth_Hodg performs polygon clipping. It is invoked four times, once for each window edge. The array variables polyin and polyout are the input and output polygon lists, respectively. The integer variable *lngth* is the number of vertices in the polyin array. Procedure Intersect is used to determine the intersection point of the line between two vertices and the clip edge. Its implementation is left as an exercise. Procedure Out and function Inside are also used, and their implementations follow.

Assume the following Pascal environment:

type

```
vertex = record
              x,y :real
         end;

varray = array[1..25] of vertex;     {vertex list}

bdy = record
              limit : real;     {window edge value}
              side : (top, bottom, left, right)
         end;
```

Function Inside (pt : vertex; edge : bdy) : **boolean**;
   {returns true if the polygon vertex, pt, is inside the window edge. This is simplified since the window has sides parallel to the x, y coordinate axis.}

```
begin
    with edge do
        case side of
            top      : Inside := pt.y <= limit;
            bottom   : Inside := pt.y >= limit;
            left     : Inside := pt.x >= limit;
            right    : Inside := pt.x <= limit
        end    {case}
end;    {Inside}

Procedure Out (pt : vertex);
    {places vertex pt in the polyout array. In performing this, it also increments
    the size of the vertices in the array}
        begin
            outlen := outlen + 1;           {number of vertices in array}
            polyout[outlen] := pt
        end;    {Out}

    Procedure Suth_Hodg (polyin : varray; var polyout : varray;
                            lngth : integer; edge : bdy);

        var
            i,                              {intersection point}
            v1,v2 : vertex;                 {line endpoints}
            j : integer;                    {array index}

        begin
            {intialize length of output array}
            outlen := 0;
            v1 := polyin[lngth];            {start with last vertex}
            for j := 1 to lngth do
                begin    {for}
                    v2 := polyin[j];
                    if Inside(v2,edge) then
                    {case 1 or 4}
                        if Inside(v1,edge) then
                        {case 1}
                            Out(v2)
                        else
                        {case 4}
                            begin    {else}
                                Intersect(v1,v2,edge,i);
                                Out(i);
                                Out(v2)
                            end    {else}
                    else
                    {case 2 or 3}
                        if Inside(v1,edge) then
                        {case 2}
                            begin    {if}
                                Intersect(v1,v2,edge,i);
                                Out(i);
```

```
                    end;   {if}
          {move on to next vertex}
              v1 := v2
        end   {for}
    end;   {Suth_Hodg}
```

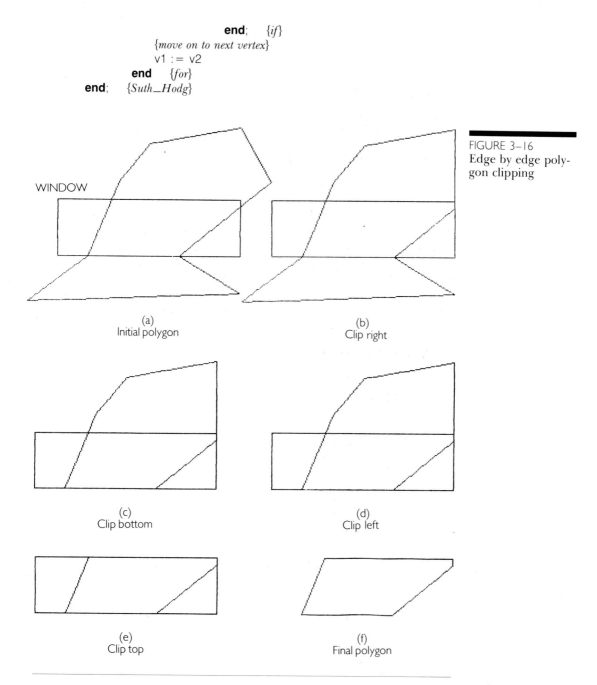

FIGURE 3–16
Edge by edge poly-
gon clipping

WINDOW

(a)
Initial polygon

(b)
Clip right

(c)
Clip bottom

(d)
Clip left

(e)
Clip top

(f)
Final polygon

3–8 TEXT IN GRAPHICS

All the images we have drawn have been composed of lines and
points. Many applications, however, require an enhanced display that

uses text in conjunction with figures. For example, a business presentation graphic image often requires a labeled graph with title and sales data.

A complete character set of one style and size is called a **font** or a type face. Computer graphics offers two distinct methods for generating character fonts: vector and raster cell.

VECTOR

A **vector-generated character** is defined by a sequence of line segments (Figure 3-17). This corresponds to the way we've been drawing our images. A font is stored in a font table, residing on disk or in read-only memory (ROM), with each character entry consisting of a line-drawing algorithm. A hardware or software **character generator** interprets these algorithms and places the character at a specified screen location. Input to the character generator is an 8-bit ASCII code that is an index into the font table (Figure 3-18).

Text generated by vectors can be displayed at any angle and scaled up or down by increasing or decreasing the length of the defining line segments. Currently, hardware plug-in cards and software modules are available for microcomputers that provide more than 10 fonts, including italics, bold, and roman types. The bold type effect in Figure 3-19 is accomplished by repeatedly displaying the vector characters *S* and *M* at neighboring locations.

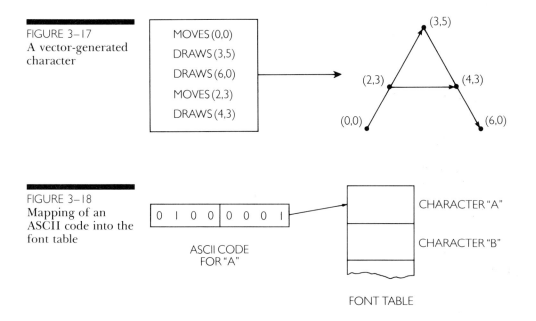

FIGURE 3–17
A vector-generated character

MOVES (0,0)
DRAWS (3,5)
DRAWS (6,0)
MOVES (2,3)
DRAWS (4,3)

(3,5) (2,3) (4,3) (0,0) (6,0)

FIGURE 3–18
Mapping of an ASCII code into the font table

0 1 0 0 0 0 0 1

ASCII CODE
FOR "A"

CHARACTER "A"

CHARACTER "B"

FONT TABLE

FIGURE 3–19
Bold vector
characters

RASTER CELL

A font can also be made of rectangular patterns of dots called **raster cells** (Figure 3-20). The size of this character raster is different for each graphics system. Sophisticated systems may have a character cell size of 10 dots wide and 20 dots high (10 × 20) in an 80-column mode and a 6 × 20 character cell size in the 132-column mode. For our purposes, we shall assume a 7-dot-wide by 8-dot-high raster. Thus, each character is represented by a raster of 8 × 7 = 56 bits. The 128 characters comprising the Apple II font are illustrated in Figure 3-21.

If the character set is stored in ROM, it is not possible to change the characters (without getting a new ROM). However, if the set is stored on disk, a character can be altered by changing bits in the two-dimensional raster cell defining that character. A **font editor** is a software program that helps the user design new fonts. It does this by displaying a greatly enlarged character, enabling the user to see clearly each dot

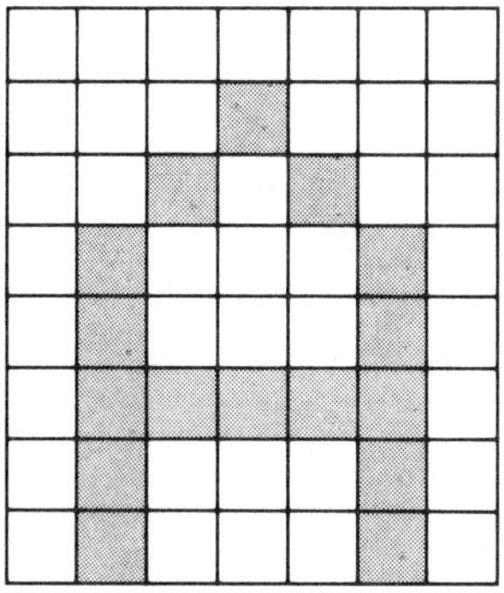

FIGURE 3–20
A raster character

FIGURE 3–21
The Apple II character set

in the raster cell. Chapter 8 describes an interactive implementation of a font editor.

Unlike vector-generated characters, raster-cell characters usually cannot be rotated or scaled, which is a severe limitation for business graphics. All microcomputers have raster-cell characters, but only some of the better display systems offer vector drawn characters. Let's now see how raster cells can be used in graphics programs.

DISPLAYING RASTER-CELL CHARACTERS

The Pascal procedure **write** displays characters, but only in the text buffer. There must be a special graphics text command that inserts character strings into the frame buffer.

Before drawing a string of characters, it is necessary to issue a **move2**(x, y) command, which positions the lower-left corner of the strings' first character raster at world coordinates (x, y). After the character string is drawn, the current pen position is returned to the start of the string.

The procedure **txt** displays all or part of a character string. Its format is

txt(string,start,length)

where string is a variable or literal character string, start is the position of the first character displayed, and length is the number of characters displayed beginning at start. Both start and length are integers. For example

txt('This is a test',2,8)

starts at the second character and is eight characters long. This displays the string

his is a

Unlike figures displayed using **move** and **draw**, the size of the character is unaffected by a change in the window or viewport parameters. This means that whenever we display a character string in a viewport, the viewport's dimensions must be large enough to contain the character string; otherwise the graphics display system clips the string. Although it is not necessary, it is best to have the window's dimensions approximately equal to the viewport's dimensions. If the start of the character string lies outside the viewport, none of the character string is drawn. Figure 3-22 illustrates the effect of clipping the two lines:

I THOUGHT IT OVER A NIGHT AND
IN ALL THIS THERE IS A MISTAKE

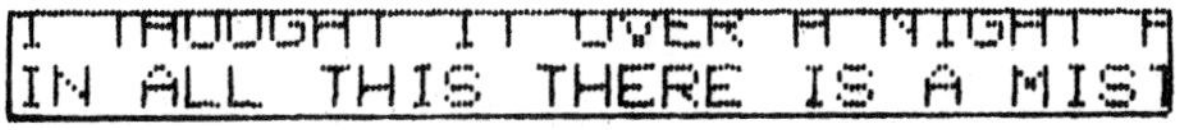

```
I THOUGHT IT OVER A MIGHT A
IN ALL THIS THERE IS A MIST
```

FIGURE 3–22
Clipping of
characters

In addition to having a procedure that has a character string as an input parameter, it is useful to have procedures that produce text with numeric input.

inum(value,count)

converts the integer value to a string of digits and displays it using "count" digits. The number count should be at least as large as the number of characters in value, including a negative sign if necessary. For example

inum(− 628,6)

is displayed as − 628 with two trailing blanks.

rnum(value,count,decimal)

displays the real number value as a character string. Count is the number of characters, including digits, decimal point, and a negative sign if needed. Decimal is the number of digits to the right of the decimal point. For example

rnum(23.14,6,3)

is displayed as 23.140.

3–9 **APPLICATIONS**

The quality of a picture drawn using computer graphics depends on conditions similar to those found in other media, such as oil or paint. In other words, creativity and artistic talent play important roles. However, computer graphics enhances the artistic ability of the nonprogrammer user by providing tools that make drawing simpler. For example, CAD systems provide graphic tablets, which closely approximate the drawing surface. A circle is drawn by indicating its center and radial distance; a rectangle is defined by a pair of diagonal endpoints.

In this section, we describe the techniques used to produce several simple pictures. Keep in mind that trial and error is always involved in any creative process, and in computer graphics more realistic pictures require several iterations before they finally look "pretty." In addition, there is a steep learning curve for the user of a graphics display system; the more one uses it, the better one becomes.

When we create a picture in a noninteractive mode, as here, we use graph paper to sketch the view. After we have something we like, we convert the graph paper drawing to world coordinate graphics commands. It is best to subdivide the picture into several parts, each part corresponding to a procedure. This technique greatly simplifies the creation and modification of the picture.

COMPUTER ART

The first set of images consists of a house and tree. Figure 3-23a illustrates a primitive house composed of two rectangles, one defining the door, and the other the frame. The roof is described by a triangle. The door is made black by drawing closely spaced horizontal lines (more on this in Chapter 5). The pine tree is constructed by a sequence of relative draw commands that are facilitated by the symmetry of the tree. Both the house and tree are described in the same world coordinate system, with origin at lower-left corner and x assuming values from 0 to 50 and y values from 0 to 25. The image lies inside one viewport framed by a rectangle.

FIGURE 3–23
House scenes

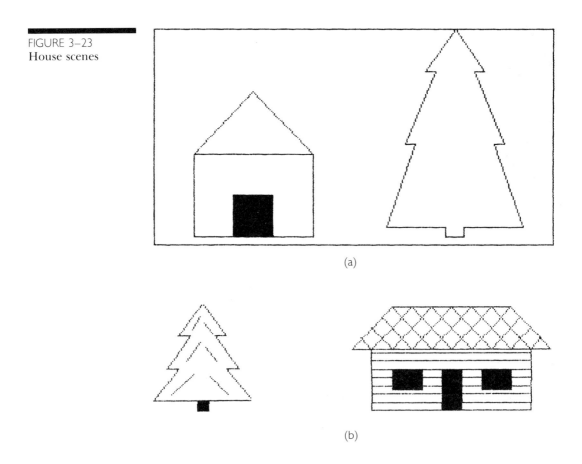

(a)

(b)

Graphics Fundamentals

Figure 3-23b illustrates a more realistic house and tree. The roof is a trapezoid shaded by intersecting diagonal lines added for realism. The house and tree were created using different windows and placed in separate viewports. Thus each object can be modified separately by changing the viewing parameters. Figure 3-23c shows the same image but in viewports having height greater than width. The final house is much more realistic (Figure 3-23d). Notice the chimney and the porch. Shading is accomplished by drawing closely spaced horizontal lines.

The cow inside the barn in Figure 3-24a on page 88 was created using three different viewports: the barn, the window, and the cow inside the open door. In addition, the cow, illustrated in Figure 3-24b, was inserted inside the barn using the reverse video command **fillscreen**(reverse).

The programs to draw these pictures are not included since they are too specialized to be adapted for other uses. The next example illustrates a more general concept, and a program listing is given.

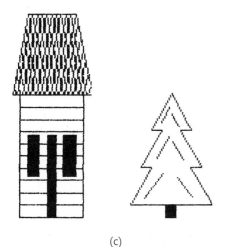

(c)

(d)

FIGURE 3–24
A cow and barn
scene

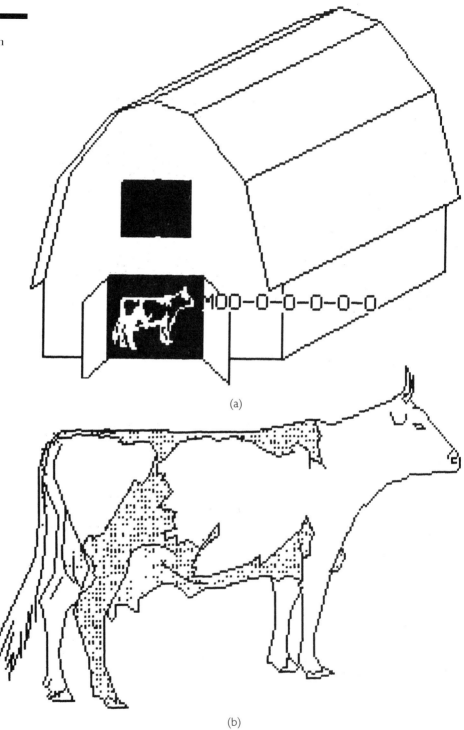

(a)

(b)

FUNCTION GRAPH

Program Graph uses four procedures to plot the function

$$y = | x^2 - 10x + 1 |,$$

as illustrated in Figure 3-25. The screen, having a resolution of 280 pixels horizontally and 192 pixels vertically, is divided into three separate viewports:

1. The area on which the function is plotted.
2. The area on which the x coordinate values are marked.
3. The area on which the y coordinate values are marked.

Each of these viewports corresponds to a separate procedure.

The fourth procedure, Find_Min_Max, determines the minimum and maximum values for the function. This data is used to set the window parameters for these procedures. The calculated values of the function are stored in an array, which is later used in the Plot_Graph procedure. For this example, we assume that x ranges from 0 to 20; these values are assigned to the variables minx and maxx, respectively.

FIGURE 3–25
A function graph

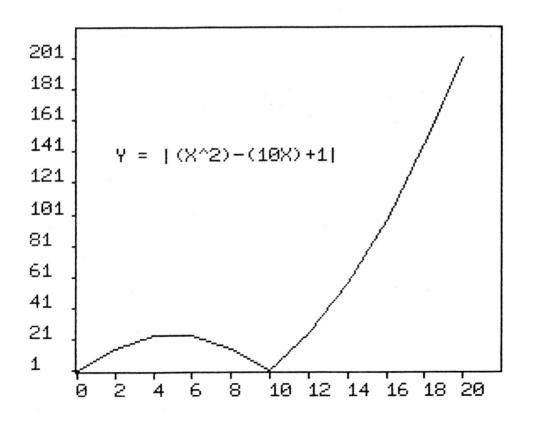

The global variables of Graph are declared by

```
var
    value : array[0..10] of integer;        {function y values}

    i,x,temp        : integer;               {temporary variables}
    miny,maxy       : integer;               {min and max y}
    minx,maxx       : integer;               {min and max x}
    xinc,yinc       : integer;               {incremental values}

Procedure Find_Min_Max;

    begin
        minx := 0;
        maxx := 20;
        {initialize min and max y}
        miny := maxint;
        maxy := −miny;
        xinc := 2;                           {size of increment in x values}
        x := minx;                           {initialize counters}
        i := 0;
        repeat
            temp := abs                      {calculate function}
                     ((x*x) − (10*x) + 1);
            value[i] := temp;                {store in array}
            if temp > maxy then
                maxy := temp;                {update max value}
            if temp < miny then
                miny := temp;                {update min value}
            x := x + xinc;                   {new x value}
            i := i + 1                       {increment index}
        until x > maxx;                      {stop at upper bound}
        yinc := maxy div 10                  {divide y-axis into 10 parts}
    end;    {Find_Min_Max}
```

Procedure Plot_y_Grid builds the viewport along the y-axis. The viewport must be wide enough for the tick marks on the axis and the numbered labels. A label can have up to three digits, where each digit, including a space, requires eight pixels. A tick requires about three pixels. Hence, a total of 28 pixels should satisfy the width requirements of the vertical y-axis viewport. Since the viewport parameters are in NDC units (0 to 1.0), this corresponds to a width of $^{28}/_{280} = 0.1$.

The bottom of this viewport must begin at the top of the horizontal x-axis viewport (built by the procedure Plot_x_Grid) and go to the top of the screen. The x-axis viewport is one digit high plus space for a blank and a 3-pixel high tick. Thus a height of 14 pixels will do. This corresponds to a height of $^{14}/_{192} = 0.073$ in NDC units.

The window parameters have values that are natural to the labeling. Horizontal values 0 to 100 were obtained by trial and error. The upper y value is greater than maxy since the last y digits start at the height of maxy, and additional space is needed for the height of the digits; without this extra height, the character digit will be clipped.

```
Procedure Plot_y_Grid;

    var
        y : real;                          {needed for drawing
                                            commands}

    begin
        viewport(0.0,0.1,0.073,1.0);
        window(0,100,miny,maxy+yinc);
        y := miny;
        repeat
            {draw ticks}
            move2(90,y);
            draw2(100,y);
            {label y-axis}
            move2(1,y);
            inum(trunc(y),3);
            y := y + yinc
        until trunc(y) > maxy
    end;    {Plot_y_Grid}
```

The procedure Plot_x_Grid is symmetric to Plot_y_Grid and we present it without any additional comments.

```
Procedure Plot_x_Grid;

    var
        x : real;

    begin
        viewport(0.1,1.0,0.0,0.073);        {up to y axis}
        window(minx,maxx+xinc,0.0,100);
        x := minx;
        repeat
            {draw ticks}
            move2(x,75);
            draw2(x,100);
            {label x-axis}
            move2(x,1);
            inum(trunc(x),2);
            x := x + xinc
        until trunc(x) > maxx
    end;    {Plot_x_Grid}
```

The final procedure, Plot_Graph, uses the values in the array to plot the graph in the center of the screen. Its viewport is derived from the previous two procedures, and the window has as its values the x and y ranges.

Procedure Plot_Graph;

```
    begin
        viewport(0.1,1.0,0.073,1);
        window(minx,maxx + xinc,miny,maxy + yinc);
        x := minx;
        i := 0;                              {array index}
        move2(2,2*maxy/3);                   {begin text}
        txt('Y =                            {to display function}
        |(X^2) – (10X) + 1|',1,20);
        move2(x,value[i]);                   {place cursor at first point}
        repeat
            x := x + xinc;
            i := i + 1;
            draw2(x,value[i])                {draw line between points}
        until x = xmax
    end;   {Plot_Graph}
```

The main program, Graph, consists of calls to these procedures

Program Graph;

```
    begin     {Graph}
        Find_Min_Max;
        Plot_Graph;
        Plot_x_Grid;
        Plot_y_Grid
    end.      {Graph}
```

3–10 COLOR

INTRODUCTION

Color is often used to enhance the realism of graphics displays. It can help the viewer differentiate between adjacent areas, as in maps and business charts. And important sections of a display can be emphasized or highlighted by displaying them in bright, vivid colors.

The most effective displays use colors that are subdued and pleasing to look at. Contrasting colors often result in a glaring and ugly display. Except for artistic images that stress realism, eight concurrent colors are usually sufficient. These eight colors may be user-selected from a palette of several thousand colors.

COLOR PROCEDURES

All drawing, up to now, has been with a white pen on a dark background. The procedure

pencolor(color)

---

sets the pen color. All pixels displayed after invoking this command will be displayed in the indicated color. The default color is white.

The viewport is erased (filled in black) by the procedure **fillscreen**(black). In general

fillscreen(color)

fills in the viewport with the specified color.

The choice and number of colors differ with each computer display system. In fact, some low-cost computers limit the use of colors by allowing specific colors only in certain areas of the screen. For the most part, we shall avoid this entanglement by refraining from using color capabilities. This does not imply, however, that a reader with a color display should refrain from experimenting with color.

3–11 **CONCLUSION**

In this chapter we introduced the concept of the world coordinate system. The primary advantage of this system is that it eliminates the dependency of drawing commands on the size of the display screen. The concept of a window and viewport introduced the need for clipping. While most inexpensive displays implement line clipping, the color and shading features of a raster-scan display require a closed region, as produced by polygon clipping.

EXERCISES

1. Determine the window dimensions for the following images:
   a. An annual sales chart, with months along the horizontal axis and dollars (0 to $100,000) along the vertical axis
   b. The flight of a spaceship, with miles along the horizontal axis and time along the vertical axis
2. Determine the NDC for your display screen. What viewports are needed to divide the screen into four equal parts?
3. Display the same figure in five different size viewports.
4. Some uses require that a screen position be converted to world coordinates. Write a procedure that does this.
5. Design the vector characters to write the character string COMPUTER GRAPHICS. Use different window/viewport settings to display the string.
6. Determine how your graphics system clips raster-cell characters. Do this by placing a character string in different parts of a fixed window while simultaneously changing the viewport dimensions.
7. Write a program to draw the house scene in Figure 3-23d.
8. Use color to enhance the realism of the scene in Figure 3-23d.

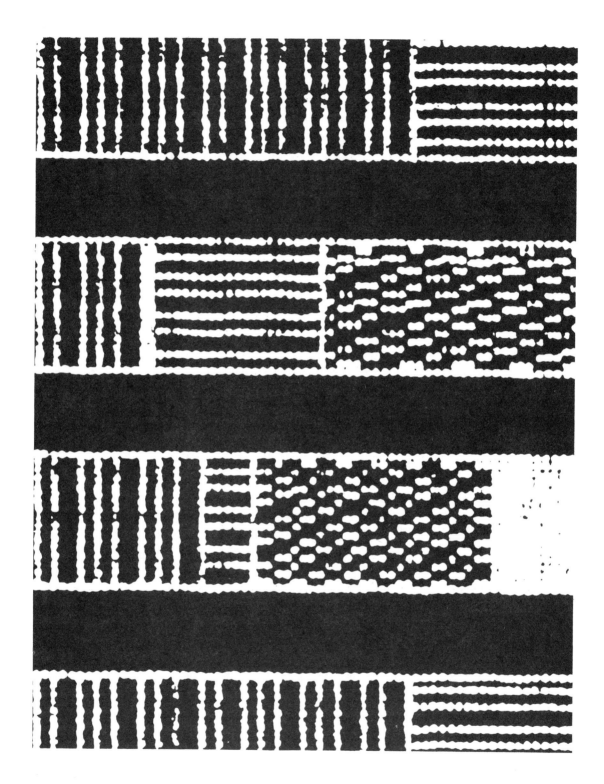

Detail of Figure 4–10

4

ELEMENTARY SHADING TECHNIQUES

4–1 **INTRODUCTION**

A primary purpose of shading is to enhance the visual realism of an image. The ability of a raster display to produce shaded and colored solid objects has been a major reason for the increase in their popularity. From its beginnings, computer graphics has been striving to produce lifelike images. Figure 4-1 illustrates a building that has different degrees of shading, depending on the amount of sunlight a side is exposed to; the less sun, the darker the shade. Another use of shading is to highlight and differentiate among parts of an image. The bar graph in Figure 4-2 illustrates this.

FIGURE 4–1

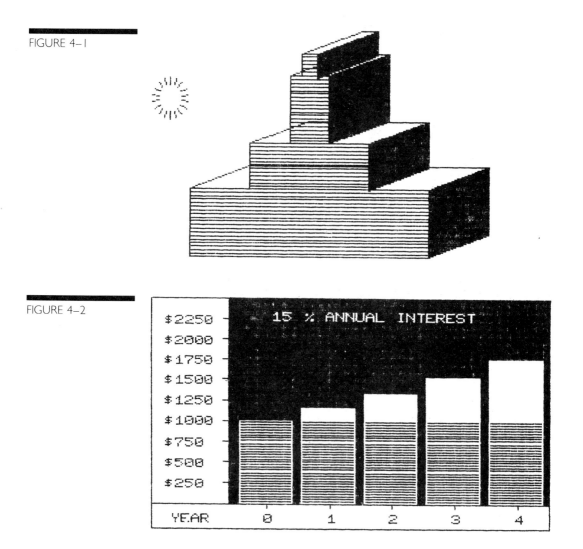

FIGURE 4–2

Elementary Shading Techniques

As described in Chapter 1, realistic black-and-white shading requires a frame buffer having eight bits/pixel, which can generate up to 256 shades of gray. Most inexpensive graphics systems do not approach this capability. A typical display system has between two and four bits/pixel, and even with this number, there are often limitations in the types of shades and colors that can be produced with these bits.

In this chapter, we examine several shading techniques that require only one bit/pixel. While these techniques do not produce high-quality shaded images, the realism of these images is significantly improved over that of a nonshaded image.[†]

4-2 RECTANGULAR SHADING

Recall that a rectangle with sides parallel to the x, y coordinate axis can be described by specifying its diagonally opposite corners. There are two standard methods of shading rectangles: lines and points. We examine line shading first.

LINE SHADING

Perhaps the simplest type of rectangular shading is produced by drawing a sequence of equally spaced horizontal or vertical lines. The spacing of these parallel lines produces different shading effects (Figure 4-3). A solid rectangle is produced by drawing very closely spaced lines.

Procedure Horizontal shades a rectangle by drawing N equally spaced horizontal lines. The choice of N depends on the degree of shading desired and the size of the rectangle. The procedure has the diagonally opposite vertices as its parameters. In this and the following two procedures, we assume that the rectangle has already been drawn and the vertex $(x1, y1)$ is the bottom-left corner, and the vertex $(x2, y2)$ is the top-right corner of the rectangle. The window's dimensions are chosen to enclose the rectangle.

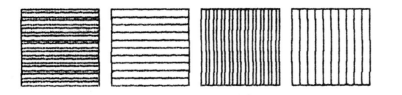

FIGURE 4–3

[†]Completely realistic images (color plates) involve a knowledge of the physics of light and reflection as well as the physiology of the human eye and brain. A discussion of these fascinating topics is beyond the scope of this book.

```
Procedure Horizontal (
          x1,y1,x2,y2:real;                    {diagonal corners}
          N:integer);                          {degree of shading}

    var
      ypt,                                      {y value to draw}
      yinc   : real;                            {y increment}

    begin
      window(x1 − 1,x2 + 1,y1 − 1,y2 + 1);
      {N lines between bottom and top of rectangle}
      yinc := (y2 − y1)/(N + 1);
      {first line above bottom}
      ypt := y1 + yinc;
      while ypt < y2 do
          begin    {while}
            {draw line}
            move2(x1,ypt);
            draw2(x2,ypt);
            {compute next line}
            ypt := ypt + yinc
          end    {while}
    end;    {Horizontal}
```

The procedure to perform vertical shading is similar and is left as an exercise.

A combination of horizontal and vertical lines produces a variety of crosshatched shadings (Figure 4-4). By varying the spacing between the lines, we obtain gradual shading (Figure 4-5). This is easily done by multiplying the previous spacing by a constant factor. A factor greater than (less than) 1 results in a shading that progresses from dark to light (light to dark). Procedure Horizontal can easily be modified to produce gradual horizontal shading. To do this, we need only assign yinc an initial spacing (since N is now meaningless) and insert the line

```
yinc := yinc∗factor;
```

after the **draw2** command.

Diagonal shading is produced by drawing equally or unequally spaced diagonal lines with positive or negative slope. Procedure Diagonal draws equally spaced diagonal lines parallel to the diagonal from $(x1, y1)$ to $(x2, y2)$ (Figure 4-6). The procedure treats separately two

FIGURE 4–4

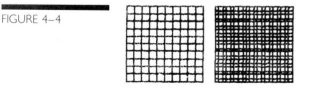

Elementary Shading Techniques

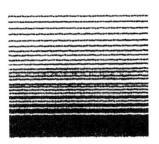

FIGURE 4–5

cases—the bottom and the top triangular regions within the rectangle. The letter N is the number of diagonal lines in each triangular region.

```
Procedure Diagonal (
        x1,y1,x2,y2 : real;              {diagonal vertices}
        N : integer);                    {degree of shading}

    var
        xinc,yinc    : real;             {incremental units}
        count        : integer;          {counter}

    begin
        window(x1 − 1,x2 + 1,y1 − 1,y2 + 1);
        xinc := (x2 − x1)/N;
        yinc := (y2 − y1)/N;
        {bottom triangle}
        for count := 1 to N do
            begin    {for}
                move2(x2 − count∗xinc,y)
                draw2(x2,y2 + count∗yinc)
            end;     {for}
        {top triangle}
        for count := 1 to N do
            begin    {for}
                move2(x1,y1 + count∗yinc);
                draw2(x2 − count∗xinc,y2)
            end      {for}
    end;     {Diagonal}
```

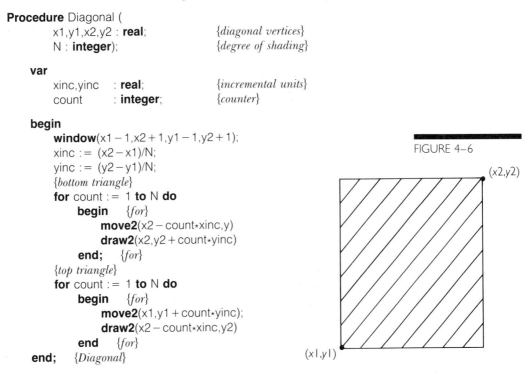

FIGURE 4–6

This procedure can easily be modified to produce diagonal lines with negative slope and varying spacing.

POINT SHADING

In addition to shading by drawing lines, shading can be produced by plotting random points in the rectangle (Figure 4-7 on page 100). Procedure Point_Shade uses the random-number generator to produce a nonuniform shade. The value of the random number is divided by its maximum value, 32767, producing a random number between 0 and 1. As

FIGURE 4–7

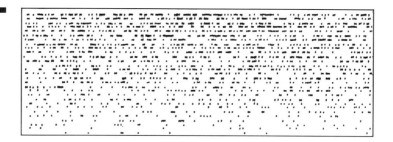

we go from the bottom to the top of the rectangle, more points are plotted, giving a graduated shading appearance. This is accomplished by adding the shading factor to the number of points plotted. In general, point shading is more time-consuming than line shading.

```
Procedure Point_Shade (
        x1,y1,x2,y2:real; )               {diagonal vertices}

   var
        x,y,                              {points plotted}
        yinc,                             {y increment}
        xwidth: real;                     {width of rectangle}
        factor,                           {shading factor}
        numbpts,                          {number of points plotted}
        count : integer;                  {counter}

   begin
        window(x1 − 1,x2 + 1,y1 − 1,y2 + 1);
        xwidth := x2 − x1;
        {assign initial spacing}
        yinc := (y2 − y1)/20;
        {assign initial number of points plotted}
        numbpts := 10;
        {assign shading increment}
        factor := 5;
        {start above bottom of rectangle}
        y := y1 + yinc;
        while y < y2 do
            begin     {while}
                for count := 1 to numbpts do
                    begin     {for}
                        {point inside rectangle}
                        x := x1 + random/32767 * xwidth;
                        {plot point}
                        point2(x,y);
                    end;     {for}
                {go up to next line}
                y := y + yinc;
```

```
                    {increase number of points}
                    numbpts := numbpts + factor
              end    {while}
     end;   {Point_Shade}
```

4-3 APPLICATIONS

GEOMETRIC IMAGES

The building in Figure 4-1 is produced by drawing four rectangular boxes (Figure 4-8), one on top of the other. Each box has three visible faces, and each face has a different shade.

A box is defined by its length, height, and width. The window for this building has coordinates 0 to 1000 in both the x and y directions. In order to center a box in the horizontal direction, vertex 1 has x coordinate $(1000 + \text{length})/2$ and vertex 2 has x coordinate $(1000 - \text{length})/2$.

The building is constructed from the top down, with the top of the lower box having the same y value as the bottom of the previous box. Thus, the edge that joins vertices 3 and 6 has a y value equal to the y value of the previous box's edge that joins vertices 1 and 2. Vertex 4 has an x value displaced $\frac{3}{4} \times$ width from the x value of vertex 3; its y value is displaced $\frac{1}{2} \times$ width from the y value of vertex 3. Vertex 5 has a similar relationship to vertex 6.

Each box can be produced by computing the five vertices 1, 3, 4, 5, and 6. However, in order to make the program easier to follow, all seven vertices will be computed.

We are going to use a Pascal record data structure to store these seven vertices. This may seem unnecessarily complex for this problem, but it is good to be exposed to this type of data structure. Then, when

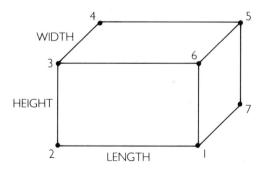

FIGURE 4–8

we solve more difficult problems, we can easily extend it to store information in addition to points.

```
type
        coords = array [1..7] of real;
        Points = record
                        x,y : coords
                    end;

var
        vertex : points
```

Using this data structure, the box in Figure 4-8 can be drawn with the following procedure.

```
Procedure Draw_Box;

    var
        count : integer;                    {counter}

    begin
        with vertex do
            begin       {with}
                move2(x[1],y[1]);
                for count := 2 to 6 do
                    draw2(x[count],y[count]);
                move2(x[5],y[5]);
                draw2(x[7],y[7]);
                draw2(x[1],y[1]);
                draw2(x[6],y[6]);
                draw2(x[3],y[3])
            end     {with}
    end;    {Draw_Box}
```

The side of the box defined by vertices 1, 6, 5, and 7 is not a rectangle since adjacent sides are not perpendicular. A special procedure, Rhombus, shades this region with equally spaced lines parallel to the bottom edge.

```
Procedure Rhombus (
        spacing : real                    {space between shade lines});

    var
        ypt1,ypt2 : real;                    {endpoints}

    begin
        {start from bottom, compute endpoints of first line}
        ypt1 := y[1] + spacing;
        ypt2 := y[7] + spacing;
        while ypt1 < y[6] do
```

Elementary Shading Techniques

```
begin    {while}
    {draw line}
    move2(x[1],ypt1);
    draw2(x[7],ypt2);
    {compute new endpoints}
    ypt1 := ypt1 + spacing;
    ypt2 := ypt2 + spacing
end    {while}
end;    {Rhombus}
```

Procedure Building begins by setting the window and viewport. For each box, the length, height, and width are used to compute the seven vertices. This program draws a shaded box by invoking Horizontal, Draw_Box, and Rhombus.

```
Procedure Building;

    type
        coords = array[1..7] of real;
        points = record
                        x, y : coords
                    end;

    var
        vertex                    : points;        {array of vertices}
        length,width,height       : real;          {box dimensions}
        top                       : real;          {top of box}
        count                     : integer;       {counter}

{insert procedures Horizontal, Draw_Box, and Rhombus}

    begin
        window(0,1000,0,1000);
        viewport(0,1,0.05,1);
        {for each of the four boxes}
        for count := 1 to 4 do
            begin    {for}
                {start at top of box}
                top := 900;    {leave space on top of window}
                {compute vertices}
                with vertex do
                    begin    {with}
                        x[1] := (1000+length)/2;
                        y[1] := top-height;
                        x[2] := x[1]-length;
                        y[2] := y[1];
                        x[3] := x[2];
                        y[3] := y[2]+height;
                        x[4] := x[3]+3*width/4;
```

```
                y[4] := y[3]+width/2;
                x[5] := x[4]+length;
                y[5] := y[4];
                x[6] := x[1];
                y[6] := y[3];
                x[7] := x[5];
                y[7] := y[5]-height
        end;     {with}
    top := y[1];     {top of next box}
    Draw_Box;
    Horizontal(x[2],y[2],x[6],y[6],4);
    Rhombus(0.1)
  end     {for}
end;     {Building}
```

BAR GRAPHS

Business data is often represented by bar graphs (Figure 4-9). This type of graph is particularly easy to read and can emphasize important trends. The effectiveness of a bar graph, however, depends on the quality of its appearance. An attractive graph should have labeled headings in large or boldface type. Both axes must be clearly identified, with their labels positioned close to the axes without interfering with the data. The width of the bars should be greater than the space separating them. The actual width depends on the number of bars and the size of the window. Enough shades and/or colors should be available to contrast the different parts of the graph. In this section, we describe the implementation of these features.

FIGURE 4–9

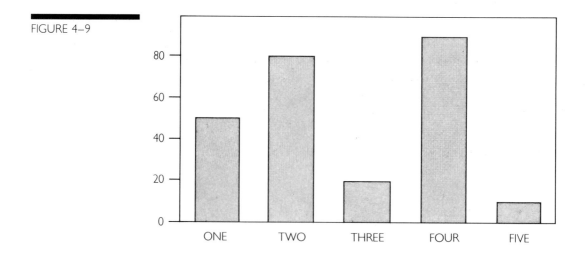

Elementary Shading Techniques

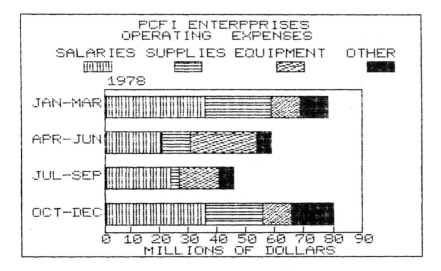

FIGURE 4-10

Two types of bar graphs are examined. Figure 4-10 uses horizontal bars that are divided into different sections, each representing millions of dollars spent on each of four operating expenses for a quarter of a year. Each section is highlighted by a distinct shade. Figure 4-11 represents a similar type of information but uses overlapping bars.

In our previous example, a rectangle was described in terms of its diagonally opposite vertices. For bar graphs this is probably not the best representation. All of the shading procedures can (easily) be modified so that a rectangle can be drawn and shaded by inputting one vertex and its length and width. Thus, if $(x1, y1)$ is the lower-left corner and

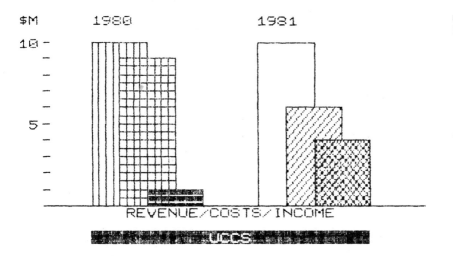

FIGURE 4-11

the length and width are known, then the upper-right corner $(x2, y2)$ has values.

$$x2 = x1 + \text{length}$$
$$y2 = y1 + \text{width}$$

NONOVERLAPPING BARS

The bar graph in Figure 4-10 uses four windows and viewports: one for the monthly quarters comprising the vertical axis, another for the millions of dollars along the horizontal axis, a third for the title and shading codes, and the fourth for the bars.

All procedures have access to the variables

var
    salaries,supplies,equipment,
    other : **array**[1..4] **of integer**;   *{one entry per quarter}*
    x,y,lngth,width : **real**;   *{define rectangle}*
    company,operation : **string**;   *{company name}*

Business graphs should be produced using interactive dialogue. Here, the user inputs the company name and operating expenses for each of the four quarters. We are now ready to describe some of the procedures required to construct this bar graph. Assume the availability of the following rectangle-shading procedures: Vert_Shade, Horz_Shade, and Diag_Shade. These shading procedures have as parameters: vertex, length, width, and spacing.

Procedure Draw_Rectangle(
    x,y,   *{lower-left corner}*
    lngth,width : **real**   *{dimensions});*

    {draws a rectangle given one vertex the length and width}

begin
    move2(x,y);
    rdraw2(lngth,0);
    rdraw2(0,width);
    rdraw2(– lngth,0);
    rdraw2(0, – width)
end;   *{Draw_Rectangle}*

Procedure Make_Heading produces the title and shading codes at the top of the bar graph. The window parameters have a width five times the height, in order to correspond, approximately, with the dimensions of the display region.

Procedure Make_Heading;
    {creates the heading viewport}

    var
        startpt : **real**;   *{x-coordinate of title}*

    Elementary Shading Techniques

```
begin
    {top third of screen}
    viewport(0,1,0.67,1);
    window(0,100,0,20);
    {title}
    company := 'PCFI ENTERPRISES';
    operation := 'OPERATING EXPENSES';
    {center company title}
    startpt := 50 - length(company)/2;
    move2(startpt,16);
    txt(company,1,length(company));
    {center operation label}
    startpt := 50 - length(operation)/2;
    move2(startpt,13);
    txt(operation,1,length(operation));
    {label shading codes}
    move2(8,8);
    txt('SALARIES',1,8);
    move2(31,8)
    txt('SUPPLIES',1,8);
    move2(54,8);
    txt('EQUIPMENT',1,9);
    move2(82,8);
    txt('OTHER',1,5);
    {draw the four shading codes}
    y := 4;     {bottom of rectangle}
    {salaries}
    x := 15;    {left side of rectangle}
    Draw_Rectangle(x,y,7,3);
    {vertical shade with spacing 0.8}
    Vert_Shade(x,y,7,3,0.8);
    {supplies}
    x := 38;    {left side of rectangle}
    Draw_Rectangle(x,y,7,3);
    {horizontal shade with spacing 0.8}
    Horz_Shade(x,y,7,3,0.8);
    {equipment}
    x := 64;    {left side of rectangle}
    Draw_Rectangle(x,y,7,3);
    {diagonal shade with spacing 0.8}
    Diag_Shade(x,y*7,3,0.8);
    {other}
    x := 87;    {left side of rectangle}
    Draw_Rectangle(x,y,7,3);
    {horizontal shade with spacing 0.2}
    Horz_Shade(x,y,7,7,0.2);
    {draw year}
    move2(21,0);
    txt('1980',1,4)
end;    {Make_Heading}
```

Procedure Make_Months labels the monthly quarters. The window has height twice the width.

Procedure Make_Months;

{*creates months viewport*}

begin

{*left part of screen*}
viewport(0,0.21,0.1,0.67);
window(0,20,0,40);
{*position text*}
move2(2,34);
txt('JAN-MAR',1,7);
move2(2,24);
txt('APR-JUN',1,7);
move2(2,14);
txt('JUL-SEP',1,7);
move2(2,4);
txt('OCT-DEC',1,7)
end;   {*Make_Months*}

Procedure Make_Grid produces the ticks, numbers, and label at the bottom of the graph. The window has width four times the height.

Procedure Make_Grid;

{*creates the dollars viewport*}

begin

{*below bar region*}
viewport(0.2,0.92,0,0.15);
window(0,100,0,25);
{*label '0'*}
move2(0,10);
inum(0,1);
{*start at label '10*}
x := 10
repeat
{*draw tick*}
move2(x,20);
draw2(x,25);
{*center digits about tick*}
move2(x − 2.5,10);
inum(trunc(x),3);
{*next digit*}
x := x + 10
until x > 91;
{*label*}
move2(15,1);
txt('MILLIONS OF DOLLARS',1,19)
end;   {*Make_Grid*}

Procedure Plot_Graph draws the shaded bars. Each bar has width 6 units and starts 10 units above the previous one. The first bar starts at $y = 2$. The updated x value starts at the end of the previous shaded part.

```
Procedure Plot_Graph;

    {produces the shaded bars}

    var
        count : integer;     {counter}

    begin
        viewport(0.21,0.85,0.1,0.67);
        window(0,90,0,40);     {to 90 million}
        frame;     {draws a rectangle just inside viewport}
        width := 6;
        {bar for each quarter of the year from top down}
        for count := 1 to 4 do
            begin
                {bottom of bar}
                y := 40 − 10*count + 2;
                {salaries}
                x := 0;
                lngth := salaries[count];
                Draw_Rectangle(x,y,lngth,width)
                Vert_Shade(x,y,lngth,width,1.2);
                {supplies}
                x := x+lngth;
                lngth := supplies[count];
                Draw_Rectangle(x,y,lngth,width);
                Horz_Shade(x,y,lngth,width,0.9);
                {equipment}
                x := x + lngth;
                lngth := equipment[count];
                Draw_Rectangle(x,y,lngth,width);
                Diag_Shade(x,y,lngth,width,7);
                {other}
                x := x+lngth;
                lngth := other[count];
                Horz_Shade(x,y,length,width,0.3)
            end     {for}
    end;     {Plot_Graph}

Procedure Produce_Chart;

    {this calls the previous procedures}

    begin
        {erase screen}
        fillscreen(black);
```

```
          Make_Heading;
          Make_Months;
          Make_Grid;
          Plot_Graph
    end;    {Produce_Chart}
```

OVERLAPPING BARS

The bar graph in Figure 4-11 illustrates the use of overlapping bars. Successive rectangles are plotted one-half a bar width to the right of a preceding rectangle. At first glance, the shading of each rectangle may seem difficult; however, this is not the case. As the rectangles move to the right, they use the same shading as the previous rectangle plus additional shading. Thus, moving right, the 1980 bars have vertical, crosshatched, and finally solid shading. The 1981 bars have none, positive diagonal, and positive-negative diagonal shading. Observe that the nonshaded large rectangle (1981) has its right side stopping at the top of the next rectangle. This is done because a vertical line would be distracting in the diagonal shading of that next rectangle. It was not a concern for the 1980 bars since the vertical shading used spacing to ensure that the rectangle's vertical line was part of the next rectangle's crosshatched shading. The coding of this bar graph is left as an exercise. **Fillscreen**(reverse) is invoked to produce reverse video.

4–4 **CIRCULAR SHADING**

CIRCLES

The interior of a circle can be shaded by using radial lines, arcs, or points. To shade a circle using arcs, it is only necessary to draw concentric circles from the center out to the circumference. The intensity of the shading depends on the radial distance between consecutive circles (Figure 4-12). Procedure Shade_Circle performs this shading. The

FIGURE 4–12

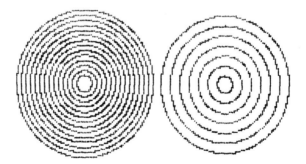

Elementary Shading Techniques

value of *factor* is the number of concentric circles. Refer back to Section 2-5 for an explanation of how circles are generated.

For the remainder of this section, we assume both that the window is set just larger than the circle size and the availability of the constant value pi:

```
const
    pi = 3.1415927;

Procedure Shade_Circle (
        xc,yc,      {center}
        radius : real;
        factor : integer {degree of shading});

var
    dtheta,                         {angle increment}
    ct,st,                          {cosine and sine}
    x,y,                            {plotted points}
    xtemp,                          {saves previous x}
    portion : real;                 {varying radius}
    count,                          {counter}
    loop : integer;                 {counter}

begin
    {draw number of circles equal to factor}
    for loop := 1 to factor do
        begin {for}
            {compute radius size}
            portion := loop*radius/factor;
            {compute angle increment}
            dtheta := 2*pi/(portion*16);
            ct := cos(dtheta);
            st := sin(dtheta);
            {initialize plot points}
            x := 0;
            y := portion;
            {draw circle having 16 × portion line segments}
            move2(xc + x,yc + y);
            for count := 1 to portion*16 do
                begin {for}
                    xtemp := x;
                    x := x*ct - y*st;
                    y := y*ct + xtemp*st;
                    draw2(xc + x,yc + y)
                end {for count}
        end {for loop}
end; {Shade_Circle}
```

To produce a shade using radial lines, we need only draw the radius at different angles of the circle. Recall that if (*xc, yc*) is the center of a circle, and θ is an angle in radians between 0 and 2π, then

$$x = xc + \text{radius} \times \cos(\theta),$$
$$y = yc + \text{radius} \times \sin(\theta)$$

is a point on the circle. To draw the radius, use the graphics commands:

move2(xc,yc);
draw2(x,y);

Using points to shade a circle presents an interesting problem. Suppose we shade by plotting points on concentric circles. Assume that the angle between consecutive points is fixed at θ. From Figure 4-13 we observe that as the radial distance of points increases, the spacing (arc) between consecutive points also increases. The reason for this is that the arc length between consecutive points is equal to the product of the radius and the angle between the points. Thus as the radius increases, so does the arc length.

To offset this problem, we should shade in a horizontal manner. Namely, as the *y* values go from the top to the bottom of the circle, a sequence of equally spaced dots is drawn from the left part, xleft, to the right part, xright, of the circle. Figure 4-14 displays two shaded circles with different spacing of dots. The values of xleft and xright are calculated from the equation

$$x = xc \pm \sqrt{\text{radius}^2 - (y - yc)^2}$$

FIGURE 4–13

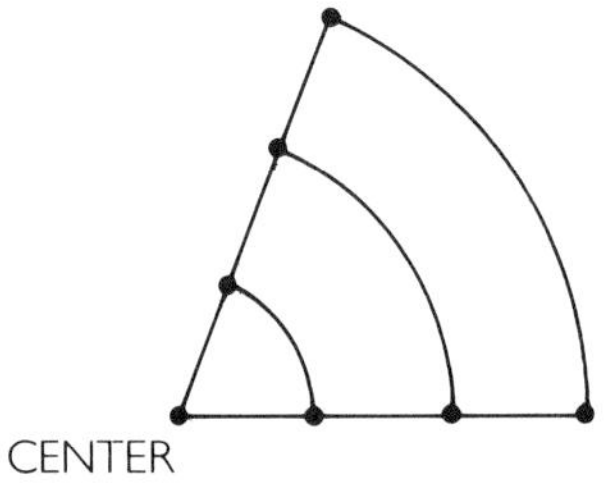

CENTER

FIGURE 4–14

Elementary Shading Techniques

Procedure Dot_Shade performs this shading. The variable yinc represents the vertical distance between the horizontally shaded rows; xinc represents the horizontal spacing between points. The coordinate pair (xright, y) is plotted outside the loop since floating point approximation prevents $x + xinc = xright$.

```
Procedure Dot_Shade (
        xinc,yinc, {spacing increments}
        xc,yc, {center}
        radius : real);

    var
        xleft,xright : real;           {points on the circle}
        x,y : real;                    {points to draw}
        radical: real;                 {square root solution for x}

    begin
        {plot top point}
        y := yc + radius;
        point2(xc,y);
        {loop to bottom of circle}
        y := y − yinc;
        while y > (yc − radius) do
            begin {while}
                {compute xleft, xright}
                radical := sqrt(radius*radius − (y−yc)*(y−yc));
                xleft := xc − radical;
                xright := xc + radical;
                x := xleft;
                {draw from xleft to xright}
                while x < xright do
                    begin {while}
                        {plot point}
                        point2(x,y);
                        x := x + xinc {x spacing}
                    end; {while x}
                {plot right-most point}
                point2(xright,y);
                y := y − yinc {y spacing}
            end; {while y}
        {plot bottom point}
        y := yc − radius;
        point2(xc,y)
    end; {Dot_Shade}
```

SECTORS

Some applications require pie-shaped sectors of a disk (Figure 4-15 on page 114). To draw these, we need the angle of the sector in

FIGURE 4–15

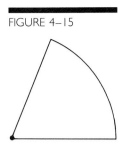

addition to the center and radius of the circle. Procedure Sector draws the boundary of a sector. It draws two radial lines and the arc connecting these lines. The arc begins at startangle radians from the horizontal and continues for theta radians. The variable numsteps is the number of line segments making up the arc. Since a circle is drawn with 16 × radius line segments,

$$numsteps = \frac{16*radius*theta}{(2*pi)}$$

The variable step is the angle subtended by each line segment.

```
Procedure Sector(
        xc,yc, {center}
        radius,
        startangle, {starting angle of sector}
        theta : real {angular size of sector} );

    var
        x,y,                        {line endpoints}
        numsteps,                   {line segments}
        inc,step,                   {angle increments}
        xend,yend : real;           {end of arc}

    begin
        numsteps := 16*radius*theta/(2*pi);
        {angle increment}
        step := theta/numsteps;
        {initialization}
        inc := 0;
        {draw first radius of sector}
        x := xc + radius*cos(startangle);
        y := yc + radius*sin(startangle);
        move2(xc,yc);
        draw2(x,y);
        {calculate end of sector}
        xend := xc + radius*cos(startangle + theta);
        yend := yc + radius*sin(startangle + theta);
        {draw arc line segments}
        while x < xend do
            begin {while}
                {increment angle}
                inc := inc + step;
                x := xc + radius*cos(startangle + inc);
                y := yc + radius*sin(startangle + inc);
                draw2(x,y)
            end; {while}
        {complete arc}
        draw2(xend,yend);
        {draw second radius}
        draw2(xc,yc)
    end; {Sector}
```

PIE CHARTS

A pie-chart program is composed of three major parts: circle draw-ing, radial line drawing, and text labeling. The interior of the circle is divided into several sectors or slices; the size of each corresponds to the percentage of that slice to the whole pie. Each slice has two radial lines marking its boundary and a descriptive label (Figure 4-16). The input to this program consists of the number of slices, the name of each slice, and the percentage of each slice. A pie chart tends to become congested and difficult to read if it has more than seven slices.

As seen in Figure 4-16, the sector label begins or ends at the middle of the sector and five units away from the circle, depending on which side of the circle the sector is on. For example, if the x value of the middle of the sector's arc is on the right side of the pie chart, the label starts just to the right of the circle. If, on the other hand, the x value of the middle of the sector's arc is on the left side of the pie chart, the label ends to the left of the circle.

The window has dimensions equal to the screen coordinates. By making it this way, a value of 8 in the world system corresponds to eight screen pixels, the height of a text character. Note that if the y value for a label is less than yc, the y value of the center of the circle, then the label begins eight units down; this prevents the label from interfering with the circle. Labels to the left of the pie chart are moved seven times the length of the label since each text character is seven pixels wide.

Procedure Chart uses the input data to compute the locations and draw the radial lines and labels for each sector. Assume screen size 280 x 192 with NDC values ranging from 0 to 1.

Each of the seven possible slices of the pie is described by the record sector:

```
type
    slice = record
                name : string;      {label}
                percent  : real     {between 0 and 1}
            end;
```

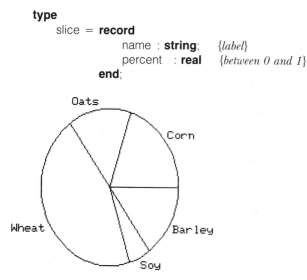

FIGURE 4–16

```
var
    sector : array[1..7] of slice;
Procedure Chart (
    xc,yc,      {center}
    radius : real;
    numsectors : integer      {number of sectors});

    {draw pie chart}

    var
        i : integer;                     {loop counter}
        prev,                            {previous angle}
        radian,                          {current angle}
        halfway,                         {middle of sector}
        xinc,                            {endpoint of}
        yinc,                            {radial line}
        xpos,                            {text label}
        ypos : real;                     {location}

    begin
        window (0,511,0,511);
        viewport(0,1,0,1);
        {initialize angle}
        prev := 0;
        {loop for each sector}
        for i := 1 to numsectors do
            begin    {for}
                {calculate radians for this sector}
                radian := 2*pi*sector[i].percent;
                {calculate end coordinates of radial line}
                xinc := radius*cos(radian + prev);
                yinc := radius*sin(radian + prev);
                {draw radial line}
                move2(xc,yc);     {center of circle}
                draw2(xc + xinc,yc + yinc);
                {calculate starting position of label}
                halfway := radian/2 + prev;
                xpos := xc + (radius + 5)*cos(halfway);
                ypos := yc + (radius + 5)*sin(halfway);
                {label ends left of circle}
                if xpos < 0 then
                    xpos := xpos − (length(sector[i].name) * 7);
                {label is below circle}
                if y pos < 0 then
                    ypos := ypos − 8;
                {label sector}
                move2(xc + xpos,yc + ypos);
                txt(sector[i].name,1,length(sector[i].name));
                prev := prev + radian     {update angle}
            end    {for}
    end;    {Chart}
```

This pie chart can be shaded using the techniques described in the previous sections.

EXPLODED PIE CHARTS

An exploded pie chart is used to highlight one or more sectors of a pie chart (Figure 4-17). The technique for drawing this chart is very straightforward. A sector that is "exploded" is drawn with its center displaced from the center of the original pie chart. This new center is also used to calculate the position of the labeled text.

Procedure Explode produces an exploded pie chart by first calculating the new center and angle of a sector. This displaced center is one-third of the radial distance and is at an angle in the middle of its sector. Explode then calls the procedure Sector, which draws the sector at the correct location. If the sector should be shaded, procedure Shade, which shades a sector using arcs, is called. The intensity of shading is controlled by its input parameter. This procedure is similar to procedure Shade_ Circle and is left as an exercise. The final part of procedure Explode uses the techniques of the procedure Chart to label the sector. The data structure record for slice is expanded to include a field indicating if the sector should be exploded and a field indicating if the sector should be shaded.

```
type
    slice =      record
                     name    : string;          {label}
                     percent : real;            {slice percent}
                     explode : boolean;         {true = explode}
                     shade                       {true = shade}
                 end;

var
    sector : array[1..7] of slice;

Procedure Explode (
    xc,yc,                          {center}
    radius: real;
    numsectors,                     {number of sectors}
    factor: integer                 {degree of shading});
```

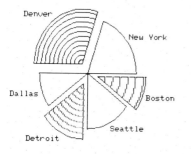

FIGURE 4–17

```
var
    i : integer;                    {counter}
    prev,                           {angle where sector starts}
    halfway,                        {middle of sector}
    radian,                         {sector angle}
    xnew,                           {coordinates of}
    ynew,                           {new center}
    xpos,                           {coordinates of}
    ypos : real;                    {start of label}
begin
    window(0,511,0,511);
    viewport(0,1,0,1);
    {initial angle}
    prev := 0;
    {loop for each slice}
    for i := 1 to 7 do
        begin    {for}
            {sector angle}
            radian := 2*pi* sector[i].percent;
            {middle of sector}
            halfway := prev + radian/2;
            {if exploded sector, then move its center coordinates radially out
             from the original center position}
            if sector[i].explode then
                begin    {if}
                    {compute new center}
                    xnew := xc + 1/3 * radius*cos(halfway);
                    ynew := yc + 1/3 * radius*sin(halfway)
                end    {if}
            else    {do not explode}
                begin    {else}
                    xnew := xc;
                    ynew := yc
                end;    {else}
            {draw sector}
            Sector(xnew,ynew,radius,prev,radian,10);
            {determine if the sector should be shaded}
            if sector[i].shade then
            {sector shade procedure}
            {different amounts for each sector}
            Shade(i * factor);
            {calculate location of start of label}
            xpos := xnew + (radius + 5)*cos(halfway);
            ypos := ynew + (radius + 5)*sin(halfway);
            {left of circle}
            if xpos < xc then
                xpos := xpos - length(sector[i].name) * 7;
            {bottom of circle}
            if ypos < yc then
                ypos := ypos - 8;
```

```
          {draw label}
          move2(xpos,ypos);
          txt(sector[i].name,1,length(sector[i].name));
          {update current angle}
          prev := prev + radian
          end     {for}
end;    {Explode}
```

4–5 **CONCLUSION**

In this chapter we described several shading techniques for rectangles and circles and then applied shading to produce artistic images and business graphics. This elementary shading is often called filling, with the term *shading* reserved for the more realistic shading models. In Chapter 10, we shall discuss those algorithms that perform arbitrary area and polygon filling.

Many display systems have commands that fill specified regions. Since these features are not always available in low-cost graphics systems, we shall not use them here. However, following is a description of several filling procedures.

fillrect(x1,y1,x2,y2,shade)

draws and fills a rectangle with diagonally opposite corners $(x1, y1)$, $(x2, y2)$ with a designated shade.

fillpoly(vertices,shade)

draws and fills a polygon with a designated shade. The parameter *vertices* is a two-dimensional array containing an ordered list of the polygon's vertices.

fillcirc(xc,yc,radius,shade)

draws and fills a circle with center (xc, yc). The shade choices can be among radial and arc with different spacing.

fillarc(xc,yc,radius,startangle,endangle,shade)

draws and fills an arc defined by a center (xc, yc), a starting and ending angle, and a radius. The angles are measured counterclockwise from the positive x-axis. The shade choices are either radial or arc.

EXERCISES

1. Write a program that performs gradual vertical shading.
2. Write a program that performs gradual diagonal shading.
3. Write a program that performs gradual radial shading.
4. Write a program that draws a polygon that has its vertices stored in a two-dimensional array.

Detail of Figure 5–20

5

TWO-DIMENSIONAL GEOMETRIC TRANSFORMATIONS

5–1 **INTRODUCTION**

Geometric transformations provide a means by which an image can be constructed or modified. Suppose, for example, we wish to move the motorcycle and driver in Figure 5-1a around the world coordinate space. To do this, we operate on the list of (x, y) coordinate pairs that define the cycle and driver and transform this list to a specified position. Each time the cycle moves, the list is transformed and the cycle must be redrawn using this new list (Figure 5-1b). In·addition to positioning the motorcycle, a transformation can make it larger or smaller, or even distort its appearance by elongating parts of the cycle in different directions. All of these changes are performed by submitting one list of (x, y) coordinates to a transformation, which produces a new list of (x, y) coordinates that is used for drawing.

Transformations can also be used to construct an image. The helicoptor in Figure 5-2a is composed of four separate subimages, as illustrated in Figure 5-2b. Each of these subimages is first constructed in its own coordinates and is then transformed to its correct position in Figure 5-2a.

The transformations we examine in this chapter are: translations, rotations, scaling, and shearing. Each one is first described geometrically, and then its matrix representation is given.

FIGURE 5–1
A transformation of a motorcycle and driver

(a)

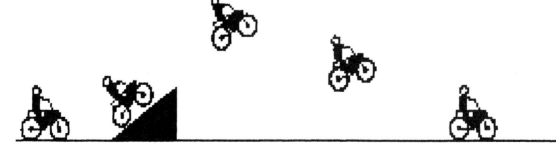

(b)

    Two-Dimensional Geometric Transformations

FIGURE 5–2
A helicopter con-
structed by
transformations

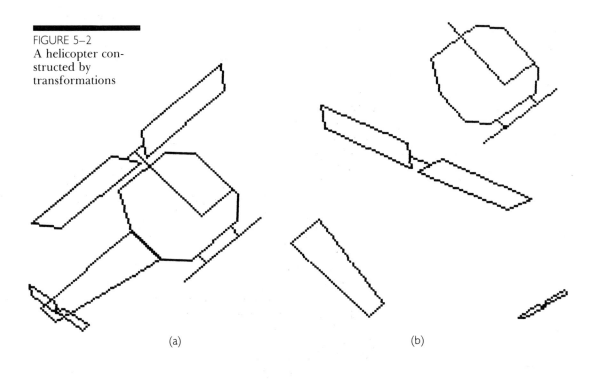

(a)   (b)

5–2 **TRANSLATIONS**

A point in the world coordinate system is transformed to another
position by modifying its x and y coordinates. In Figure 5-3, a point at
location (x, y) has been moved 10 units up and and 5 units to the left.

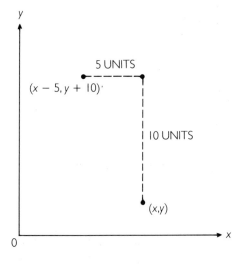

FIGURE 5–3
Point (x, y) trans-
lated 10 units up
and 5 units to the
left

FIGURE 5–4
Horizontal and ver-
tical displacement

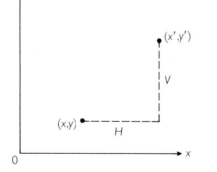

In general, a point (x, y) is **translated** to a new position (x', y') by moving it H units in the horizontal direction and V units in the vertical direction (Figure 5-4). Mathematically this can be represented as

$$(5-1) \quad \begin{aligned} x' &= x + H \\ y' &= y + V. \end{aligned}$$

The H and V represent the horizontal and vertical displacement or distance that the point has moved. If H is positive, the point moves to the right; if H is negative, the point moves to the left. Similarly, a positive V moves the point up; a negative V moves it down.

In most cases, we want to translate not just a point but one or more objects in an image. To perform this, we must translate every point defining the object(s). When doing this, all points are displaced the same distance, and the object is redrawn using these transformed points (Figure 5-5).

FIGURE 5–5
A translation of a
spaceship

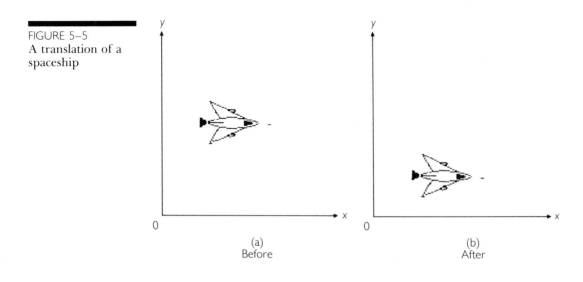

(a)
Before

(b)
After

Two-Dimensional Geometric Transformations

5-3 **ROTATIONS**

Another useful transformation is the **rotation** of an object about a specified pivot point (Figure 5-6). After the object has been rotated, it is still the same distance away from the pivot point, however its orientation has been changed. It is possible to rotate one or more objects, or the entire image, about any point in world space in either a clockwise or counterclockwise direction. Figure 5-7a on page 126 illustrates a rotation where the pivot point is inside the owl. Figure 5-7b has the pivot point outside the dog.

We want to examine the mathematics of a counterclockwise rotation about an arbitrary pivot point. In order to make this derivation a little more understandable, let's first examine a rotation where the pivot point is the origin of the world space.

As discussed in Chapter 2, any point (x, y) can be represented by its radial distance, r, from the origin and its angle, ϕ, off the x-axis. In Figure 5-8 on page 127, the point (x, y) is represented as

$$x = r \times \cos(\phi)$$
$$y = r \times \sin(\phi).$$

If (x, y) is rotated an angle θ in the counterclockwise direction, the transformed point (x', y'), as illustrated in Figure 5-9 on page 127, is represented as

$$x' = r \times \cos(\phi + \theta)$$
$$y' = r \times \sin(\phi + \theta).$$

Using the laws of sines and cosines from trigonometry, the above equations become

$$x' = r \times \cos(\phi) \times \cos(\theta) - r \times \sin(\phi) \times \sin(\theta)$$
$$y' = r \times \sin(\phi) \times \cos(\theta) + r \times \cos(\phi) \times \sin(\theta).$$

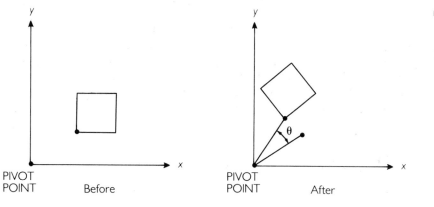

FIGURE 5-6
Rotation about a pivot point

FIGURE 5–7
Rotation about piv-
ot points

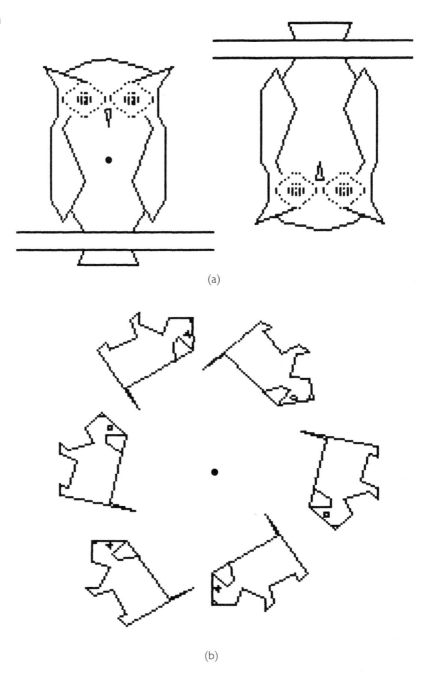

(a)

(b)

From the definition of x and y, these equations reduce to

$(5–2)$ $\quad x' = x \times \cos(\theta) - y \times \sin(\theta)$
$\qquad\quad y' = y \times \cos(\theta) + x \times \sin(\theta).$

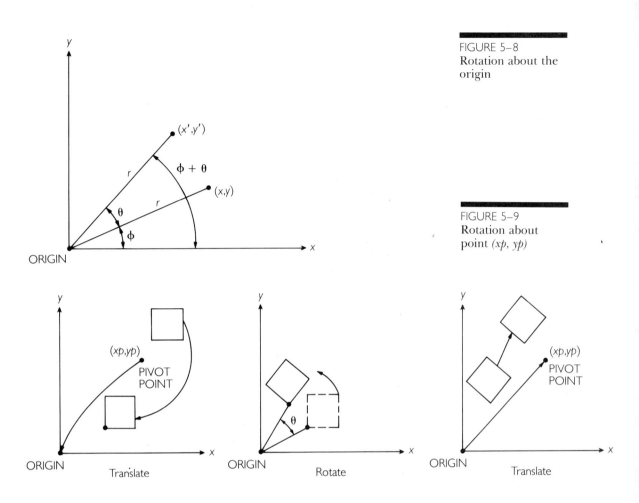

FIGURE 5–8
Rotation about the
origin

FIGURE 5–9
Rotation about
point *(xp, yp)*

ORIGIN

ORIGIN   Translate

ORIGIN   Rotate

ORIGIN   Translate

Equations 5-2 are the transformation that rotates a point an angle θ
about the origin in the counterclockwise direction. To rotate an object,
each point defining that object must be transformed using these equations. The object is then redrawn using the list of transformed points.

It is often necessary to rotate an object an angle θ about a pivot
point other than the origin. To perform this, three steps are required
(see Figure 5-6).

1. Translate the pivot point *(xp, yp)* to the origin. When doing this,
    every point *(x, y)* defining the object is translated to a new point *(x',
    y')* where

    $$x' = x - xp$$
    $$y' = y - yp.$$

    Observe that, as required above, this translation sends the pivot
    point *(xp, yp)* to (0,0).

2. Rotate these translated points (x', y') θ degrees about the origin to obtain the new point (x'', y''), where

$$x'' = x' \times \cos(\theta) - y' \times \sin(\theta)$$
$$y'' = y' \times \cos(\theta) + x' \times \sin(\theta).$$

Substituting the above values for x' and y' into these equations, we get

$$x'' = (x - xp) \times \cos(\theta) - (y - yp) \times \sin(\theta)$$
$$y'' = (y - yp) \times \cos(\theta) + (x - xp) \times \sin(\theta).$$

3. Translate the center of rotation back to the pivot point (xp, yp). Thus the point (x'', y'') is translated to (x''', y''') where

$$x''' = x'' + xp$$
$$y''' = y'' + yp.$$

Substituting the values of x'' and y'' from the previous equations, we obtain the desired equation for a counterclockwise rotation of angle θ about the point (xp, yp):

(5–3)
$$x''' = (x - xp) \times \cos(\theta) - (y - yp) \times \sin(\theta) + xp$$
$$y''' = (y - yp) \times \cos(\theta) + (x - xp) \times \sin(\theta) + yp.$$

You may reasonably ask why we are rotating an object in the counterclockwise direction and not in the clockwise direction. The answer is that in mathematics, counterclockwise is usually considered the positive rotation direction. If you like your directions clockwise, just change the angle θ to $-\theta$ in the above equations. Remember that $\cos(-\theta) = \cos(\theta)$ and $\sin(-\theta) = -\sin(\theta)$.

5–4 **SCALING**

In Chapter 3, we saw how to change the size of the image by changing the dimensions of the window and the viewport. This technique in not satisfactory for all cases, however. For example, we may only want to alter the size of a single object in the window. If the window's dimensions are changed, all objects within the window are affected. In this section, we describe how scaling allows us to change the size of a specified object.

An object can be made larger by increasing the distance between the points describing the object (Figure 5-10). In general, we can change the size of an object, or the entire image, by multiplying the distances between points by an enlargement or reduction factor. This factor is called the **scaling factor**, and the operation that changes the size is called **scaling**. If the scaling factor is greater than 1, the object is enlarged; if

y

FIXED POINT

x

FIGURE 5–10
Scaling

the factor is less than 1, the object is made smaller; a factor of 1 has no effect on the object.

Whenever a scaling is performed, there is one point that remains at the same location. This is called the fixed point of the scaling transformation (Figure 5-10). If the fixed point is at the origin (0, 0), as in Figure 5-10, a point (x, y) can be scaled by a factor Sx in the x direction and Sy in the y direction to the new point (x', y') by the multiplications

(5–4) $$\begin{aligned} x' &= x \times Sx \\ y' &= y \times Sy. \end{aligned}$$

Sx and Sy are called the horizontal and vertical scale factors, respectively. If $Sx \neq Sy$, the resulting object is a distortion of the original (Figure 5-11).

If both the scaling factors are greater than 1, the scaled object is enlarged and moved further away from the fixed point. A scaling factor

FIGURE 5–11
Scaling distortion

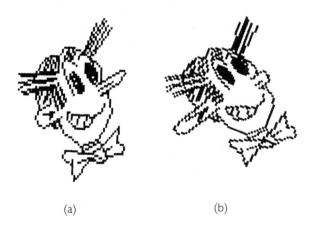

(a)   (b)

less than 1 brings the object closer to the fixed point while reducing it. Figures 5-12a and 5-12b illustrate these features, with the fixed point at the origin.

It is possible to choose any point (xp, yp) as the fixed point of scaling. To do this, we perform three steps similar to those described in rotating about an arbitrary point.

1. Translate the point (xp, yp) to the origin. Every point (x, y) is moved to a new point (x', y'):

$$x' = x - xp$$
$$y' = y - yp.$$

2. Scale these translated points with the origin as the fixed point:

$$x'' = x' \times Sx$$
$$y'' = y' \times Sy.$$

FIGURE 5–12
Scaling changes the distance from a fixed point

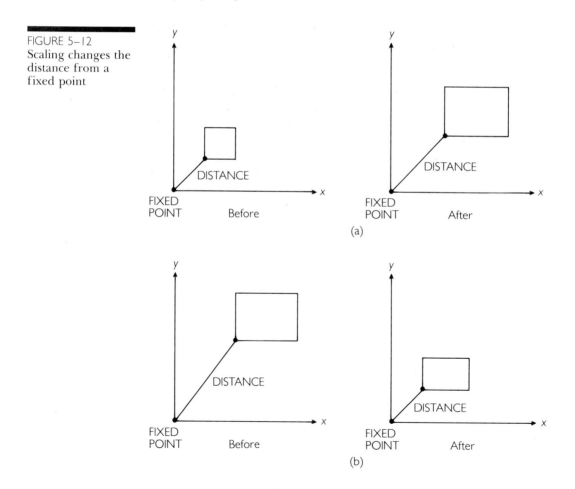

(a)

(b)

3. Translate the origin back to the fixed point (xp, yp):

$$x''' = x'' + xp$$
$$y''' = y'' + yp.$$

Substituting the values of x', y', x'', and y'' into these last equations, we obtain the desired scaling transformation, with (xp, yp) as the fixed point:

$$(5\text{--}5) \quad \begin{aligned} x''' &= (x - xp) \times Sx + xp \\ y''' &= (y - yp) \times Sy + yp. \end{aligned}$$

We can verify that (xp, yp) is a fixed point of this transformation by equating x''' to x and y''' to y and solving for x and y, respectively. That is

$$x = x''' = (x - xp) \times Sx + xp \qquad \text{or}$$
$$x = x \times Sx - xp \times Sx + xp \qquad \text{or}$$
$$x \times (1 - Sx) = xp \times (1 - Sx) \qquad \text{or}$$
$$x = xp, \qquad \text{assuming } Sx \neq 1.$$

We can perform a symmetric sequence of steps to show that yp is the y coordinate of the fixed point.

5–5 SHEARING

A **shearing** transformation produces a distortion of an object or the entire image. We examine two types of shears: y-shear and x-shear. A y-shear transforms the point (x, y) to the point (x', y'), where

$$(5\text{--}6) \quad \begin{aligned} x' &= x \\ y' &= Shy \times x + y, \qquad Shy \neq 0. \end{aligned}$$

A y-shear moves a vertical line up or down, depending on the sign of the shear factor Shy (Figure 5-13 on page 132). A horizontal line is distorted into a slanted line with slope Shy. Combining these two observations, we see that a y-shear distorts a rectangle into a parallelogram (Figure 5-14 on page 132).

An x-shear has the opposite effect. That is, the point (x, y) is transformed to the point (x', y'), where

$$(5\text{--}7) \quad \begin{aligned} x' &= x + Shx \times y, \qquad Shx \neq 0 \\ y' &= y. \end{aligned}$$

Vertical lines become slanted with slope Shx and horizontal lines are shifted to the right or left, depending on the sign of Shx (Figure 5-15 on page 132).

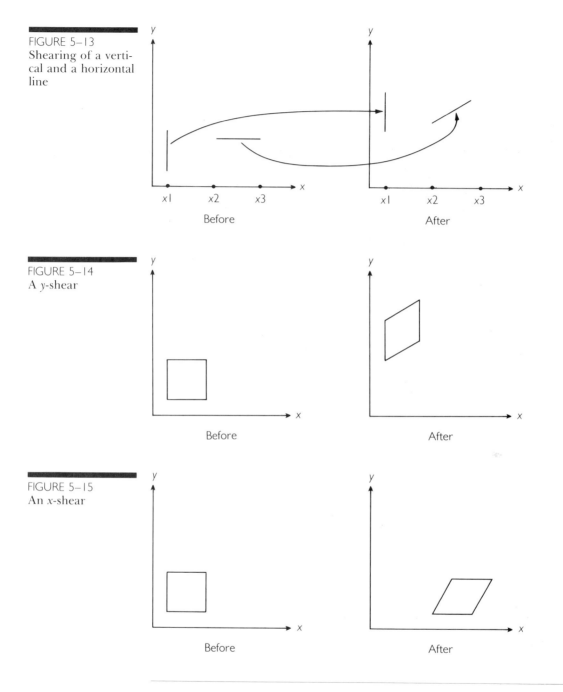

FIGURE 5–13
Shearing of a verti-
cal and a horizontal
line

y

y

x1   x2   x3   x

x1   x2   x3   x

Before

After

FIGURE 5–14
A *y*-shear

y

y

x

x

Before

After

FIGURE 5–15
An *x*-shear

y

y

x

x

Before

After

5–6 **INVERSE TRANSFORMATIONS**

To undo a transformation, we must perform the inverse of that transformation. The inverse of a transformation is a transformation of the same type but with inverse parameters. These parameters are:

Translate: $-H$, $-V$
Rotate: $-\theta$
Scale: $1/Sx$, $1/Sy$
Shear: $-Shx$, $-Shy$.

5–7 MATRICES

A **matrix** is a rectangular array of numbers such as the following:

$$[1\ 4] \quad \begin{bmatrix} 2 & 0 \\ 3 & 8 \end{bmatrix} \quad \begin{bmatrix} 6 & -1 & 2 \\ 0 & 3 & 7 \\ 5 & 8 & 1 \end{bmatrix}.$$

The horizontal and vertical subarrays within the matrix are called its rows and columns, respectively. A matrix having m rows and n columns is said to be an $m \times n$ matrix. If m equals n, the matrix is square. The above matrices, from left to right, are 1×2, 2×2, and 3×3.

A **vector** is a special matrix having one row or one column—that is, m or n, but not both—that equals 1. Vectors are important since a coordinate pair (x, y) can be expressed as a row vector

$$[x\ y]$$

or a column vector

$$\begin{bmatrix} x \\ y \end{bmatrix}.$$

The product of two matrices, $A \times B$ is defined only when the number of columns in A equals the number of rows in B. In this chapter, the second matrix B will always be a 3×3 square matrix. If A is a 1×3 row vector (matrix), then $A \times B$ is also a 1×3 row vector. If A is a 3×3 square matrix, then $A \times B$ is also a 3×3 square matrix.

Matrix multiplication is a sum of products operation, where, loosely speaking, the rows of A are multiplied by the columns of B. Let's look at some examples.

Example 1:
Let

$$A = [2\ 1\ 3] \quad \text{and} \quad B = \begin{bmatrix} 1 & 0 & 2 \\ -2 & 3 & 1 \\ 4 & 6 & 3 \end{bmatrix}$$

$$A \times B = [12\ 21\ 14]$$

where

$$12 = 2 \times 1 + 1 \times (-2) + 3 \times 4 \qquad \text{(row 1 of } A) \times \text{(col 1 of } B)$$
$$21 = 2 \times 0 + 1 \times 3 + 3 \times 6 \qquad \text{(row 1 of } A) \times \text{(col 2 of } B)$$
$$14 = 2 \times 2 + 1 \times 1 + 3 \times 3 \qquad \text{(row 1 of } A) \times \text{(col 3 of } B)$$

Example 2:

Let

$$A = \begin{bmatrix} 0 & 2 & -1 \\ 3 & 1 & 2 \\ 1 & 2 & 1 \end{bmatrix} \quad \text{and} \quad B = \begin{bmatrix} 1 & 0 & 2 \\ -2 & 3 & 1 \\ 4 & 6 & 3 \end{bmatrix}$$

$$A \times B = \begin{bmatrix} -8 & 0 & -1 \\ 9 & 15 & 13 \\ 1 & 12 & 7 \end{bmatrix}$$

where

$$-8 = 0 \times 1 + 2 \times (-2) + (-1) \times 4 \qquad \text{(row 1 of } A) \times \text{(col 1 of } B)$$
$$0 = 0 \times 0 + 2 \times 3 + (-1) \times 6 \qquad \text{(row 1 of } A) \times \text{(col 2 of } B)$$
$$-1 = 0 \times 2 + 2 \times 1 + (-1) \times 3 \qquad \text{(row 1 of } A) \times \text{(col 3 of } B)$$
$$9 = 3 \times 1 + 1 \times (-2) + 2 \times 4 \qquad \text{(row 2 of } A) \times \text{(col 1 of } B)$$
$$15 = 3 \times 0 + 1 \times 3 + 2 \times 6 \qquad \text{(row 2 of } A) \times \text{(col 2 of } B)$$
$$13 = 3 \times 2 + 1 \times 1 + 2 \times 3 \qquad \text{(row 2 of } A) \times \text{(col 3 of } B)$$
$$1 = 1 \times 1 + 2 \times (-2) + 1 \times 4 \qquad \text{(row 3 of } A) \times \text{(col 1 of } B)$$
$$12 = 1 \times 0 + 2 \times 3 + 1 \times 6 \qquad \text{(row 3 of } A) \times \text{(col 2 of } B)$$
$$7 = 1 \times 2 + 2 \times 1 + 1 \times 3 \qquad \text{(row 3 of } A) \times \text{(col 3 of } B)$$

Matrix multiplication is not commutative; that is, $A \times B$ may not equal $B \times A$. The reader should verify that for the two matrices in Example 2.

$$B \times A = \begin{bmatrix} 2 & 6 & 1 \\ 10 & 1 & 9 \\ 21 & 20 & 11 \end{bmatrix}$$

Observe that $B \times A$ is not defined for the matrices in Example 1.
Matrix multiplication is associative:

$$A \times (B \times C) = (A \times B) \times C$$

A square matrix with 1s along the diagonal from top left to bottom right, called the main diagonal, and 0s everywhere else is the **identity** matrix, denoted by I:

$$I = \begin{bmatrix} 1 & 0 & 0 \\ 0 & 1 & 0 \\ 0 & 0 & 1 \end{bmatrix}$$

The **inverse** of a square matrix A is the matrix A^{-1} having the property

$$A^{-1} \times A = A^{-1} \times A = I.$$

The inverse of a square matrix may not exist, but when it does, the general method for finding it can require many floating-point operations. The inverse of the product of two square matrices is the product of the inverse in reverse order:

$$(A \times B)^{-1} = B^{-1} \times A^{-1}.$$

The **transpose** of a matrix A is the matrix A^T, which is formed from A by interchanging its rows and columns. The matrix B in Example 1 has transpose

$$B^T = \begin{bmatrix} 1 & -2 & 4 \\ 0 & 3 & 6 \\ 2 & 1 & 3 \end{bmatrix}$$

The transpose of the product of two matrices is the product of the transpose of the matrices in reverse order:

$$(A \times B)^T = B^T \times A^T.$$

5–8 MATRIX REPRESENTATION OF TRANSFORMATIONS

Each of the transformations we have discussed, except for the translation, can be represented as a product of the row vector $[x\ y]$ and a 2×2 matrix. We can, however, represent all four transformations as a product of the 1×3 row vector and an appropriate 3×3 matrix. The advantage of using this uniform (homogeneous) representation will become clear in the next section when transformations are combined.

Since we are going to use 3×3 matrices, it is necessary to convert the two-dimensional coordinate pair (x, y) into a three-dimensional **homogeneous vector.** This is accomplished by associating (x, y) with the homogeneous row vector $[x\ y\ 1]$. After multiplying this vector by a 3×3 matrix, we obtain another homogeneous row vector, one having three components with the last component equal to 1: $[x'\ y'\ 1]$. The first two terms in this vector are the coordinate pair (x', y') which is the transform of (x, y). This (nonunique) three-dimensional representation of the two-dimensional plane is called a representation of **homogeneous**

coordinates. We are now ready to give the matrix representation of the four transformations: translation, rotation, scaling, and shearing.

Translation:

$$[x'\ y'\ 1] = [x\ y\ 1]\begin{bmatrix} 1 & 0 & 0 \\ 0 & 1 & 0 \\ H & V & 1 \end{bmatrix}$$

Rotation:

$$[x'\ y'\ 1] = [x\ y\ 1]\begin{bmatrix} \cos\theta & \sin\theta & 0 \\ -\sin\theta & \cos\theta & 0 \\ 0 & 0 & 1 \end{bmatrix}$$

Scaling:

$$[x'\ y'\ 1] = [x\ y\ 1]\begin{bmatrix} Sx & 0 & 0 \\ 0 & Sy & 0 \\ 0 & 0 & 1 \end{bmatrix}$$

y-Shear:

$$[x'\ y'\ 1] = [x\ y\ 1]\begin{bmatrix} 1 & Shy & 0 \\ 0 & 1 & 0 \\ 0 & 0 & 1 \end{bmatrix}$$

x-Shear:

$$[x'\ y'\ 1] = [x\ y\ 1]\begin{bmatrix} 1 & 0 & 0 \\ Shx & 1 & 0 \\ 0 & 0 & 1 \end{bmatrix}$$

The inverse matrices are readily obtained by substituting the appropriate inverse parameters (given in Section 5-6) into the 3×3 transformation matrix.

5–9 COMBINING TRANSFORMATIONS

Any of the above transformations can be combined to produce new transformation. For example, a rotation about an arbitrary pivot point requires a translation, followed by a rotation, followed by another translation (the inverse of the first). Figure 5-16 illustrates the effect of combining rotations and translations. Having the matrix representation of a transformation, the transformations can be combined by multiplying their corresponding matrices. (This is the reason all two-dimensional transformations are represented as 3×3 matrices.) This association between combining transformations and multiplying matrices make the matrix representation particularly attractive. It is far easier to perform matrix multiplication than to perform the substitutions necessary to combine transformations.

There are two different ways to combine transformations. Each produces the same result, but one is considerably more efficient. To illustrate, suppose that a rotation Rot is followed by a translation Tr. Therefore

$$[x' \; y' \; 1] = [x \; y \; 1] \times Rot \times Tr.$$

The first method multiplies the row vector by the rotation matrix, obtaining the intermediary vector:

$$[x''' \; y''' \; 1] = [x \; y \; 1] \times Rot.$$

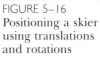

FIGURE 5–16
Positioning a skier using translations and rotations

This matrix multiplication requires nine multiplications and six additions. The final vector is obtained by multiplying this intermediary vector by the translation matrix:

$$[x'\ y'\ 1] = [x'''\ y'''\ 1] \times Tr.$$

This step requires an additional nine multiplications and six additions, giving a total of 18 multiplications and 12 additions. These two steps must be applied to each (x, y) pair in the list defining the transformed object(s). For lists containing hundreds or thousands of points, a considerable amount of floating-point arithmetic must be performed.

The second method reduces the number of arithmetic operations by first combining the two 3×3 matrices. The multiplication, $Rot \times Tr$, requires 27 multiplications and 18 additions. The important observation to make is that this multiplication is performed one time only, and not for each (x, y) pair in the object list. The combined matrix is now multiplied by the row vector:

$$[x'\ y'\ 1] = [x\ y\ 1] \times (Rot \times Tr).$$

This matrix multiplication requires nine multiplications and six additions. Therefore, except for the one-time multiplication of $Rot \times Tr$, the second method of combining transformations can reduce by one-half the number of arithmetic computations.

Since matrix multiplication is not commutative, whenever we combine different types of transformations we must be careful of the order in which they are performed. Figure 5-17 illustrates that a translation followed by a rotation produces a different effect than a rotation followed by a translation.

FIGURE 5–17
Changing the order
of a translation and
a rotation

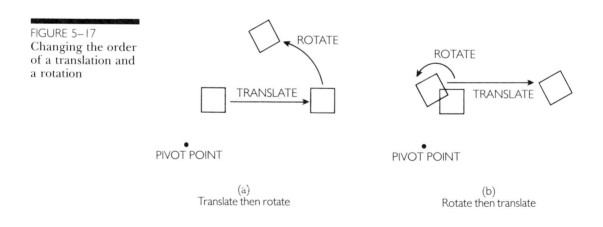

(a)
Translate then rotate

(b)
Rotate then translate

Two-Dimensional Geometric Transformations

5–10 **TRANSFORMATION PROCEDURES**

Anyone who has tried writing his or her own matrix multiplication procedure quickly realizes that matrix multiplication is a slow operation. For this and other reasons, most graphics systems provide these transformations and perform the matrix multiplication in low-level code or special-purpose hardware. These transformations are designated by the world coordinate system commands:

translate(H,V)

H units horizontally, *V* units vertically;

rotate(θ)

in a counterclockwise direction about the origin; θ is in radians;

scale(Sx,Sy)

Sx units along the *x*-axis, *Sy* units along the *y*-axis, with the origin as the fixed point.

Few systems provide the user with the shear transformations, and therefore we will assume that it is not available in the graphics package. The importance of the shear transformation will be evident when three-dimensional transformations are examined.

Before using these transformations, it is necessary to comment on how they affect the drawing commands. First, all transformations are cumulative in that they act not on the initial coordinates but on the transformed coordinates. For example, if we had previously performed a translation and now issue a rotation, the translation matrix is multiplied by the rotation matrix, and this new matrix is used for future transformations.

Second, if we display an object on the screen and then issue a transformation, expecting to see the object move, we will be disappointed. All transformations operate only on world coordinate graphics commands (such as **draw2**), which are invoked *after* the invocation of the transformation. Thus if we want to draw a square and then rotate it, it is necessary to reinvoke the square-drawing procedure after issuing the rotate command. Forgetting either of these two restrictions produces undesired (and sometimes startling) results.

Let's also include in the graphics package the command

identity,

which resets the transformation matrix to the identity matrix *I*. This cancels all previous transformations.

5–11 APPLICATIONS

It is possible to produce striking pictures by using simple objects and transformations. Figure 5-18 shows the effect of rotating two boxes about two circles. This is equivalent to placing the two boxes at different distances from the origin of the world coordinate system and applying the rotation command. The following code produces this effect. We use the Draw_Box procedure from Chapter 4, where the (x, y) coordinates are in the lower-left corner of the box. The constant identifier pi equals 3.1415927.

```
for count := 1 to N do     {N rotations}
    begin
        Draw_Box(x1,y1,len1,wid1);
        Draw_Box(x2,y2,len2,wid2);
        rotate(2*pi/N)
    end;
```

FIGURE 5–18
Rotating two boxes
about two circles

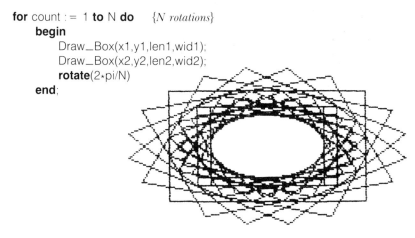

Figure 5-19 depicts a plane flying in a spiral pattern. This effect is achieved by incrementing the x value of the plane's position and then rotating the plane. As the spiral grows, successive planes are rotated less from the previous one. The following code assumes the existence of a Procedure Draw_Plane(x), which draws the plane at a specified location. (Use graph paper to construct the plane.)

```
{initial plane position}
x := 0;
y := 0;
{initial rotation angle}
theta := pi/2;
while x < limit do     {inside window}
    begin     {while}
        Draw_Plane(x);
        {spiral effect}
        x := x + 5;
        rotate(theta);
        {decrease successive rotations}
        theta := theta − pi/25
    end;     {while}
```

FIGURE 5-19
An airplane flying
in a spiral pattern

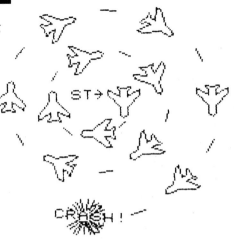

The final illustration (Figure 5-20), shows a diamond that has first been sheared in the *x* direction, then scaled, and finally rotated about a circle. Since our graphics package does not have an *x*-shear procedure, one is created in the program. We use an *x*-shear factor of − 1 to produce this image. The entire program is listed below.

```
Program Diamond;

type
    coords = array[1..7] of real;
    points = record
                x,y: coords
             end;

var
    vertex : points;    {seven vertices of diamond}
    i : integer;    {loop counter}

Procedure Get_Diamond;
    {assign vertex values of diamond}

begin
    with vertex do
        begin    {with}
            x[1] := 5 y[1]     : = 30;
            x[2] := −5; y[2]   : = 30;
            x[3] := −11; y[3] : = 24;
            x[4] := −5; y[4]   : = 18;
            x[5] := 5; y[5]    : = 18;
            x[6] := 11; y[6]   : = 24;
            x[7] := 0; y[7]    : =  0
        end    {with}
end;    {Get_Diamond}
```

FIGURE 5–20
Rotation and shear-
ing of a diamond

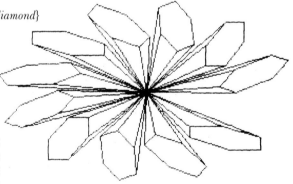

```
Procedure Draw_Diamond;
    {draws the diamond figure}

var
    i: integer;    {loop counter}

begin
    with vertex do
        begin    {with}
            move2(x[6],y[6]);
            for i := 1 to 6 do
            draw2(x[i],y[i]);
            draw2(x[7],y[7]);
            draw2(x[5],y[5]);
            move2(x[7],y[7]);
            draw2(x[4],y[4]);
            move2(x[7],y[7]);
            draw2(x[3],y[3])
        end    {with}
end;    {Draw_Diamond}

Procedure Xshear(
    factor: real    {shear factor});

    {perform x-shear transformation}

begin
    with vertex do
        for i := 1 to 7 do
            x[i] := x[i] + factor*y[i]
end;    {Xshear}

begin    {Diamond}
    {make window large enough for rotated diamonds}
    window(-45,45,-50,50);
    viewport(0,1,0,1)
    Get_Diamond;
    {build transformation}
    Xshear(-1);    {shear factor -1}
    scale(2,1,0);    {scale factor 2 in x direction}
    {11 copies of transformed diamond}
    for i := 1 to 11 do
        begin    {for}
            Draw_Diamond;
            rotate(pi/6)
        end{for}
end.    {Diamond}
```

5–12 CONCLUSION

An image is created by placing its component subimages at specified locations in the world coordinate system; this is a process referred to as instancing. These subimages are often created separately, necessitating the use of geometric (modeling) transformations to position the sub-images correctly in the image. Any part of the image, or the entire image itself, can be moved or distorted by applying a transformation to the list of points defining the image. Three by three matrix representation is an efficient and homogeneous technique for performing these types of two-dimensional transformations.

EXERCISES

1. Write a program that
   a. first rotates and then translates a rectangle
   b. first translates and then rotates a rectangle.
2. For the matrices in Example 2 of Section 5-7, show that
   $(A \times B)^T = B^T \times A^T$.
3. Write a program that rotates about an arbitrary pivot point.
4. Determine the matrix that performs the following sequence of transformations

   scale$(2, -1)$
   rotate(pi/6)
   translate$(-3,4)$

5. How many multiplications and additions are required to compute the transformation matrix in exercise 4? Reduce this number by using the 2 × 2 submatrices to multiply the scale, and rotate and append the fourth row and column prior to multiplying by the translation matrix.
6. Rotate, scale, and shear the character string generated in exercise 5 of Chapter 3.
7. Verify that the matrix of a reflection in the x-axis is formed by replacing the first entry in the identity matrix with a -1. What is the transformation matrix of a reflection in the y-axis?
8. A reflection about the line $y = x$ sends a point (a, b) to (a', b') where

   $a' = b \qquad b' = a.$

   Show how a reflection can be performed by a rotation followed by a scale.

9. Create an image similar to Figure 5-2 by defining several subimages in their own coordinate system and then placing these subimages in one image using translations, scales, and rotations.

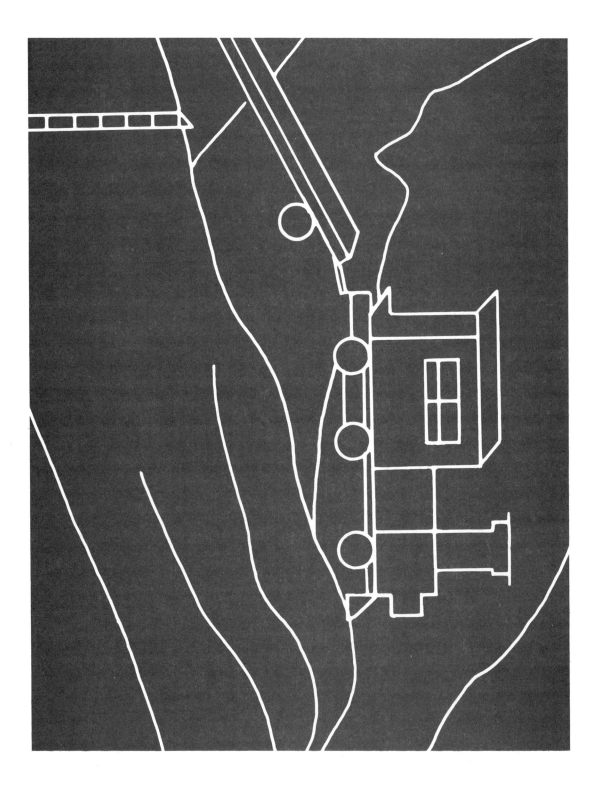

Detail of Figure 6-1a

6

DISPLAY
FILE
SEGMENTATION

6-1 **INTRODUCTION**

Complex images are often composed of simpler subimages, some of which may be transformations of each other. For example, an image depicting a busy intersection has cars of different sizes in different locations heading in different directions. In addition, there are people, street signs, and buildings. As the day progresses, we want to alter the image by increasing or decreasing the number of cars and people at this intersection. Hence, we would like to have the capability of changing parts of an image while keeping other parts fixed.

A natural way of providing this feature is to allow an image to be subdivided or **segmented** into a collection of independent objects or

FIGURE 6-1
A sequence of a
segmented image

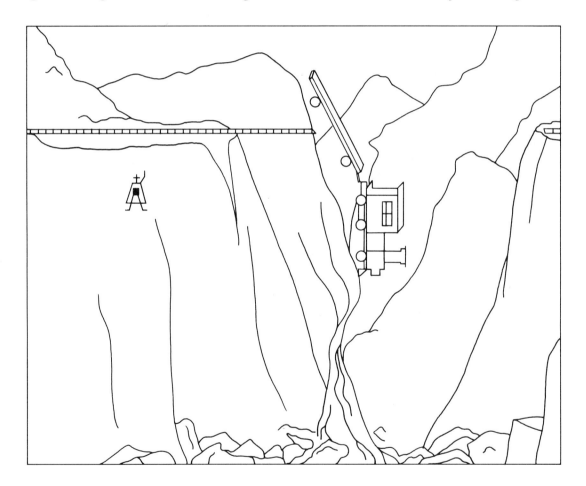

(a)

subimages. Each subimage is a sequence of graphics commands packaged into one unit. This segmentation allows the user to reference parts of the image independently of the rest of the image. The subimages can be deleted, transformed to another part of the image, altered in shape, or even reproduced throughout the image. The process of segmenting an image into logical units is similar to the modularization process in programming: A large program is divided into procedures and functions that are invoked with different values (parameters) when needed.

Figures 6-1a and 6-1b illustrate two sequences of a train falling off the railroad tracks. The train, the tracks, the mountain range, and the super hero trying unsuccessfully to save the train are distinct subimages. By creating the image this way, it is relatively easy to produce the two-image sequence.

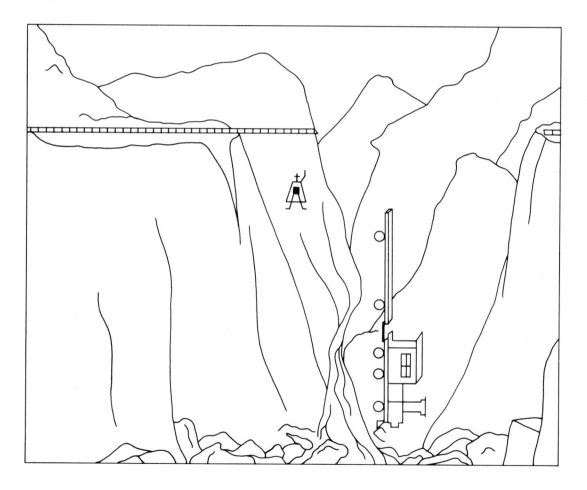

(b)

This chapter examines how to implement graphics display segmentation, a process available in sophisticated display systems. Segmentation has a natural setting in a random-vector system. For example, an animation sequence might require the movement of a line from one part of the display to another. If this line is placed in a separate segment in the display file, the display controller need only redraw the transformed line in the next refresh cycle. A raster-scan system performing the same task requires two actions: First, the original line must be erased by redrawing it in the background color, and second, the line is drawn in its new location. Even if the display system hardware and software perform this erasure fast enough, there may be other problems since this technique may produce a "hole" in other lines that the erased line intersected. Figure 6-2 illustrates this problem by erasing the horizontal line.

6–2 DISPLAY FILE

Recall that an image is described by a sequence of primitive graphics commands such as **move2**(x, y) and **draw2**(x, y). Each command is interpreted by the appropriate scan conversion algorithm, which calculates the correct pixels to illuminate. This collection of graphics commands that represent the image is called a **display file**.

An entry in the display file can be represented by a record, with one field representing the name of the command and the other fields the operands of the command. The number of operand fields should be the maximum number of operands for a legal graphics command. The display file consists of an array of these records. For illustrative purposes, we shall assume that each record has three fields: a command field and two operand fields. This is sufficient if we use only the four basic commands: **draw2**, **move2**, **rdraw2**, **rmove2**.

The Pascal record data type provides a convenient construct with which to create this display file. In order to differentiate the user-defined drawing commands from the system-defined ones (which are key words), we have omitted the vowels from their spelling. The command

FIGURE 6–2

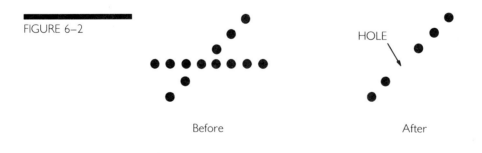

Before   After

Display File Segmentation

stop indicates the end of the file and will be explained in more detail later.

```
const
     size = 500;    {maximum length of display file}

type
     {user-defined drawing commands}
     commands = (drw2,mve2,rdrw,rmve2,stop);
     {display file entry}

     entry = record
                    cmd : commands;
                    opand1 : real;    {x value}
                    opand2 : real    {y value}
             end;

var
     display_file : array[1..size] of entry;
```

A display file is illustrated in Figure 6-3. Using this data structure, the graphics command **move**2(1.5, −6.8) is inserted into the fifth entry of the display file array by the code:

```
with display_file[5] do
    begin
        cmd := Mve2;
        opand1 := 1.5;
        opand2 := −6.8
    end;
```

There are other, and better, ways to represent a display file in Pascal, however. Since a display file often changes size as the display changes, using dynamic variables is a natural choice for implementation

	CMD	OPAND1	OPAND2
1			
2			
3			
4			
5	MOVE 2	1.5	−6.8
. . .			
SIZE			

FIGURE 6–3
A display file

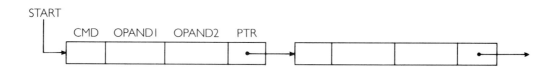

START

CMD   OPAND1   OPAND2   PTR

FIGURE 6–4
A dynamic display
file

(Figure 6-4). A dynamic display file list can grow as new records are needed. If part of the image is no longer needed, the corresponding records in the display file can be deleted, returning unused memory to the memory allocator. However, many students do not feel comfortable using pointers, and what is gained in efficiency might be lost in clarity. Another reason for choosing arrays is that we often wish to locate a particular entry in the display file. Using arrays, we need only reference it by its index. Locating a specific node with link lists requires a time-consuming search.

6–3 SEGMENTED DISPLAY FILE

FIGURE 6–5
Display file
segments

Since the display file consists of the graphics commands necessary to construct an image, dividing the display file into distinct logical units, or **segments,** partitions the image into distinct parts. Each display file segment consists of a sequence of graphics commands treated as one unit. The portion of the image represented by a segment can be translated, rotated, scaled, not displayed, or transformed in any other manner without affecting any other segments (Figure 6-5). (Of course, if we move an object described by one segment into that part of the screen

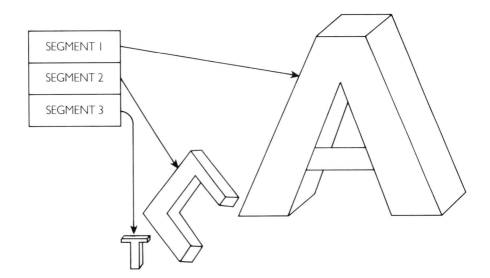

SEGMENT 1

SEGMENT 2

SEGMENT 3

described by another segment, the object that is moved may overwrite the other. However, the two segments in the display file remain disjoint and unaffected.)

In order to display the subimage represented by a segment, we must assign to it some **attributes,** or modeling commands. One attribute places the corresponding subimage at a specified position by translating it a certain number of units. Another attribute indicates a rotation, and still another, a shear. A subimage can be deleted by changing the visibility attribute of the corresponding segment. Each of these attributes transforms the subimage to world coordinates. Since the order of a sequence of modeling transformations affects the shape and orientation of the image, another attribute specifies this order.

Several versions of the same subimage can be displayed by copying the corresponding segment and displaying it with different attribute values. For example, we can invoke the segment representing the letter *T* to create a *T* in one part of the screen (Figure 6-6). If we copy this segment and change the scaling, translation, and rotation attributes, a different size *T* appears in another part of the screen without affecting the original *T*.

6–4 SEGMENT TABLE

The display file is usually composed of several segments. In order to reference the correct segment, a unique name is assigned to each. Once we have the name of the segment, we must find the segment's location in the display file. We also need to know the number of display

FIGURE 6–6
Multiple invocations of the segment representing the alphabet letter *T*

file entries for this segment—otherwise, we would not know where a particular segment ends. The location and length of a segment are two additional attributes of a segment. It is convenient to store the names of the segments and their corresponding attributes in a data structure called a **segment table**. We can reference and manipulate a segment by locating its entry in the segment table (Figure 6-7).

The segment table can be implemented as an array of records. Each field corresponds to an attribute of the segment. If the name of a segment is an integer, this number can be used as an index into the array. The segment table can be implemented in Pascal as the following:

```
const
    num_seg = 50;    {maximum number of segments}

type
    {entry in segment table}
    table_entry = record
                    segstart,                      {start in display file}
                    seglength :      integer;      {length of segment}
                    visible :        boolean;      {display = true}
                    cmdorder :       integer;      {transformation order}
                    trans_x,                       {translations}
                    trans_y :        real;
                    scale_x,                       {scale}
                    scale_y :        real;
                    shear_x,                       {shear}
                    shear_y :        real;
                    rotate_angle :   real          {rotation}
                  end;

var
    segment_table : array[1..num_seg] of table_entry;
```

With the data structure in Figure 6-7, the fifth segment can be made visible and translated three units in the *x* direction with the code

```
with segment_table[5] do
    begin {with}
        visible := true;
        trans_x := 3
    end; {with}
```

6–5 OPERATIONS ON DISPLAY FILE SEGMENTS

Display file segments are made up of contiguous entries in the display file array. Creating a segment requires first locating an available block of entries in the display file. Once we are given a block, we con-

SEGMENT NAME	SEGSTART	SEGLENGTH	VISIBLE	CMDORDER	TRANS_X	. . .
1						
2						
3						
4						
. . .	. . .	. . .	. . .	. . .	. . .	

struct the segment by entering a sequence of values into the command and operand fields of the display file records for the segment.

After a segment has been constructed, the attributes for it must be assigned in the segment table. Prior to this, the segment must be assigned a number (integer). The segment is now ready to be referenced in the graphics program.

In this section we describe the procedures necessary to construct segments and update the display file. Although these operations are straightforward, some crucial error checking must be performed. The overriding concern is that one segment does not accidentally overwrite another. The details of error checking are described in the discussion of the procedures in which they are used.

Three global variables are declared in the main program that are available to all segment procedures:

Segopen—A boolean variable that has the value true while a segment is being constructed.

Free—An integer variable that contains the index of the next available entry in the display file array.

Error—A boolean variable that is true if an error has occurred.

These variables are declared as

```
var
    segopen : boolean;
    free :    integer;
    error :   boolean;
```

CREATE_SEG

This procedure creates a segment with its number (name) passed as a parameter. Prior to creating the segment, Create_Seg performs some error checking. It uses the boolean variable segopen to determine if another segment is still being constructed. If one is, an error message is generated since two segments cannot be constructed simultaneously.

(An alternative action is to close the old segment.) If segopen is false (that is, if no other segment is being created), Create_Seg next checks that the segment number is within the range 1 to num_seg, the segment table array indices. If the number is not within the range, it does not have a valid segment number, and an error is reported. The last error check determines if any segment already has this number. This is the case if the seglength field for this numbered segment is greater than zero. Creating a segment with the same number as another destroys the first, an action we may want to take.

If there are no errors, the next free space in the display file, indicated by the variable free, is placed in the field segstart of the record for this segment in the segment table. All the other attributes in this segment table record are assigned default values and the variable segopen is assigned the value true. It is important to note that Create_Seg does not place the graphics commands into the display file segment.

```
Procedure Create_Seg (number : integer);

    begin
        if segopen then
            begin    {if}
                writeln ('Error: Another segment is open');
                error := true;
                exit(Create_Seg)
            end;    {if}
        if (number < 1) or (number > num_seg) then
            begin {if}
                writeln('Error: Invalid segment number');
                error := true;
                exit(Create_Seg)
            end;    {if}
        with seg_table[number] do
            begin    {with}
                if seglength > 0 then
                    begin    {if}
                        writeln('Error: Segment already created');
                        error := true;
                        exit(Create_Seg)
                    end;    {if}
                {starting place in display file for segment}
                segstart := free;
                {set default attributes values}

                visible    := true;
                cmdorder := 1;
                trans_x    := 0;
                trans_y    := 0;
                scale_x    := 1;
                scale_y    := 1;
                shear_x    := 0;
```

```
            shear_y    := 0;
            rotate_angle := 0
            end;    {with}
        segopen := true
    end;    {Create_Seg}
```

GET_COMMAND

After a segment has been created by Create_Seg, we place the graphics commands into the display file segment. The Procedure Get_Command does this. The commands may come from a file stored on disk or from keyboard input. In either case, the command is passed as parameters to this procedure. Prior to invoking this procedure, the commands should be checked to determine if they are valid. Get_Command first tests that the index of the free block is within the display file array. When it finishes, it increments by one the index of the free block in the display file.

```
Procedure Get_Command (
    com : commands; param1,param2 : real);

    begin
        if free > size then
            begin    {if}
                writeln('Error: Display file full');
                error := true;
                exit(Get_Command)
            end;    {if}
        with display_file[free] do
            begin    {with}
                cmd := com;
                opand1 := param1;
                opand2 := param2
            end;    {with}
        free := free + 1
    end;    {Get_Command}
```

CLOSE_SEG

Once all the commands have been entered into the current segment, that segment must be "closed." Close_Seg first checks that a segment is open (segopen = true), and then enters the length of the segment in the seglength field in the segment table record. Finally, the variable segopen is set to false.

```
Procedure Close_Seg (number : integer);
    begin
```

```
            if not segopen then
                begin    {if}
                    writeln('Error: No segment to be closed');
                    error := true;
                    exit(Close_Seg)
                end;    {if}
            with segtable[number] do
                begin    {with}
                    seglength := free − segstart;
                    segopen := false
                end    {with}
        end;    {Close_Seg}
```

MAKE_SEG

The Make_Seg procedure consists of calls to the preceding procedures. Its main loop reads the commands from the input file. To ascertain whether the last graphics command for that segment has been entered, a special nongraphics command, stop (0, 0), is used that denotes the end of a segment. After an above procedure is invoked, the global error variable is checked. If it is true, an error routine is called and an appropriate action is taken. Implementation of this routine is left as an exercise for the reader. In most cases the error routine simply branches to the next read command instruction.

```
    Procedure Make_Seg (number : integer);

    begin
        Create_Seg(number);
        if error then erroutine(create);
        {read_command reads the command from the keyboard or a file and
          checks that the command and operands are valid}
        read_command(cmd,opand1,opand2);
        if error then erroutine(read);
        while cmd <> Stop do
            begin    {while}
                Get_Command(cmd,opand1,opand2);
                if error then erroutine(get);
                read_command(cmd,opand1,opand2);
                if error then erroutine(get);
            end;    {while}
        Close_Seg(number);
        if error then erroutine(close)
    end;    {Make_Seg}
```

SET_TRANSFORM

Each segment has a set of transformation attributes in its segment table record. We want to be able to change these attributes at will. Procedure Set_Transform does this. All the transformation parameters must be passed to the procedure. If there are many transformation attributes, however, this may become awkward. In that case, separate procedures can be used to set the attributes of each type of transformation.

```
Procedure Set_Transform (number : integer;
            trx,try,scx,scy,shx,shy,rot : real);

    begin
        if (number < 1) or (number > num_seg) then
            begin     {if}
                writeln('Error: Invalid segment number');
                error := true;
                exit(Set_Transform)
            end;     {if}
        with segment_table[number] do
            begin     {with}
                trans_x  := trx;
                trans_y  := try;
                scale_x  := scx;
                scale_y  := scy;
                shear_x  := shx;
                shear_y  := shy;
                rotate_angle := rot
            end     {with}
    end;   {Set_Transform}
```

SET_ORDER

The order of the transformations is set by the Set_Order Procedure. Since there are four different types of transformations, there are a total of 4!, or 24, distinct orders. For simplicity, shearing will always be performed last, reducing the number of distinct orders to 3!, or 6. (An alternative implementation is to keep a running total transformation matrix for each segment. Whenever a new transformation is invoked for that segment, it is combined with this matrix. This enhancement is left as an exercise.)

```
Procedure Set_Order(number,order : integer);
    begin
        segment_table[number].cmdorder := order
    end;   {Set_Order}
```

CONSTRUCT_TRANSFORM

Once the transformation parameters have been entered into the segment table record, procedure Construct_Transform builds the transformation according to cmdorder.

```
Procedure Construct_Transform(number : integer);

   begin
      with seg_table[number] do
         begin    {with}
            case cmdorder of
               1: begin
                     translate(trans_x,trans_y);
                     scale(scale_x,scale_y);
                     rotate(rotate_angle)
                  end;
               2: begin
                     translate(trans_x,trans_y);
                     rotate(rotate_angle);
                     scale(scale_x,scale_y)
                  end;
               3: begin
                     scale(scale_x,scale_y;
                     translate(trans_x,trans_y);
                     rotate(rotate_angle)
                  end;
               4: begin
                     scale(scale_x,scale_y);
                     rotate(rotate_angle);
                     translate(trans_x,trans_y)
                  end;
               5: begin
                     rotate(rotate_angle);
                     scale(scale_x,scale_y);
                     translate(trans_x,trans_y);
                  end;
               6: begin
                     rotate(rotate_angle);
                     translate(trans_x,trans_y);
                     scale(scale_x,scale_y)
                  end
            end;    {case}
            {perform shear}
            xshear(shear_x);
            yshear(shear_y)
         end    {with}
   end;    {Construct_Transform}
```

VISIBLE

A segment can be made visible or invisible by changing its visibility attribute. Procedure Visible performs this.

```
Procedure Visible(number : integer;
            see : boolean    {is it visible});
```

```
      begin
          if (number < 1) or (number > num_seg) then
              begin    {if}
                  writeln('Error: Invalid segment number');
                  error := true;
                  exit(Visible)
              end;    {if}
          segment_table[number].visible := see
      end;    {visible}
```

COPY_SEG

If the image has several transformed versions of a subimage, the display file, correspondingly, has several identical segments with different attribute settings in the segment table. The Copy_Seg procedure copies the information from one segment table entry to another. This segment now has two numbers referencing it in the segment table, which is equivalent to, and more efficient than, having multiple copies of the segment in the display file.

```
      Procedure Copy_Seg(from,too : integer );

          begin
              if (from < 1) or (from > num_seg) or
                  (too < 1) or (too > num_seg) then
                  begin    {if}
                      writeln('Error: Invalid segment number(s)');
                      error := true;
                      exit(Copy_Seg)
                  end;    {if}
              if seg_table[from].seglength <> 0 then
                  begin    {if}
                      writeln('Error: Segment does not exist');
                      error := true;
                  end;    {if}
              if seg_table[to].seglength > 0 then
                  begin    {if}
                      writeln('Error: Segment already exists');
                      error := true;
                      exit(Copy_Seg)
                  end;    {if}
                  {copy the entire segment table record}
                  seg_table[to] := seg_table[from]
          end;    {Copy_Seg}    ⁊too
```

CONVERT

Each entry in the display file must be converted into a graphics procedure (command). Procedure Convert performs this by stepping through a display file segment. The last statement of the procedure invokes the identity transformation, which cancels all previous transformations. Without this, the next invocation of Construct_Transform would incorrectly build on the previous transformations.

```
Procedure Convert(number:integer);

    var
        index,                          {array index}
        count : integer;                {segment length}

    begin
        index := segment_table[number].segstart;
        count := segment_table[number].seglength;
        while index <=
                    (segment_table[number].segstart + count − 1) do
            begin    {while}
                with display_file[index] do
                    begin    {with}
                        if cmd = mve2 then move2(opand1,opand2);
                        if cmd = drw2 then draw2(opand1,opand2);
                        if cmd = rmve2 then
                            rmove2(opand1,opand2);
                        if cmd = rdrw2 then rdraw2(opand1,opand2)
                    end;   {with}
                index := index + 1    {location of next command}
            end;   {while}
        identity
    end;    {Convert}
```

DISPLAY_IMAGE

We are now ready to display the image. Procedure Display_Image is the main driver. It steps through the segment table and invokes the two procedures Construct_Transform and Convert whenever a segment has nonzero length and is visible.

```
Procedure Display_Image;

    var
        number : integer;

    begin
        for number := 1 to num_seg do
            with segment_table[number] do
                if seglength > 0 and (visible) then
                    begin    {if}
                        Construct_Transform(number);
                        Convert(number)
                    end    {if}
    end;    {Display_Image}
```

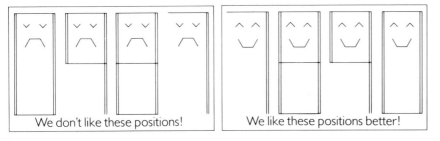

FIGURE 6–8
Sad and happy dig-
its created by using
segments

6–6 **CONCLUSION**

Whenever there is an attribute change using the Set_Transform, Set_Order, or Visible Procedure, it may be necessary to redraw the entire image due to lack of a selective erase procedure. Such a procedure is not difficult to construct; however, we shall put it off until we examine interactive techniques in Chapter 8.

In a dynamic environment, certain display file segments may no longer be needed. Since the size of the array allocated to the display file is fixed, it is preferable to recombine all unused entries in the array, placing them in one contiguous block at the end of the display file, and set the variable free equal to the start of this block. This "garbage collection" is performed by moving up all segments in the display file array below a deleted segment by the number of entries that equal the length of the deleted segment. Since we are not performing "garbage collection," its implementation is left as an exercise.

Figure 6-8 illustrates several sad and happy digits that are created using segments. A menu-driven program prompts the user to input the necessary values to create and/or change the segments. This is implemented via a case statement that calls the appropriate segment table procedure after obtaining the input from the user.

EXERCISES

1. Redo exercise 9 in Chapter 5 using segments.
2. What other attributes might be associated with a display file segment?
3. Draw a face using different segments for the head, nose, eyes, ears, and mouth. Distort the face by changing the scale attributes of some features.
4. Draw a car using different segments for the body and wheels. Move the car by translating the body and rotating and translating the wheels.
5. Change procedure Construct_Transform by maintaining a running total transformation matrix.

Detail of Figure 7–2

7
GRAPHICS PROGRAM DESIGN

7-1 INTRODUCTION

The design of an interactive graphics program follows the same design principles used in interactive text programs. These principles are probably more important for graphics programs, however, since the end user may be inexperienced not only with computers but also with graphics concepts and devices. The goal is a "user-friendly" graphics system that emphasizes user efficiency and ease of use. The programmer of a graphics system must also consider computer display system efficiency and ease of programming.

The graphics program should help the novice user through every step by providing a prompt, such as a cursor or a list of choices, that suggests the next action to take. In addition, the graphics program should provide different levels of prompting, which would allow the experienced user to interact with the system without unwanted prompts or directions. Equally important is feedback that acknowledges what, if any, action has been taken as a response to the user's.

The study of user-computer interaction is still in its early stages of development. The computing community has a lot to learn about the needs of noncomputer professionals. For example, what is the most natural input device and screen format for a commercial artist? This chapter uses several features of UCSD Pascal to describe several of the known techniques that make an interactive graphics program user-friendly. First, however, let's examine some hardware limitations placed on the graphics programmer.

7-2 MEMORY VS. SPEED

As we write graphics programs, we are soon confronted with one of the fundamental problems of interaction: space vs. time. Microcomputer memories are small (although the use of a 24-bit address is changing this) and some of the techniques of saving memory, such as swapping code between memory and disk, are time-consuming. This problem is more acute in animation since smooth motion techniques (discussed in Chapter 9) often require additional memory through their use of multiple frame buffers.

Good programming style must follow the methods of structured programming. This requires a top-down approach that divides the program into separate modules, each with its own task to perform. Unfortunately, though, extensive use of modules can significantly reduce program speed while requiring additional memory because of the stack mechanism used to invoke subroutines. A partial solution to this problem is to identify, early in the program design, which modules are best as independent units and which modules can be combined. Similar problems exist in recursion, and the graphics programmer should be careful in using it.

7–3 REQUIREMENTS OF USER-FRIENDLY SYSTEMS

In the early days of computer graphics, the graphics system was primarily used as an output device. The technology that enabled the system to maintain a running dialogue between user and machine did not exist. Today, however, computer graphics is heavily dependent on user-machine interaction. A joystick or mouse is used to move a cursor around the screen; a light pen is used for picking objects. These input devices give the user flexibility in entering information in a natural and convenient way.

There are several features the programmer should incorporate into a user-friendly graphics program. Certainly the conversation between the user and the computer should be in a language that is natural to the user. In addition, the computer should give helpful information if the user has made a mistake, and it should also notify the user that certain actions have been taken. These are both examples of feedback. Menus, when used as a command language and for operand selection, are especially helpful for the inexperienced user. The inclusion of sophisticated error-handling routines allows the user to recover gracefully from input mistakes. In this chapter, we examine some user-friendly techniques and describe several features available in UCSD Pascal that help the application programmer develop user-friendly graphics programs.

ERROR HANDLING

Only rarely do we find a user who never makes errors when inputting data from the keyboard or some other input device. One component of a user-friendly system is an easy and convenient way for users to recover from and correct a mistake. The graphics program should not try to correct an error by guessing what the user had in mind. First, it should not terminate, and, second, it should provide information that will help the user correct the error. Suppose a user has accidentally entered a character value when the program requires numeric input. Most systems executing a Pascal program will abort the execution of the program. This too frequent occurrence requires the user to start over from the beginning, wasting a lot of time reentering data. The graphics program should instead verify that the data entered by the user is of the correct type before it is used in the program. If it is incorrect, the program should go no further, but should prompt the user to reenter the data. Similar action should be taken to ensure that the input data is in the correct range.

The following Pascal program Get_Real prompts the user to enter a valid real number, which is stored in a character string. Function Get_Char gets a character from the keyboard and determines if it is a member of a specified character set. If it is, the character appears on the screen and is returned to Get_Real; otherwise the bell rings and Get_Char waits for another character to be entered.

The set, validset, consists of those characters comprising a real number. This set changes throughout the program since a plus or minus sign can only be the first character, and at most one decimal point is allowed. The blank character is included since entering a blank or striking the Return key signifies the end of a real valued number. The plus sign (+), while valid at the beginning of the number, is not valid when entered in the character string.

```
Program Get_Real;

    const
        blank = ' ';

    type
        setofchar = set of char;

    var
        validset: setofchar;
        numeric,                        {real character string}
        valid : string;                 {valid input character}

Function Get_Char ( okset : setofchar) : char;

    const
        bel = 7;     {ASCII code for the bell}

    var
        ch : char;

    begin
        repeat
            {"keyboard" is a nonechoing input channel}
            read(keyboard,ch);
            if not ( ch in okset) then
            write(chr(bel))
        until ch in okset;
        write(ch);      {writes valid character}
        Get_Char: = ch
    end;     {Get_Char}

    begin     {main}
        writeln('enter real valued number');
        validset := ['0'..'9','+','−','.',blank];
```

```
        {initialize string valid to length one}
        valid := blank;
        valid[1] := Get_Char(validset);
        if valid[1] <> '+' then
            {include in string}
            numeric := valid;
        {remove '+' and '-' from validset}
        validset := validset - ['+','-'];
        repeat
            valid[1] := Get_Char(validset);
            if valid[1] <> blank then
                {place at end of numeric string}
                numeric := concat(numeric,valid)
        until (valid[1] = blank) or (valid[1] = '.');
        if valid[1] = '.' then
        begin    {if}
            {remove '.' from valid set}
            validset := validset - ['.'];
            {continue entering digit}
            repeat
                valid[1] := Get_Char(validset);
                if valid[1] <> blank then
                    numeric := concat(numeric,valid)
            until valid[1] = blank
        end    {if}
    end.    {Get_Real}
```

The character string consisting of a real number must be converted into a real data type. The following function, Val, returns a real value for a valid character string.

```
Function Val( s : string ) : real;
    {returns the real number value of the string s}

        var
            neg          : boolean;
            i,
            tens         : integer;
            temp_val     : real;

begin
    temp_val:=0.0;
    if length(S) > 0 then
        begin    {if}
            {check for negative number}
            neg:=s[1] = '-';
            if neg then
            {get rid of '-' if there}
            delete(s,1,1);
            tens:=pos('.',s);
            if tens > 0 then
```

```
             begin    {if}
                 {get rid of '.' if there}
                 delete(s,tens,1);
                 {determine power}
                 tens: = (length(s) − tens) + 1;
             end;    {if}
         for i: = 1 to length(s) do
         {determine value of the string}
             temp_val: = (10 * temp_val) +
                         (ord(s[i]) − ord('0'));
         if neg then
             {set correct sign}
                 temp_val: = −(temp_val / exp(tens*ln(10)))
         else
             temp_val: = temp_val / exp(tens*ln(10))
     end;    {if}
 val: = temp_val    {return the value}
end;    {Val}
```

An error that often appears occurs when the user is asked to enter into the program the name of a file to be read. If the file does not exist or there is something wrong with the file (such as bad block) or the disk driver, the program will usually terminate. In some implementations of UCSD Pascal, it is possible to turn off the system's I/O error checking and perform our own test using the **IO_Result** function, which returns a positive integer if there has been an I/O error. The advantage in this is that an unsuccessful I/O does not then terminate the graphics program. Procedure Get_File performs error checking while procedure IO_Error prints the cause of an I/O error.

```
Procedure IO_Error(
         err_num : integer    {I/O error number});

     begin
         case err_num of
             1 : writeln('Diskette has a bad block: Try another one.');
             2 : writeln('Bad device (volume) number: Try another one.');
             3 : writeln('Illegal I/O request.');
             4 : writeln('Unknown hardware error.');
             5 : writeln('Device is no longer on-line.');
             6 : writeln('File has been lost.');
             7 : writeln('Illegal file name: Check file name and re-enter');
             8 : writeln('No room on diskette: Use another one.');
             9 : writeln('Volume is not on line.');
            10 : writeln('File was not found: Check file name and re-
                         enter');
            11 : writeln('File already exists: Check file name and re-
                         enter');
            12 : writeln('File not closed.');
            13 : writeln('File not open.');
```

```
            14 : writeln('Bad input format.');
            15 : writeln('Ring buffer overflow.');
        end;    {case}
    end;    {IO_Error}

Procedure Get_File;

    var
        s               : string;
        ior             : integer;
        name            : string;

    begin
        repeat    {until valid file}
            write('Enter name of file to print: ');
            readln(name);
            {turn off system response to I/O}
            {$i-}
            reset(in_file,name);
            {get result of I/O test}
            ior: = io_result;
            if ior <> 0 then
                {I/O error}
                IO_Error(ior);
        until (ior = 0) or (name = '');
        close(in_file)
    end;    {Get_File}
```

MENUS

A menu is typically composed of text and/or graphics symbols that represent several different processing options. The menu is usually displayed across the top, bottom, or side of the display screen. Larger menus may take up the entire screen (Figure 7-1). The user selects a menu item either by inputting a short string of characters from the keyboard or by "picking" a string or symbol with an input device. A major advantage in using menus is that they reduce user error and save time by replacing memorization with visual recognition.

FIGURE 7-1
Different types of menus

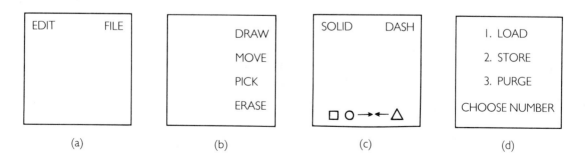

(a)   (b)   (c)   (d)

The design of a menu is an important part of a user-friendly graphics program. A menu that fills the entire screen must be erased after the selection is made. This full-screen menu is often used at the start of a graphics program. However, once there are objects on the screen, it is better not to erase them when bringing up a menu. Instead, a shorter menu is placed in a small section of the screen.

Menus can form a multilevel hierarchical structure (Figure 7-2). That is, a menu may have one or more submenus that, in turn, may have submenus. Figure 7-3a illustrates this nesting with a main menu that lists four types of figures to be drawn: rectangle, circle, ellipse, or triangle. If we choose "circle," a submenu appears (Figure 7-3b) that lists three different sizes: small, medium, or large. Selecting one of these choices causes another menu to appear (Figure 7-3c) that lists two display modes: solid or dashed.

Once the user has made a menu selection, the system provides some type of feedback that indicates which item was selected. For example, the selected item may be displayed in reverse video or in blinking mode. After an item is selected, the processing of that request (for example the transfer of a large file from disk to memory) may take a significant amount of time. In this case, a message should be displayed informing the user of the delay; otherwise, the user may think no action is being taken and may attempt to abort the run or reenter his or her choice.

It is important to reiterate that once a user has become experienced with a graphics program, a menu consisting of prompt messages may no longer be needed. Indeed, experienced users will consider prompts to be a deterrent to generating an image efficiently. The user should have an option that either eliminates or reduces the occurrence of these menu prompts.

A menu-building function, Menu_Select, has a menu_record as input. This record consists of the title of the menu, the number of items in the menu, and the actual items. This can be represented in Pascal as:

```
type
    item_range = 1..max_items;
    menu_record = record
                    title      : string;
                    num_items  : item_range;
                    item       : array[item_range] of string
                  end;
```

Menu_Select displays the menu on the video screen. This function returns the choice of the menu item to the user. In order to have the menu centered on the display screen, a function Longest_Line is accessed that determines the length of the longest menu line. In addition, there is a procedure Write_String, which writes a character string at a specified screen position.

Once these procedures are written, they can be invoked from procedure Build_Menu, which reads the menu_record fields and con-

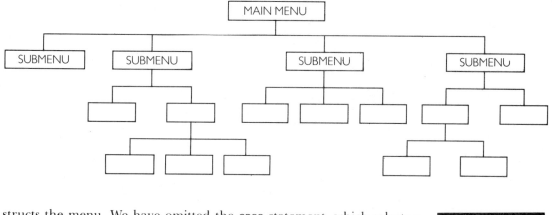

structs the menu. We have omitted the **case** statement, which selects a course of action based on the user's choice.

```
Procedure Write_String (
        x,y               : integer;    {screen position}
        message           : string;)

    begin
        gotoxy(x,y);    {screen location}
        write(message)
    end; {Write_String}

Function Longest_Line (menu :menu_record) : integer;

    var
        i   : integer;
        len : integer;

    begin
        len := 0;
        with menu do
            for i := 1 to num_items do
                if length(items[i] > len then
                    len := length(items[i]);
                    longest_line := len;
    end;    {Longest_Line}
```

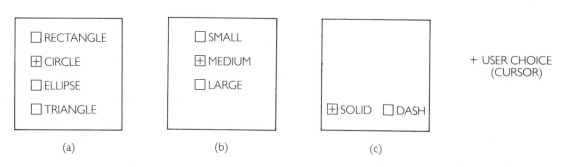

(a)   (b)   (c)

```
Function Menu_Select (menu :menu_record) : item_range;

    var
        choice          : integer;
        xpos,                           {location of the}
        firstline       : integer;      {first item entry}
        choice          : char;         {menu choice}

    begin
        with menu do
            begin   {with}
                {display menu title on 80-character line}
                write_string((80 − length(title)) div 2,0,title);
                {determine values for centering menu selections}
                xpos := (80 − (longest_line(menu) + 3)) div 2;
                {skip four lines after title}
                firstline := 4;
                {display menu}
                for i := 1 to num_items do
                    begin   {for}
                        gotoxy(xpos,firstline + (i − 1));
                        write(i:2,' ',items[i]);
                    end;    {for}
                gotoxy(24,22);    {bottom of 24-line screen}
                write('Enter your choice (1 to ');
                write(num_items:3,'): ');
                readln(choice);
                menu_select := choice
            end   {with}
        end;    {Menu_Select}

Procedure Build_Menu

    var
        menu : menu_record;
        choice,    {menu selection}
        count : integer;

    begin
        {get menu title and selections}
        with menu do
            begin   {with}
                write('Enter number of menu choices: ');
                readln(num_items:3);
                writeln;
                writeln('Enter menu title as it should be printed');
                readln(title)
                writeln('On a separate line, enter the menu choices');
                for count := 1 to numitems do
                    readln(items[count])
            end;    {with}
```

```
        {build menu and get selection}
        choice := Menu_Select(menu)
    end;   {Build_Menu}
```

The following interactive dialogue uses these procedures to produce the menu in Figure 7-4.

Enter number of menu choices: 4
Enter menu title as it should appear
***** GRAPHICS PROGRAMS AVAILABLE *****
On a separate line, enter the menu choices
Paint System
Business Graphics
Computer_Aided Design
Solid Modeling

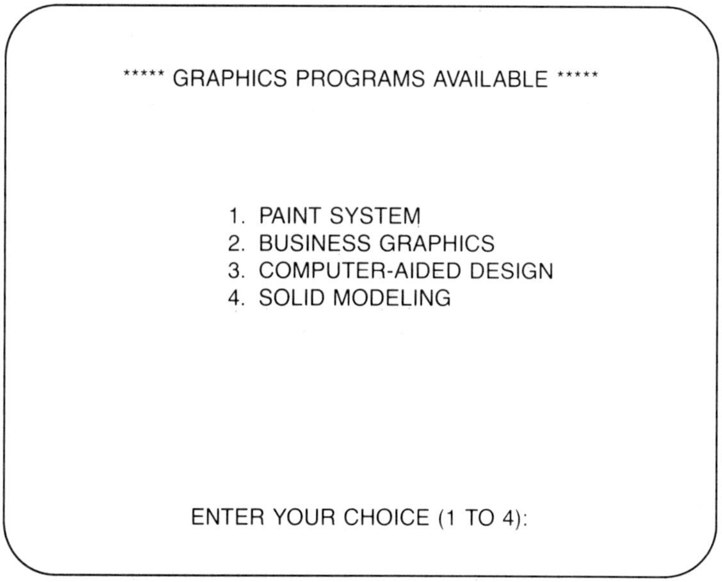

***** GRAPHICS PROGRAMS AVAILABLE *****

1. PAINT SYSTEM
2. BUSINESS GRAPHICS
3. COMPUTER-AIDED DESIGN
4. SOLID MODELING

ENTER YOUR CHOICE (1 TO 4):

FIGURE 7–4

7–4 CONCLUSION

Programmers are strongly encouraged to incorporate the procedures described in this chapter in all graphics programs. Indeed, the code presented here is only a rudimentary collection of error-handling and menu-generating routines. The programmer, therefore, should enhance them according to the needs of the program and the users. In order to make the graphics programs and procedures less wordy and redundant and, hopefully, more readable, the menu and error-handling routines have been left out of future programs reproduced in this text.

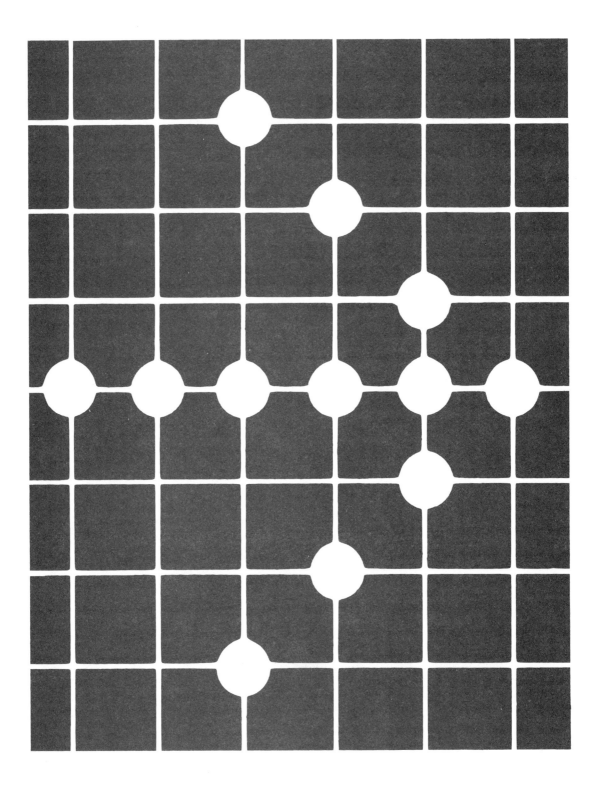

Detail of Figure 8–10

8

TECHNIQUES IN INTERACTION

8–1 **INTRODUCTION**

The graphic techniques discussed in previous chapters are sufficient to produce quality two-dimensional images. Although the algorithms that have been presented are efficient, however, the amount of processing time required to generate these images is disappointingly large. In addition, the user has no means of controlling or modifying the image. In interactive graphics, the user controls and responds to an image by means of an appropriate input device such as a joystick. The image does not change until the user takes a specific action, such as moving an object about the screen. Figure 8-1 illustrates the display screen for a menu-driven, interactive computer-aided design (CAD) program.

Animation, which we shall discuss in Chapter 9, differs from interaction in that the image can change even while the user is not responding to the system. For example, in video arcade games, the player may control only the defending spaceship while the graphics program itself manipulates several attacking spaceships.

If interaction is to be useful for the user, a fast response time is essential. When a system responds to a user input within $1/10$ of a second the user notices no delay. However, a user may accept a delay longer than that for certain applications. For example, a user inputting two endpoints of a line can wait (with annoyance) while the line is being drawn. The response time depends directly upon the complexity of the action taken: Moving a line is considerably easier than moving an entire car. This chapter examines several techniques used for interactive graphics. Many of these can be used to produce animated images as well.

An interactive graphics system presents to the user several input devices. These can include a keyboard, light pen, paddles, joystick, or a mouse. Each device has certain attributes that make it suitable for a specific interactive task. A light pen can be used to pick an object whereas a joystick is best used to move an object around the screen.

Most inexpensive microcomputer systems do not yet offer the necessary hardware and software for light pen and mouse interaction. (Apple Macintosh is a notable exception.) For that reason, our implementation will be restricted to paddles and joysticks. However, the interactive techniques we present can be used for any of the interactive devices noted. If your system has several interactive input devices attached to it, use the one that is most natural for your current needs. Notice that keyboard character input is not natural for most graphic interaction. A user should not be required to move an object by entering the present and new coordinates of the object to be transformed. However, a keyboard with arrow keys can be used to manipulate a special symbol, such as a cursor, about the screen.

Techniques in Interaction

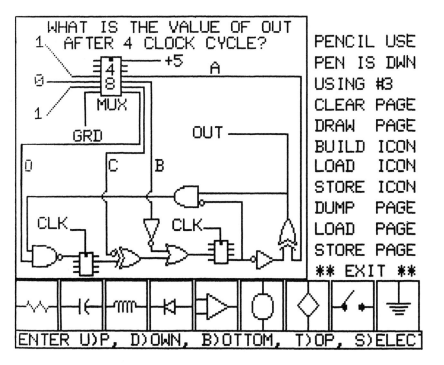

FIGURE 8–1
A computer-aided
design screen

8–2 **INPUT DEVICES**

The interactive techniques and applications we shall examine are often divided into two classifications: **positioning** and **selecting**, or **pointing**. In the former, the computer receives from a user-controlled input device the position or location of a screen pixel. In the latter, the input device is used to select or point to an object without information being transferred as to the coordinates of that object. In this text we discuss both techniques without formally separating the two. After all, in many circumstances an object is first selected and then positioned to a new screen location.

Input devices are divided into several logical categories (for details see Appendix: Graphical Kernel System). In this chapter, only two types will be examined: **valuator** or **button (choice)**. A valuator returns an integer value. A joystick is a pair of valuators. A button, however, returns one of the boolean values true or false.

Each input device is assigned a unique name or number. Whenever a device changes state, the application program must observe this event. In most inexpensive display systems, input devices are **polled** (interrogated) by the application program, returning its state at the time it is polled. Polling must be performed often enough so that a change of state or event is detected; otherwise, quick events may get lost.

On some systems, an event caused by an input device results in an entry made in an **event queue**. At any time, the application program can query the queue for an event, thus preventing the loss of an event. One problem with the event queue is the time involved in searching for a particular event. One advantage of a queue is that devices need not be polled if nothing is going on.

Sophisticated display systems allow the application programmer to decide which devices are queued and which are polled. For simplicity, we shall assume that all devices are polled, the default case for some of the better systems.

A final note: We shall use screen coordinates since there is a significant additional delay when the system must use the viewing mapping to convert from world to NDC or screen coordinates.

8–3 **CURSOR MOTION**

A **cursor** is a special symbol such as a cross or plus sign that is displayed on the screen at a specified location. The cursor is used as feedback; it provides the user with visible information as to the current screen location. We could draw the cursor using a procedure. However, every time we wished to move the cursor, it would be necessary to reinvoke that procedure and draw the lines defining the cursor, which would be a time-consuming method. Luckily, most graphics systems provide a better way.

A **shape table**, or **raster**, is a rectangular pattern of bits (pixels) that can be referenced and manipulated as one unit (similar to a raster-cell character). These shapes are usually defined as a two-dimensional array of type boolean. A logically true value in the array will cause a corresponding pixel to be illuminated and a logically false value will cause the corresponding pixel to be turned off (Figure 8-2). Assume the following declarations:

```
type
    shape = array[1..5,1..5] of boolean;

var
    cursor : shape;
    row, col :integer;
```

The following segment of Pascal code creates a plus sign in the cursor array.

```
for row := 1 to 5 do
    for col := 1 to 5 do
        cursor[row,col] := (row = 3) or (col = 3)
```

After this shape (cursor) is defined in memory, we want to be able

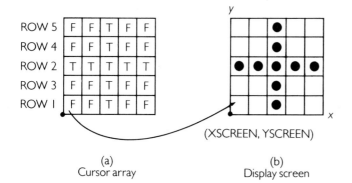

ROW 5 | F | F | T | F | F
ROW 4 | F | F | T | F | F
ROW 2 | T | T | T | T | T
ROW 3 | F | F | T | F | F
ROW 1 | F | F | T | F | F

(a)
Cursor array

(XSCREEN, YSCREEN)

(b)
Display screen

FIGURE 8–2
A shape table

to move it to any location in the frame buffer, thus enabling the user to move the cursor about the screen. The graphics procedure

blockmove(cursor,xscreen,yscreen)

places the first row, first column entry of the cursor array at screen location (xscreen, yscreen) (Figure 8-2). Thus the first row of the array is copied to the bottom row of the screen. We should think of the shape array as having its first row at the bottom and the row numbers going up.

As the cursor is moved about the screen, it is necessary to first erase it from its previous location, then draw it at its new location. In order to move the cursor from position $(x1, y1)$ to position $(x2, y2)$, the following two sequence commands are necessary

erase(cursor,x1,y1);
blockmove(cursor,x2,y2);

Although this looks easy enough to implement, there are several sticky issues that must be examined. To do this, we first discuss the "**exclusive or**" mode.

The "exclusive or" logic is used to determine if two bits are different. For example, suppose we have the declaration

var
        bit1,bit2: **boolean**;

Denoting "exclusive or" by XOR, we can define it by the following truth table:

BIT1	BIT2	BIT1 XOR BIT2
true	true	false
true	false	true
false	true	true
false	false	false

According to this table, the "exclusive or" of two bits is true only if both bits are neither true nor false—that is, if bit1 or bit2 is true but not both.

The "exclusive or" can be applied to the bit pattern shape representing the cursor. To explain how it works, both the screen background and the cursor, which corresponds to true and false values in the frame buffer, will be represented as a string of Ts and Fs.

If we XOR the cursor with a blank screen, we produce the cursor.

	F	F	F	F	F	blank screen
XOR	T	F	T	T	F	cursor
	T	F	T	T	F	result (cursor)

If we XOR the cursor with itself, we erase the cursor.

	T	F	T	T	F	cursor on screen
XOR	T	F	T	T	F	cursor
	F	F	F	F	F	blank screen

What happens when the cursor comes into contact with another object on the screen?

	F	F	T	F	T	object
XOR	T	F	T	T	F	cursor
	T	F	F	T	T	distorted cursor

Figures 8-3a and 8-3b illustrate that we have lost the third pixel (F) and gained an extra pixel in the fifth position (T) of the cursor. The pixel gained is of no consequence since it is part of the object and was initially displayed. However, the deletion of the third pixel results in a "hole" in the object and the cursor. This is usually acceptable since the next step removes the hole. This step eliminates this distortion by using the OR mode instead of XOR (see exercise 6 in this chapter.)

If this distorted cursor is now XORed with the original cursor, the distorted cursor is erased and the object is restored to its original shape (Figure 8-3c).

	T	F	F	T	T	distorted cursor
XOR	T	F	T	T	F	original cursor
	F	F	T	F	T	original object

This discussion has illustrated how XOR is used to erase and move the cursor without permanently changing any other object or the display screen. In order to use these ideas, we shall add a mode parameter to the **blockmove** procedure.

blockmove(cursor,xscreen,yscreen,mode)

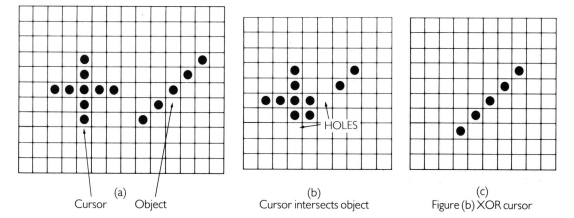

(a)	(b)	(c)
Cursor Object	Cursor intersects object	Figure (b) XOR cursor

If mode equals XOR, the cursor will be XORed at the given screen location. If mode equals normal, **blockmove** places the cursor at the screen location (which is equivalent to using the OR mode).

FIGURE 8–3
The exclusive OR results of a cursor moving through an object

The cursor is placed at its original screen position ($x1, y1$) by issuing the graphics command

blockmove(cursor,x1,y1,xor)

To erase it and move it to a new position ($x2, y2$), use the sequence of commands

```
blockmove(cursor,x1,y1,xor);    {erase old}
blockmove(cursor,x2,y2,xor);    {draw new}
```

To describe how to move the cursor about interactively, we assume the availability of two paddles (or one joystick). The rotation of the knob on a paddle results in an integer in the range 0 to 255. This integer is returned via a Pascal graphics function

paddle(I) ,

where $I = 0$ or 1 corresponding to two paddles.

Suppose we wish to move the cursor about the screen, which is described by x, y integer coordinate values ranging from 0 to 191 in the y direction and 0 to 279 in the x direction. The first step is to convert the integer paddle values 0 to 255 into screen coordinates. The following code does this:

```
const
    xval = 279/255;
    yval = 191/255;

    xscreen := trunc(paddle(0)*xval);
    yscreen := trunc(paddle(1)*yval);
```

Now, whenever the knob on **paddle**(0) is rotated, a valid xscreen position is returned; similarly, a yscreen position is returned by **paddle**(1).

In several of our interactive applications, it is necessary to inform the system when the cursor is at a certain location on the screen. We do this by using the function

button(I) ,

where $I = 0$ or 1, which returns the boolean value true whenever the button on the corresponding paddle is pressed; otherwise, it is false. The cursor can now be moved about the screen until the button on paddle 0 is pressed, using the following code:

```
    {get initial screen position}
xscreen := trunc(paddle(0)*xval);
yscreen := trunc(paddle(1)*yval);
    {display cursor the first time}
blockmove(cursor,xscreen,yscreen,xor);
repeat    {erase and redraw cursor}
    blockmove(cursor,xscreen,yscreen,xor);    {erase cursor}
    xscreen := trunc(paddle(0)*xval);    {new screen}
    yscreen := trunc(paddle(1)*yval);    {location}
    blockmove(cursor,xscreen,yscreen,xor)    {display cursor}
until button(0);
```

Before leaving this discussion of cursor motion there are several enhancements we should make to the preceding code segment. The first concerns the fact that the hardware in most inexpensive display systems is not fast enough to keep up with successive paddle reads. Thus a wait loop must be inserted between two successive calls to the paddle function; otherwise, the same paddle may be read twice. We should insert a delay such as

```
for i := 1 to 5 do;    {does nothing}
```

between each xscreen and yscreen assignment statements.

We further note that the code produces a flashing cursor. That is, if the paddle knob is not moved, the cursor flashes on and off in the current screen position. If this is distracting, the code should be altered to test if the knob has been turned prior to erasing and redrawing the cursor. This idea, combined with the previous observation, produces the following enhanced procedure.

```
Procedure Move_Cursor (cursor:shape);

    var
        count        : integer;    {delay loop counter}
        xpt,ypt      : integer;    {old screen position}

    begin
        xscreen := trunc(paddle(0)*xval);
        for count := 1 to 5 do;    {nothing}
        yscreen := trunc(paddle(1)*yval);
```

```
{display cursor the first time}
blockmove(cursor,xscreen,yscreen,xor);
repeat
    xpt := xscreen;      {get previous}
    ypt := yscreen;      {position}
    {get new screen position}
    xscreen :=        trunc(paddle(0)*xval);
    for count := 1 to 5 do;
    yscreen :=        trunc(paddle(1)*yval);
    {has the cursor moved?}
    if (xpt <> xscreen) or (ypt <> yscreen) then
    {move cursor}
    begin    {if}
        blockmove(cursor,xpt,ypt,xor);      {erase}
        blockmove(cursor,xscreen,yscreen,xor)    {display}
    end    {if}
    until button(0)
end;    {Move_Cursor}
```

Inexpensive paddles or joysticks are often "noisy"; that is, a small change in input values occurs even when the device is not moved. If this occurs, the procedure should be modified so the cursor is moved only if the new screen location is greater than some minimum distance away from the old screen location. This is left as an exercise for the reader.

If your system does not have the equivalent of a **blockmove** procedure, it may be possible to implement it yourself. However, your implementation may be slower than a graphics system's implementation since a system programmer will have written the procedure in assembly language or microcoded it in ROM (read-only memory). A possible implementation uses the graphics procedure

pencolor(mode)

that, when mode equals XOR, draws all subsequent pixels in the XOR mode. When mode equals normal, the pixels are written in white; and when mode equals erase, subsequent pixels are written in the background color (black).

Assume the following Pascal environment:

```
const
    xmax = 10;    {array limits}
    ymax = 10;

type
    shape = packed array[1..xmax,1..ymax] of boolean;
    color = (normal,xor,erase);
```

Recall that the screen procedure **plotpoint**(x,y) illuminates a pixel on the screen at location (x, y). Observe that the rows correspond to the scan lines—that is, to the *y* values—and the columns correspond to the *x* values.

```
Procedure Blockmove(
    cursor:shape; xscreen,yscreen:integer; mode:color);

var
    row,col :integer;      {indices in cursor array}

begin
    pencolor(mode);
    for row := 1 to xmax do
    for col := 1 to ymax do
    {if pixel is illuminated}
    if cursor[row,col] then
    {(xscreen, yscreen), the lower-left corner of the cursor, corresponds to the
    first entry of the cursor array}
    plotpoint(xscreen + col −1,yscreen + row − 1)
end;     {Blockmove}
```

8–4 BUILDING TECHNIQUES

This section describes several techniques that can be used to create an image interactively. Many of these methods can be applied to other interactive tasks, such as selecting (identifying) an object on the screen.

LINE DRAWING

A line can be drawn between any two points on the screen by first using the paddle knob to move the cursor to one endpoint of the line. When we depress the paddle button, the coordinates of that point are used as the initial point of the line. We then move the cursor to the other endpoint, and once again depress the paddle button. Now we use a line-drawing procedure to draw the line between these two endpoints (Figure 8-4).

If we want to draw a horizontal or vertical line, we may encounter some difficulty in aligning the two endpoints. Constraints can be used to simplify this task. For example, a vertical line can be drawn by retaining the *x* value of the initial position and moving the cursor to the *y* value of the other endpoint. The vertical line is drawn using the initial point and the *x* value of the initial point and the *y* value of the other point (Figure 8-5). A horizontal line is drawn using a similar technique.

Another line-drawing task is to attach one line to another at a point (Figure 8-6). We assume that a line *AB* has already been drawn between points (*x*1 *y*1) and (*x*2, *y*2). The new line to be attached to line *AB* has its initial position off of line *AB*. The cursor is now moved to the approximate location on line *AB* where the line is to be attached. If line *AB* is vertical, its constant x value and y value of the cursor are the coordinates of the intersection point. If line *AB* is nonvertical, the x value of the cursor is used as the x coordinate value of the endpoint of this new line. The y coordinate is obtained using, for example, the two-point equation of a line

$$y = \frac{(x - x1)(y2 - y1)}{(x2 - x1) + y1}.$$

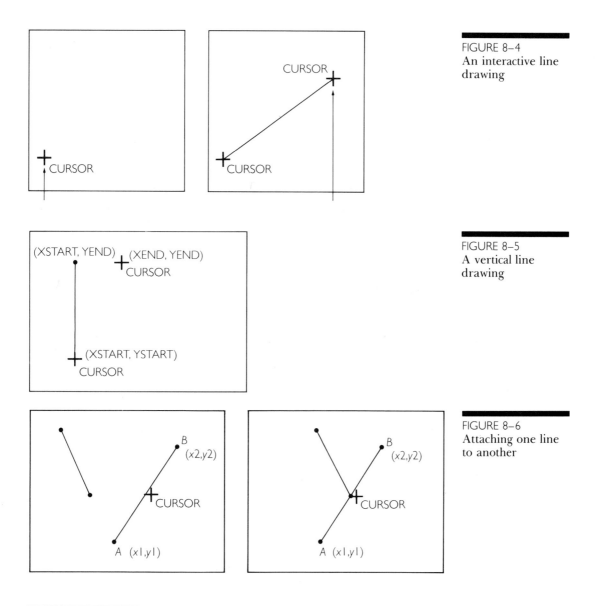

FIGURE 8–4
An interactive line drawing

FIGURE 8–5
A vertical line drawing

FIGURE 8–6
Attaching one line to another

GEOMETRIC DRAWINGS

A rectangle can be drawn by positioning the cursor at its bottom-left and top-right (or bottom-right and top-left) corners (Figure 8-7). The rectangle-drawing procedure in Chapter 3 uses this input to construct the rectangle with that diagonal.

A circle is drawn interactively by first moving the cursor to its center (xc, yc) and then placing the cursor on any point on its circumference (x, y). The radius is obtained by using the equation for the distance between two points

$$radius = \textbf{trunc}(\textbf{sqrt}((xc - x)(xc - x) + (yc - y)(yc - y)))$$

A circle can also be specified by the two endpoints of its diameter. The center is the point equidistant between the endpoints. The radius is half the distance of the diameter.

Three points can define a circle. In this case we would have to solve for the center (xc, yc) and the radius, an operation involving the solution of three simultaneous equations in three unknowns. Several standard techniques in numerical analysis can be used. We leave this as an exercise.

Any of the standard conic sections—ellipse, parabola, hyperbola—can also be drawn given correct input values. Simply use the techniques of analytical geometry to solve for the unknowns. Although these methods are not difficult, they can get mathematically messy. The interested reader is urged to refer to any standard geometry textbook.

CREATING SHAPE TABLES

In Section 8-3, we observed that it is faster to move objects defined in shape tables than to transform a vector-drawn object defined by a procedure. Recall that a shape table object can only be translated about the screen (using **blockmove**) and not scaled or rotated, as a vector-drawn object can be.

FIGURE 8–7
Specifying a rectangle by its diagonally opposite corners

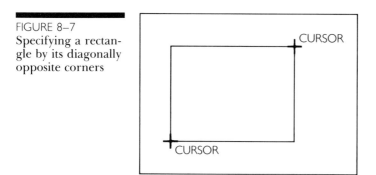

Techniques in Interaction

A shape table symbol can be created using graph paper to help determine which bits should be displayed. While this method gets the job done, it becomes laborious even for moderately simple images. In addition, an interactive user should not have to step away from the display system to create an image.

GRAPHICS EDITOR

A graphics editor provides the user with the means to create graphic symbols (shape tables) interactively. In fact, a graphics editor can even be used as a font editor to design a raster font.

The editor we present enables the user to manipulate the cursor around an enlarged graph paper–type grid with, in our illustration, 10 cells in each of the horizontal and vertical directions. Whenever the user wishes to fill in a cell in this grid, he or she depresses the paddle button. Figure 8-8 illustrates the definition of the symbol for pi on the enlarged grid; next to it is its actual raster-cell representation. Since this editor is so crucial to any graphics package, we have included the entire listing.

```
Program Shape_Table;
    {creates a graphics editor}

    type
        {Define a 10 × 10 shape}
        shape = packed array [0..9,0..9] of boolean;

    var
        figure   : shape;      {the actual symbol}
        block    : array [0..17,0..17] of boolean;    {fills a cell}
        cursor   : array [0..8, 0..8 ] of boolean;    {screen cursor}
        row,col  : integer;    {figure indices}
```

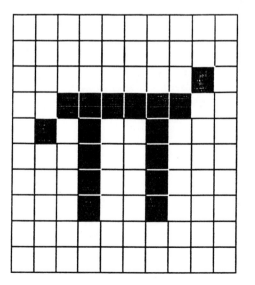

π

FIGURE 8–8
A graphics editor
display screen

Procedure Set_Cursor;
{sets up the plus sign cursor}

```
    var
        i : integer;      {row}
        j : integer;      {column}
    begin
        for i: = 0 to 8 do
            for j: = 0 to 8 do
                cursor[i,j]: = (i = 4) or (j = 4)
    end;    {Set_Cursor}
```

Procedure Set_Block;
{sets up the 18 × 18 block used to fill in a cell in the grid; all true since we want a solid block to turn on and off}

```
    var
        i : integer;
        j : integer;
    begin
            for i: = 0 to 17 do
            for j: = 0 to 17 do
            block[i,j]: = true;
    end;    {Set_Block}
```

Procedure Get_Shape(**var** s : shape);
{draws the grid, filling in the current value of the shape passed in. The paddles are used to move a cursor to any cell in the matrix. Button(1) moves the value for that cell back and forth. That is, whenever the button is pressed, the cell is filled or unfilled. Button(0) exits from this procedure.}

```
    var
        oldx  : integer;     {previous}
        oldy  : integer;     {cell location}
        newx : integer;      {current}
        newy : integer;      {cell location}
```

Procedure Draw_Grid;
{draws a 10 × 10 grid and fills in the cells depending on the current value of the shape passed to the procedure. The cells in the matrix are 19 pixels by 19 pixels. The grid has dimensions 191 × 191.}

```
    var
        i : integer;
        j : integer;
    begin
        for i: = 0 to 10 do
        {draws horizontal lines}
                begin{for}
                    moves(0,i*19);
                    draws(190,i*19);
                end;    {for}
        for i: = 0 to 10 do
```

{*draws vertical lines*}
```
        begin    {for}
            moves(i*19,0);
            draws(i*19,190);
        end    {for}
end;    {Draw_Grid}
```

Procedure Delay(n : **integer**);
{*adds delay between successive reads of the paddles*}

```
    var
        i : integer;
    begin
        for i: = 0 to n do;
    end;    {Delay}
```

Procedure Put_Cursor;
{*moves cursor about grid*}

```
    begin
```
{*maps the paddle values (0..255) to values in the range (0..9) corresponding to the 10 cells in the x and y directions. Note that the cursor is now moved only when the paddle value is changed by at least 26.*}
```
        newx: = paddle(0) div 26;
        Delay(5);
        newy: = paddle(1) div 26;
```
{*erases cursor in cell (oldx,oldy) and places it in the new cell. The cell values (0..9) are converted to x, y screen values by multiplication by the cell size of 19. The cursor is placed in the middle of the cell by an addition of 5.*}
```
        blockmove(cursor,(oldx*19) + 5,(oldy*19) + 5,xor);
        blockmove(cursor,(newx*19) + 5,(newy*19) + 5,xor);
```
{*retains the current position*}
```
        oldx: = newx;
        oldy: = newy;
    end;    {Put_Cursor}
```

Procedure Fill_Area;
{*turns on and off the cell over which the cursor is placed when button(1) is pressed. Also, moves the actual value in the shape table back and forth. Recall that the x values are the columns and the y values are the rows.*}

```
    begin
        blockmove(block,(newx*19) + 1,(newy*19) + 1,xor);
        s[newy,newx]: = not(s[newy,newx]);
    end;    {Fill_Area}
```

Procedure Show_Shape;
{*shows the new shape to the right of the matrix*}

```
    begin
        blockmove(s,230,85,normal);
    end;    {Show_Shape}
```

```
begin    {Get_Shape}
         Draw_Grid;
         {gets and shows the initial position of the cursor}
         oldx: = paddle(0) div 26;
         delay(5);
         oldy: = paddle(1) div 26;
         blockmove(cursor,(oldx*19) + 5,(oldy*19) + 5,xor);
         repeat
               Put_Cursor;
               {checks if button(1) pressed. If so, moves that position in the matrix
               and the shape table back and forth and displays new configuration
               of both.}
               if button(1) then
                    begin    {if}
                        Fill_Area;
                        Show_Shape;    {after each change}
                    end;    {if}
         until button(0)
end;    {Get_Shape}

begin    {Shape_Table}
         {initializes entire shape table to false}
         for row : = 0 to 9 do
             for col : = 0 to 9 do
                   figure[row,col] : = false;
         Set_Block;
         Set_Cursor;
         Get_Shape(figure)
end    {Shape_Table}
```

Program Shape_Table can also be used to create new fonts. Figure 8-9a illustrates user-designed characters that produce the Christmas greeting in Figure 8-9b.

VECTOR DRAWING

Another technique for creating a shape table is to use a function that determines whether a screen pixel is illuminated. The graphics function

screenbit(xscreen,yscreen)

returns the boolean value true if the screen location (xscreen,yscreen) is illuminated; otherwise, it returns false. Let's examine how **screenbit** can be used to create a shape table. Procedure Draw_Arrow produces the arrow in Figure 8-10.

Procedure Draw_Arrow;

```
begin
    moves(0,5);
    draws(12,5);
    draws(9,8);
```

(program continues on page 192)

𝔐 e r y   𝕮 h i s t m e
a ! n d 𝕳 p o n w 𝖄 𝕴

FIGURE 8–9
User-designed
characters

(a)

𝔐erry 𝕮hristmas
and a
𝕳appy 𝕹ew 𝖄ear!

(b)

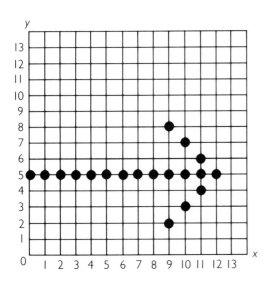

FIGURE 8–10
A vector-drawn
arrow

```
        moves(12,5);
        draws(9,2)
    end;    {Draw_Arrow}
```

The following procedure, Copy_Shape, copies this vector-drawn arrow into the boolean shape table "arrow." Observe, again, that the screen rows correspond to the *y* values and the screen columns to the *x* values. Assume the following Pascal environment:

```
var
    arrow : array[0..13,0..10] of boolean;    {shape table}
    row,col: integer;

Procedure Copy_Shape;

    begin
        for row := 0 to 13 do
            for col := 0 to 10 do
                arrow[row,col] := screenbit(col,row)
    end;    {Copy_Shape}
```

8–5 SELECTING AND POSITIONING

We not only want to create objects, but also to manipulate and modify existing objects. In doing this, the first task is to identify (select) a particular object on the screen. The technique we describe to do so requires us to place the center of the cursor within the bounding rectangle of the shape table–defined object (Figure 8-10).

In order to make the identification task simple, we shall define an object by a record of type "objdescrib," which contains the boolean shape array and the diagonal corners of the bounding rectangle:

```
type
    shape = array[0..20,0..20] of boolean;
    objdescrib = record
                    lowx,lowy,                      {lower-left corner}
                    highx,highy : integer;          {upper-right corner}
                    image : shape
                 end;
var                                                 {10 objects}
    object : array [1..10] of objdescrib;
```

The following function, Select, tests if the cursor is within the bounding rectangle of each object. Since the center of the cursor is displaced two units in the *x* and *y* direction from its lower-left corner (xcursor,ycursor), it is necessary to subtract 2 from the corner coordinates. Select returns the number of the object found, or zero if none of the 10 objects have been selected.

```
Function Select(xcursor,ycursor:integer):integer;

var
    objectfound            : 0..10; {object number found}
    number                 : 1..10: {list of objects}

begin
    {initialization}
    number := 1;
    objectfound := 0;
    while (objectfound = 0) and (number <= 10) do
    {test each object}
    begin    {while}
        with object[number] do
            if (xcursor – 2 > lowx) and (xcursor – 2 < highx) and
            (ycursor – 2 > lowy) and (ycursor – 2 < highy) then
                objectfound := number;
        number := number + 1;
    end;    {while}
    Select := objectfound
end;    {Select}
```

Once we have selected an object, the next step may position it on the screen. One technique for doing this has the object follow the cursor about the screen until the new location has been reached. This is referred to as *dragging*. To perform dragging, the center of the cursor is first positioned at the lower-left corner of the object's bounding rectangle. We then use the **blockmove** procedure in the "exclusive or" mode to move both the object and the cursor. Procedure Follow_Cursor performs this task. Its parameter, icon, is the object that has been identified by the function, Select. The house scene in Figure 8-11 was created

FIGURE 8–11
An image created by selecting and positioning objects

using procedure Follow_Cursor and function Select. Notice that the frame of the house was drawn using vectors.

Procedure Follow_Cursor(icon:objdescrib);

```
    var
            xnew,ynew : integer;                {new screen position}
            count : integer;                     {delay loop}
    begin
        with icon do
        begin     {with}
        {move the center of cursor to lower-left corner of icon}
        blockmove(cursor,xcursor,ycursor,xor);     {erase old}
        blockmove(cursor,lowx − 2,lowy − 2,xor);     {draw new}
        {move cursor and icon until paddle button is pressed}
            repeat
                xnew := trunc(paddle(0)*xval);
                for count := 1 to 5 do;
                ynew := trunc(paddle(1)*yval);
                if (xnew<>lowx − 1) or (ynew<>lowy − 2) then
                {cursor has moved}
                    begin     {if}
                    {erase old cursor and icon}
                    blockmove(cursor,lowx − 2,lowy − 2,xor);
                    blockmove(image,lowx,lowy,xor);
                    {draw new cursor and icon}
                    blockmove(cursor,xnew − 2,ynew − 2,xor)
                    blockmove(image,xnew,ynew,xor);
                    lowx := xnew;     {update present location}
                    lowy := ynew
                    end     {if}
                    until button(0)
        end     {with}
    end;     {Follow_Cursor}
```

8–6 **PAINTING**

In the previous section, an object was moved about the screen following the cursor. Before drawing the new object, the previous one was erased using the "exclusive or" mode. Now recall from Chapter 1 that painting is a technique that mimics the creation of an image using a painter's brush and palette. A paint brush (shape) is moved about the screen by an input device. However, unlike in the previous discussion, the shape is not erased from its previous location (Figure 8-12).

Painting is usually menu driven. Typically, a viewport offers several choices, including a variety of brushes displayed (Figure 8-13 on page 196). An input device is used to select the type of brush and to maneuver the brush about the screen. Clearly, the subroutines Select and Follow_

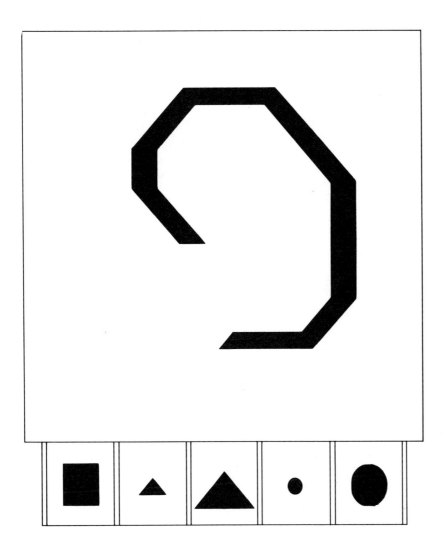

FIGURE 8–12
Moving a triangular
brush around the
screen

Cursor can be used to perform this task. The brush can follow a pre-defined curve—for example, a circle—by using the coordinate values of the curve as input. The brush can also serve as an eraser by drawing in the background color (black). This is usually done by using **blockmove** in the erase mode:

blockmove(brush,x,y,erase).

There is one problem that a user of a painting algorithm encounters. If the input device is moved too quickly, there will be gaps between successively drawn brushes. This can be prevented by using a line-drawing DDA as in Chapter 2 to determine the points between successive input values. The brush is then applied to these intermediary points. If the brush is convex (that is, any line between any two points on the

BRUSHES					ERASERS			OPTIONS		MODE
▪	■	⬟	╱	╲	▪	◻		■	PRINT	READY

FIGURE 8–13
A menu-driven
paint program

brush is entirely within the brush), it is only necessary to compute these points when the distance between successive input points is greater than the width of the brush.

8–7 **CONCLUSION**

Interactive graphics display systems require special hardware and software technologies that give the system a fast response to user-controlled input devices. Since speed is of the essence, many software routines are written in low-level code. This chapter used Pascal to examine some of the more common interactive concepts and algorithms.

EXERCISES

1. Use the graphics editor to create several cursor symbols. These may include an arrow, an hourglass, or a plus sign.
2. Redo exercise 1 using the **screenbit** function to place the cursor in a shape table.
3. Implement procedure Move_Cursor on your computer.
4. Implement dragging, using the procedure Follow_Cursor and the function Select.
5. Write a painting program that allows the user to select a brush size and, if your system has color, a paint color. Use the line DDA in Chapter 2 to fill in gaps in all line drawing.
6. Use the "or" mode to eliminate a temporary hole caused by a moving cursor.
7. If your system has two buffers, use them to draw and erase lines rapidly and to perform dragging.
8. Draw a circle given three noncollinear points lying on the circle.

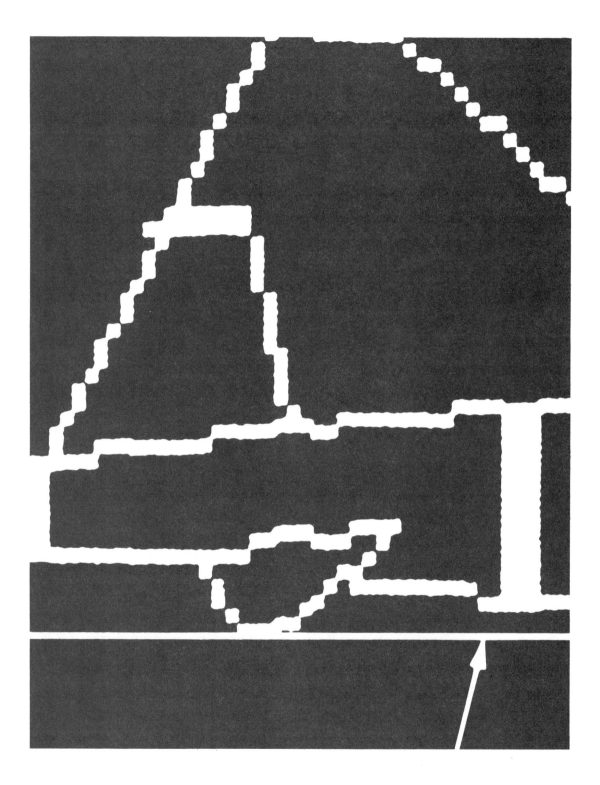

Detail of Figure 9–5

9
ANIMATION

9–1 INTRODUCTION

Computer-generated animated images are used in entertainment, such as in video arcade games and movies, and in instruction, such as in flight simulators for pilots and astronauts. Both of these applications require, in varying degrees, that the image appear realistic and behave in a natural manner. Any significant deviation from what our senses perceive as natural gives an unwanted, artificial flavor to the animation. As an example, a pilot flying a plane in a flight simulator has to be able to change course smoothly without any loss of detail. This stringent requirement for exactness has frustrated many good programmers, while those who have mastered the techniques of animation have reaped the rewards of their talents.

As discussed in Chapter 1, real-time flight simulators use special-purpose, high-performance hardware that is still too expensive for most graphics display systems. Consequently, in this chapter we examine only some of the techniques that can produce video arcade–quality animated images. Many of these techniques are no more than "tricks" that have been discovered over the years. In fact, a large part of animation skills is simply a fine tuning of the interactive methods studied in Chapter 8.

Before going on, it is only fair to note that Pascal procedures cannot

FIGURE 9–1
A low-resolution
animated sequence

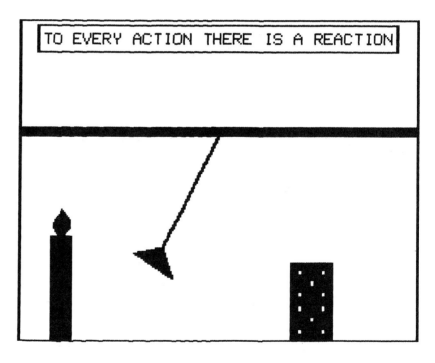

(a)

produce even the low-quality animation of video arcade games. These games owe their fast response time to the use of clever assembly language programming. These machine-level arcade programmers rely on exacting knowledge of the processor and memory that can be used only with low-level instructions. Be aware, too, that the design of a successful arcade game can require thousands of programming hours.

Figure 9-1 illustrates two frames in a simple animated sequence produced on a low-resolution display. While not of very good quality, the design of this game can be just as demanding and exciting as producing an arcade game. To speed up animation as much as possible, we shall continue to use display screen coordinates and commands.

9–2 SPEED CONSIDERATIONS

There are two fundamental speed considerations in animation: screen update rate and screen erase time. In an animated sequence, each displayed image is called a **frame**. Animation requires that at least 15 frames/sec be displayed; otherwise, motion becomes jumpy and discontinuous. (Flight simulators have a 30-frame/sec update rate.) For this chapter, we assume a display screen resolution of $280 \times 192 = 43,760$

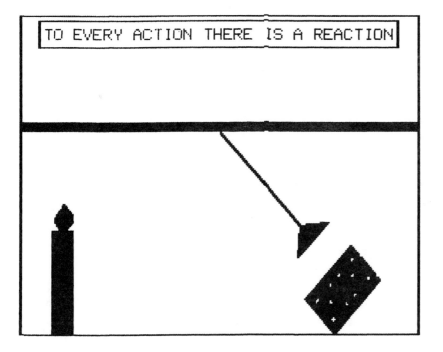

TO EVERY ACTION THERE IS A REACTION

(b)

pixels. In order to generate a sequence having smooth motion, all of these 43,760 pixels must be updated within $\frac{1}{15}$ of a second. This minimum **screen update rate**, however, is currently beyond the power of most microcomputer processors, especially when executing a Pascal program.

One solution to the problem is **selective updating**. This technique is based on the observation that in most animated sequences only a small portion of the image changes in subsequent frames. We can speed up the motion by updating only those objects or areas of the screen that have changed. For example, a spaceship may be the only object moving in a star-filled sky. We have already seen in Chapter 8 how the "exclusive or" mode can be used to perform this type of selective update.

The second concern, **screen erase time**, is related to the update rate. Before a new frame is displayed, all or part of the old frame must be erased. If the time required to erase a screen is longer than one-quarter of the frame rate, a perceptible flicker is produced. There are several methods available to decrease the length of this blank period.

First, the technique of selective updating requires that only a small area of the screen be changed. The time it takes to erase this area, instead of the entire screen, can be fast enough to eliminate the flicker.

Another technique, called **screen ping-ponging** or **double buffering**, requires two frame buffers. As the display controller displays an image from one buffer, the display processor erases and redraws the image in the second buffer. When this new image is ready, the display controller displays the contents of the second buffer. This switch between buffers is performed instantaneously without any noticeable flicker. One disadvantage with this technique is the extra memory required for the second frame buffer. However, the low cost of memory is making this option attractive to newer display systems.

Another flicker-reduction technique is available on some display systems. In generating a raster-scan image, approximately one-quarter of the scan refresh time is spent during vertical retrace—that is, in moving the electron beam from the bottom of the screen back to the top of the screen. During this vertical blanking time, no scan lines are being displayed, and we can take advantage of this inactivity by performing selective erase and redraw.

9–3 PADDLE TECHNIQUES

In Chapter 8, we converted paddle values from 0 to 255 into x, y screen coordinates ranging from 0 to 279 horizontally and 0 to 191 vertically using the equations

```
xscreen := trunc(paddle(0)*1.09);
yscreen := trunc(paddle(1)*0.74);
```

For most interactive usage, these equations are satisfactory. However, they do not work too well for animation. Let's examine some of the problems encountered using these equations.

Animation has more stringent requirements for real-time response than does interaction. An acceptable delay of ½ sec in interaction can be unacceptable in animation. Thus we must eliminate time-consuming operations whenever and wherever possible. For example, the preceding equations have two necessary calls to the paddle function; but they also involve a multiplication, and an invocation of the truncate function. All of this can consume valuable processor time.

Alternatively, for many applications it is not necessary to access each pixel on the display screen. Consider the fish in Figure 9-2. It is described by a boolean shape array of size 25 in each of the x, y screen coordinates. If we assign to xscreen location the value of **paddle**(0), the left-most part of the fish moves from position 0 to 255 in the horizontal direction. Thus, the 256-integer paddle values (0..255) are all that are needed to move the 25-pixel-wide fish shape across the screen.

The maximum vertical position for the lower-left corner of the fish is the top of the screen less the height of the shape—that is, $191 - 25 = 166$. Thus, we must limit the yscreen value of this corner to 166. The following code does this:

```
yscreen := paddle(1);
if yscreen > 166 then
    yscreen := 166;
```

It may appear that we can take advantage of this method only in the horizontal direction when the width of the object plus 255 is about 280, the width of the screen. This is not necessarily the case, however.

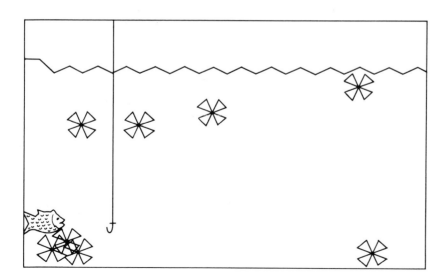

FIGURE 9–2
An animation frame of a fish under water

Suppose an object is four pixels wide. Using the paddle value as the xscreen position, this object moves from screen location 0 to location 259. The missing 20 horizontal pixels may seem like a lot, but if we offset the xscreen value by 10 units

xscreen := **paddle**(0) + 10;

the xscreen locations now range from 10 to 269. The unused 10 pixels on each side of the screen are scarcely noticeable, and the loss of these pixels is more than compensated for by the reduced computational time.

Another technique is to precompute the x and y screen coordinates using the xscreen and yscreen equations and to store these values in arrays of size 256.

var
    xval,yval : **array**[0.255] **of integer**;

Then xval[**paddle**(0)] and yval[**paddle**(1)] accesses the screen coordinates. This technique is fast and accurate but does require additional storage space. We shall examine this method in more detail in the next section.

Another and more pressing concern is the demand for smooth motion. If the paddle knob is rotated too much, the object will jump from one location to the next, producing an artificial appearance in the animation. There should be a predetermined maximum distance an object can move from frame to frame. Suppose, for example, that an object is allowed to move across the screen in 2 sec. For a frame rate of 15 frames/sec, $15 \times 2 = 30$ frames are needed to move the object across the entire 280-pixel screen in 2 sec. Thus for each frame, the object should move no more than $^{280}/_{30} = 9.3$ pixels.

To achieve this smooth motion, we should compare the current xscreen location with the new paddle-determined location, xnew. If xscreen < xnew, xscreen is incremented either by nine pixels or by xnew − xscreen, whichever is smaller. If xscreen > xnew, xscreen is decremented by a similar amount.

This technique works well except for the times when we wish to move an object across the screen at a much faster rate. In those cases, when the new paddle-input value is much larger than the current xscreen position, we want to move the object a maximum of 18 pixels, doubling the rate of motion.

The following procedure, Move_Across, implements slow and fast motion in the horizontal direction. The parameter xscreen is the location of the left side of the shape describing the object and xnew is the x value obtained from the paddle input.

Procedure Move_Across (**var** xscreen, xnew, : **integer**);

    var
        xdif : **integer;**   *{difference between screen values}*

```
begin
    xdif := xnew − xscreen;
    if xdif > 0 then
    {increment horizontal position}
        if xdif < 9 then
            {little motion}
            xscreen := xnew
        else
            if xdif < 30 then
                {slow motion}
                    xscreen := xscreen + 9
            else
                {fast motion}
                xscreen := xscreen + 18
    else    {decrement position}
        if −xdif < 9 then
        {little motion}
        xscreen := xnew
        else
            if −xdif < 30 then
                {slow motion}
                xscreen := xscreen − 9
            else
                {fast motion}
                xscreen := xscreen − 18
end;    {Move_Across}
```

Similar code produces movement in the vertical, y direction. This is left as an exercise.

9–4 PATH LOOK-UP TABLE

Many objects in an animated sequence are not controlled by the user but follow a specified path, such as a trigonometric curve. For example, an arcade game airplane might be following the path of a sine curve $(y = \sin x)$ (Figure 9-3 on page 206). If the plane is represented by a boolean shape table, then the sine function must be invoked every time the plane moves along the curve. More complicated motion might require several function calls combined with complex arithmetic and logical operations. All of this can consume precious processor time, thus degrading the animation performance.

Since the path of the object is known in advance—$(x, \sin x)$ in the airplane example—we should precompute this path and store its coordinate values in a **look-up table**. Then, whenever the object moves, it is only necessary to access the look-up table to determine the screen coordinates. This technique is based on the principle that it is quicker to

FIGURE 9–3
An airplane follow-
ing a curve defined
in a path look-up
table

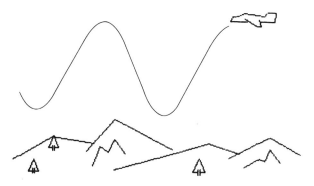

look a value up in a table than to calculate it. Of course, the table does consume memory; but that is becoming a rather cheap commodity.

A look-up table can be implemented using an array of records. Each record entry consists of the screen coordinates of a point on the specified path.

```
type
    table_entry = record
                        x,y : integer
                    end;
var
    {path coordinates}
    table : array[1..100] of table_entry;
```

The following code moves an object about the path defined in a look-up table:

```
{draw object}
blockmove(figure,table[1].x,table[1].y,xor);
for i := 1 to 99 do
    begin
        {erase object}
        blockmove(figure,table[i].x,table[i].y,xor);
        {draw object}
        blockmove(figure,table[i + 1].x,table[i + 1].y,xor);
    end;
```

Generally, before the pair of **blockmove** commands in the for loop, there will be many lines of code that perform other tasks required for the animation sequence.

An object that moves along a path at a constant speed is too predictable for most arcade–type games. A spaceship can be speeded up or slowed down by an acceleration term. To accelerate an object moving across the screen, it is necessary to increase the difference between successive x values by the acceleration value. However, in doing this we must be careful not to have the spaceship fly across the screen at an alarming rate. For example, suppose an acceleration value of one pixel is used. Then the following sequence consists of successive x coordinates of the object starting at zero:

0 1 3 6 10 15 21 28 36 45 55 ...

Here, the fifth coordinate has x value $5 \times \frac{1}{2} = 10$. In general, the nth coordinate value is $n(n - 1)/2$. This would allow a total of 24 moves ($24 \times \frac{23}{2} = 276$) with a large jump of 24 pixels from the twenty-third to the twenty-fourth move.

To smooth out acceleration, a better technique is to have constant velocity (no acceleration) for, say, four frames and apply acceleration only during the fifth frame. This often results in a more natural looking motion. The following code implements this for an acceleration constant of four pixels:

```
{initial position}
table[1].x := 0;
{remaining moves}
for i := 2 to 100 do
    if 0 = i mod 5 then
        {accelerate every fifth move}
        table[i].x := table[i-1].x + 4
    else
        {no acceleration}
        table[i].x := table[i-1].x + 1;
```

One type of motion that is often displayed is that of an object being thrown up into the air, or equivalently, a bomb being dropped from a plane. Both objects follow the path of a parabola (Figure 9-4) with the equation

$$y = -s(x - k)^2 + h.$$

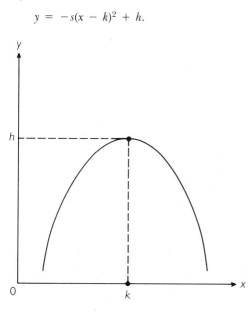

FIGURE 9–4
Parabolic motion

The values k and h represent the x and y coordinates, respectively, of the vertex of the parabola. The value s describes the parabolic shape: A small value of s spreads the parabola out, and a large s results in a narrow curve. By varying these parameters, we can simulate the object thrown at a specified initial speed and angle from the horizontal. Once these values are determined, the equation for a parabola is used to load the x, y coordinate values into a look-up table. We leave this as an exercise for the reader.

9-5 COLLISION

Two objects collide when part of one object occupies the same screen coordinate as part of another object. Our eyes can detect collision easily and instantaneously. Unfortunately, the computer has a more difficult time observing this phenomenon.

It would seem easy to detect collision by comparing the screen coordinates of the two shapes: If any of these coordinates were equal, collision would occur. The problem with this naive approach is the potentially enormous amount of computing that must take place to perform these tests. For example, suppose that each shape is represented by a 10×10 array. Since each pixel of one shape is compared with each pixel of the other shape, $100 \times 100 = 10,000$ comparisons would be necessary to detect collisions. And if this weren't bad enough, suppose we were trying to determine if one object (a missile) would collide with any of a hundred other objects (attacking spaceships, for example). This scenario would require $10,000 \times 100 = 1,000,000$ comparisons, which is totally out of the question for real-time performance.

One technique used to speed up detection is to use the defining rectangles of the object. As an example, suppose a missile has its tip at location $(x1, y1)$, and a spaceship is represented by a 20×100 shape array with its lower-left corner at location (x, y), as in Figure 9-5. From the shape table definition, the bounding rectangle of the spaceship has upper-right corner $(x + 99, y + 19)$. Therefore, the tip of the missile is within this rectangle only if the following inequalities are valid:

$$x <= x1 <= x + 99 \quad \text{and}$$
$$y <= y1 <= y + 19.$$

If this is the case, we have collision.

This bounding rectangle method has the advantages of being easy to code and of detecting collisions in real time. Unfortunately, it has the severe disadvantage of producing inaccurate results. That is, the tip of the missile may be in the spaceship's rectangle without actually hitting the spaceship. Also, we only tested for the tip of the missile. What happens if the tip misses the spaceship but one of the sides of the missile

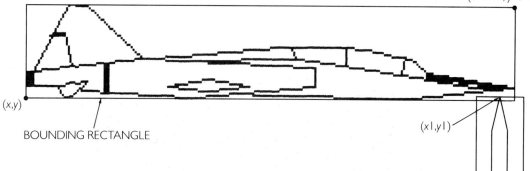

(x + 99, y + 19)

(x,y)

BOUNDING RECTANGLE

(x1,y1)

BOUNDING
RECTANGLE

collides with the spaceship? We could test to determine if the bounding rectangle of the missile (actually we need only check its width) intersects the spaceship's rectangle. This test would solve the second problem but would compound the difficulty with the first problem since these rectangles can overlap without the missile or the spaceship intersecting each other (Figure 9-5).

If one of the objects is not too complex, there is an efficient method that accurately detects collision. Suppose that the boundary of a missile (not its bounding rectangle) presently occupies the following screen coordinates (Figure 9-6):

$(x, y)\ (x-1, y-1)\ (x+1, y-1)\ (x-1, y-2)\ (x+1, y-2)$.

We wish to determine if this missile collides with any object in the next frame. Assume, then, that the missile moves up four pixels in the y direction in each frame. In this case, the missile will collide with some object in the next frame if part of an object in this subsequent frame occupies any of the screen locations that the missile will occupy—namely, the screen locations:

$(x, y+4)\ (x-1, y+3)\ (x+1, y+3)\ (x-1, y+2)\ (x+2, y+2)$.

In order for this to work, it is important that the missile be drawn last and the test performed prior to redrawing the missile in its new position.

FIGURE 9–5
The bounding rectangles of a spaceship and a missile

FIGURE 9–6
A simplified missile

(x,y)

Otherwise, the missile will be tested against itself—guaranteeing a collision!

If hit is a boolean variable, this test can be implemented using the **screenbit** function:

```
hit := screenbit(x,y + 4)      or screenbit(x − 1,y + 3) or
       screenbit(x + 1,y + 3) or screenbit(x − 1,y + 2) or
       screenbit(x + 1,y + 2);
if hit then . . .    {collision}
```

What happens when a collision is detected? One of the first tasks is to determine which object collided with the missile. This can be done by comparing the collision coordinates with the present coordinates of all the objects. That object having coordinates closest to these values is the one that collided. Of course, we may identify the wrong object. However, most of the time we will be correct, and an exact identification is messy and time-consuming. In any case, both the object selected and the missile are erased using XOR, and an explosion shape or sequence is placed at the location of the collision. This enhancement is left as an exercise for the reader.

9–6 PROGRAMMING EXAMPLE

Program Sailboat is a simple animated video arcade-type game consisting of a ship moving along a path and a bird whose flight is controlled by two paddles (Figure 9-7). If the bird lands on the ship's mast, the ship stops. Failing to land the bird on the mast allows the ship to hit the rock and sink. The game repeats until the paddle's button is depressed.

The following is an explanation of the procedures:

Plot_Course	: Enters points for the ship's path into a look-up table.
Draw_Bird	: Draws a bird and uses **screenbit** to enter it into the shape table.
Draw_Ship	: Draws a ship in upright and rotated (sunk) position. Enters both ships into the shape table using the **screenbit** function. Drawing is performed in world coordinates so that the rotate function can be used.
Ocean	: Draws a repetitive zig-zag pattern for waves. Since this is quickly drawn, no shape table is needed.
Moon_Shine	: Uses world coordinates to rotate a line segment, producing a shaded disk. Creates a shape table for the moon.
Rock	: Draws the rock; again no shape table is needed.
Hit_Test	: Uses **screenbit** to test two points near the top of the mast. If either of these pixels is lit, then the bird is on the mast and the variable "landed" is set to true.

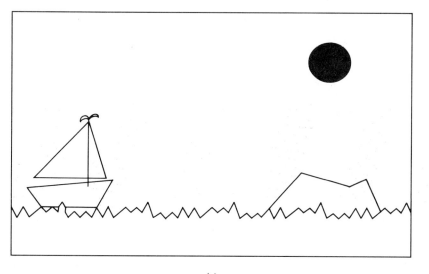

(a)

FIGURE 9–7
An animation se-
quence of a sailboat

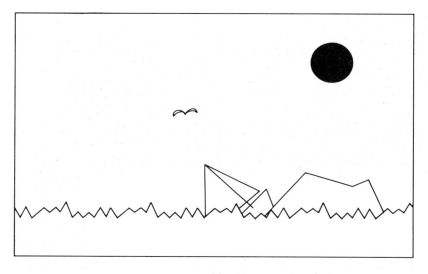

(b)

```
Program Sailboat;

const
    pi = 3.1415928;

type
    table_entry = record
                    x,y : integer
                  end;
```

```
var
    table : array [1..13] of table_entry;                    {ship path}
    moon : array[1..56,1..56] of boolean;                    {shape table}
    bird : array [1..5,1..15] of boolean;                    {shape table}
    landed : boolean;     {bird on mast = true}
    titanic : array [1..68,1..61] of boolean;    {upright ship}
    sink : array [1..66,1..55] of boolean;    {sinking ship}
    i,j,    {counters in the for loop}
    xpt,ypt : integer;    {screen coordinates}

Procedure Plot_Course;
    {enters the points into look-up table}

    begin
        table[1].x := 0;
        table[1].y := 38;
        table[2].x := 11;
        table[2].y := 38;
        table[3].x := 22;
        table[3].y := 44;
        table[4].x := 39;
        table[4].y := 38;
        table[5].x := 50;
        table[5].y := 44;
        table[6].x := 66;
        table[6].y := 38;
        table[7].x := 83;
        table[7].y := 32;
        table[8].x := 89;
        table[8].y := 44;
        table[9].x := 100;
        table[9].y := 38;
        table[10].x := 111;
        table[10].y := 44;
        table[11].x := 116;
        table[11].y := 38;
        table[12].x := 122;
        table[12].y := 45;
        table[13].x := 133;
        table[13].y := 38
    end;    {Plot_Course}

Procedure Draw_Bird;

    var
        i,j, : integer;    {counters}

        begin
            moves(0,0);
            rdraws(4,4);
            rdraws(3, -3);
```

```
                    rdraws(3,3);
                    rdraws(4, − 4);
                    rdraws(− 4,3);
                    rdraws(− 3, − 2);
                    rdraws(− 3,2);
                    rdraws(− 4,3);
                    rdraws(4,2);
                    rdraws(3, − 1);
                    rdraws(3,1);
                    rdraws(4, − 2);
                    {copy into shape table}
                    for i := 0 to 14 do
                        for j := 0 to 5 do
                            bird[j + 1,i + 1] := screenbit(i,j)
            end;    {Draw_Bird}

Procedure Draw_Ship;

        var
            i,j : integer;      {loop counters}

Procedure Ship;
        {draw ship}
        begin
            move(11,0);
            rdraw2(39,0);
            rdraw2(11,22);
            rdraw2(− 61, − 6);
            rdraw2(11, − 16);
            rdraw2(33,19);
            rdraw2(0,49);
            rdraw2(− 38, − 44);
            rdraw2(50,0);
            rdraw2(− 12,44)
        end;    {Ship}

begin   {Draw_Ship}
    window(− 140,140, − 96,96);
    fillscreen(black);
    {draw ship}
    Ship;
    {copy into shape table}
    for i := 1 to 61 do
        for j := 1 to 68 do
            titanic[j,i] := screenbit(i + 139,j + 95);
    fillscreen(black);
    {draw sinking ship}
    rotate(pi/4);
    Ship;
    {copy into shape table}
    for i := 1 to 55 do
```

```
                    for j := 1 to 66 do
                        Sink[j,i] := screenbit(i + 123,j + 118)
        end;      {Draw_Ship}

Procedure Ocean;
        {draw zig-zag shape}

        var
            xpt,ypt : integer;

        begin
            {initialization}
            xpt := 0;
            ypt := 38;
            while xpt < 279 do
                begin      {while}
                    moves(xpt,ypt);
                    rdraws(4, − 8);
                    rdraws(4,8);
                    rdraws(4, − 8);
                    rdraws(8,8);
                    rdraws(4, − 4);
                    rdraws(4,4);
                    rdraws(4, − 4);
                    rdraws(4,8);
                    rdraws(4, − 12);
                    rdraws(4,4);
                    rdraws(4, − 4);
                    rdraws(4,4);
                    rdraws(4, − 4);
                    rdraws(4,8);
                    {repeat zig-zag}
                    xpt := xpt  + 60
                end
        end;      {Ocean}

Procedure Moon_Shine;

        var
            i,j : integer;                                      {loop counters}
            theta : real;                                      {rotation angle}

        begin
            {top right of screen}
            viewport(0.7,0.9,0.45,1);
            window( − 20, 20, − 20,20);
            theta := 0.06;
            j := 1;
            {rotate line 360 degrees}
            while j < = 360 do
                begin      {while}
                    rotate(theta);
```

```
                move2(0,0);
                draw2(0,11);
                j := j + 3
            end;    {while}
        {copy into shape table}
        for i: = 1 to 56 do
            for j := 1 to 56 do
                {0.7 × 279 = 196, 0.45 × 191 = 86}
                moon[j,i] := screenbit(i + 195,j + 85);
        {reset viewport to entire screen}
        viewport(0,1,0,1);
        fillscreen(black)
    end;    {Moon_Shine}

Procedure Rock;

    begin
        moves(176,33);
        rdraws(27,33);
        rdraws(33, − 11);
        rdraws(11,6);
        rdraws(11, − 28)
    end;    {Rock}

Procedure Hit_Test;

    var
        testx,testy : integer;    {points above mast}

    begin
        testx := table[i].x + 48;
        testy := table[i].y + 68;
        {is bird on mast?}
        if screenbit(testx,testy) then
            landed := true
        else
            {test two other points above mast}
            begin
            testx := table[i].x + 43;
            testy := table[i].y + 70;
            landed := screenbit(testx,testy)
            end    {else}
    end;    {Hit_test}

    begin    {Sailboat}
        landed := false;    {bird not on mast}
        {construct path and shape tables}
        Plot_Course;
        Draw_Ships;
        Moon_Shine;
        Draw_Bird;
        {start the game}
```

```
while not button(0) do
    begin    {while}
        viewport(0,1,0,1);
        fillscreen(black);
        frame;
        {draw ocean}
        Ocean;
        {draw moon}
        blockmove(moon,195,132,xor);
        {draw rock}
        Rock;
        {initial bird position}
        xpt := 260;
        ypt := 90;
        {draw bird}
        blockmove(bird,xpt,ypt,xor);
        {initial point on ship path}
        i := 1;
        repeat
            {draw ship}
            blockmove(titanic,table[i].x,table[i].y,xor);
            {erase bird}
            blockmove(bird,xpt,ypt,xor);
            {use paddles to move bird}
            xpt := paddle(0);
            {wait between paddle reads}
            for j:= 1 to 5 do;
            ypt := paddle(1);
            if ypt > 175    then {bird height = 15}
                ypt := 175;
            {draw bird}
            blockmove(bird,xpt,ypt,xor);
            {delay before redrawing ship}
            for j:= 1 to 100 do;
            {erase ship}
            blockmove(titanic,table[i].x,table[i].y,xor);
            {is bird on mast?}
            Hit_Test;
            {next point on ship path}
            i := i+1;
        until (i = 14) or landed;
    if not landed then
        {bird not on mast}
        begin    {if}
            {draw sinking ship}
            blockmove(sink,133,38,xor);    {draw}
            blockmove(sink,133,38,xor);    {erase}
            blockmove(sink,133,38,XOR);    {draw}
        end    {if}
    else    {bird on mast}
```

{draw ship, with bird on mast}
          blockmove(titanic,table[i – 1].x,table[i – 1].y,xor)
     end   *{while}*
  end.   *{Sailboat}*

9–7 **CONCLUSION**

This chapter has presented only a few of the many techniques currently in use in animation. In particular, we have steered our discussion toward arcade–type games since this is a familiar type of animation that can be displayed effectively on an inexpensive display system. Animation as seen in movies, television commercials, and flight simulators uses special-purpose, high-resolution display hardware to generate realistic images quickly. While significant progress has been made over the past 10 years, there is still room for improvements in hardware and software design. The reader is encouraged to learn more about animation by discovering and analyzing the graphics techniques in arcade games and movies.

EXERCISES

1. Create shape tables of spaceships and missiles. Write a collision detect procedure to determine when these shapes collide.
2. Perform animation by having a car remain in its location while its wheels are rotating and the background moves.
3. Write a procedure that has an airplane flying in a spiral pattern.
4. Write a procedure that bounces a ball around the sides of a box. Have the ball accelerate whenever it bounces off the top and bottom sides.
5. Create several shape tables, each depicting different stages of a person walking. Simulate walking by cycling through these shapes, displaying one shape at a time in a slightly different screen location. Use two frame buffers if your system has this capability.
6. Simulate a bombing mission using parabolic motion.
7. Write a postcollision routine that puts parts of an exploded spaceship throughout the display screen. To do this, have each part defined separately in a separate shape table.

Detail of Figure 10–1

10
POLYGON FILLING

10-1 **INTRODUCTION**

Many complex objects that are computer-generated can be represented by one or more polygons. Even if an object is not polygonal in nature, a polygonal approximation of it can be used. For example, a circle is displayed as a polygon with many sides. The more sides the polygon has, the more it looks like a circle. Once a polygon is displayed, we can use the features of our raster display system to fill the interior region of this polygon. If all the pixels inside the polygon's boundary are illuminated, a solid-fill is performed. It is also possible to illuminate the pixels on every other scan line, or every third scan line, and so on. We can even fill the polygon with an arbitrary predefined pattern. These different types of fillings can enhance the realism of a polygon-defined object, or highlight different features of several polygons. Figure 10-1 illustrates several polygon fillings.

In this chapter, we examine several techniques and algorithms to fill polygons. We begin with a discussion of different polygon representations.

10-2 **POLYGON REPRESENTATION**

Perhaps the most natural way to represent a polygon is by listing its n vertices in an ordered list: $P = \{(x1, y1),(x2, y2), \ldots ,(xn, yn)\}$. The polygon can be constructed by moving the pen to the first vertex, $(x1, y1)$, and then issuing draw commands to the remaining $n - 1$ vertices. In order to close up the polygon, a final draw command from the last vertex to the first vertex is needed (Figure 10-2).

FIGURE 10–1
Several filled polygons

Polygon Filling

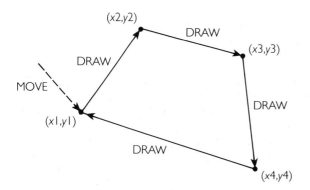

FIGURE 10–2
Polygon
construction

One problem with this representation is that if we wish to translate the polygon, it is necessary to apply the translation transformation to each vertex in order to obtain the translated polygon. For objects described by many polygons with many vertices, this can be a time-consuming process. One method for reducing the computational time is to represent the polygon by the (absolute) location of its first vertex $(x1, y1)$ and represent subsequent vertices as relative positions from the previous vertex. This enables us to translate the polygon simply by changing the coordinates of the first vertex. Let's look at an example using this idea.

Polygon P in Figure 10-3 is represented in **absolute coordinates** by

$$P = \{(-1, -1), (-1, 1), (3, 1), (3, -1)\}.$$

To translate P three units in the x direction and five units in the y direction, it is necessary to add 3 to each of the x coordinates and 5 to each of the y coordinates of P. This requires a total of eight additions. If, however, we represent the same polygon P in **relative coordinates**

$$P = \{(-1, -1), (0, 2), (4, 0), (-4, 0)\},$$

where the first pair is the initial vertex and the other pairs are directed distances, we can translate the polygon by the same amount simply by

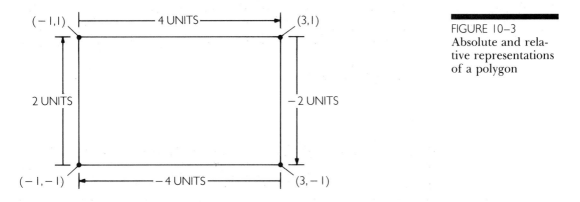

FIGURE 10–3
Absolute and relative representations of a polygon

adding three units to the *x* coordinate and five units to the *y* coordinate of the first coordinate $(-1, -1)$. Their other vertices remain the same since their displacement from the new first coordinate (2, 4) is the same. This method requires only two additions.

Polygons can also be represented by listing their edges and vertices. This operation makes it easier to determine geometric properties such as which polygons share a common edge. This representation requires more storage but reduces the computational time spent in determining the geometric properties.

In order to simplify the discussion of filling polygons, we shall represent polygons using their actual vertex coordinates. Having made this decision, we must now choose an appropriate data structure for representing the vertices that define the polygon. Here we also have two choices. Each representation is composed of records and arrays but used in a different way. Let's examine both of these data structures.

Assume that a polygon has a maximum of 20 vertices. The following constant declaration is used for both representations:

```
const
    maxvert = 19;    {one less than the number of vertices in the polygon}
```

The first representation creates one record with two fields: *x* and *y*. Each field is an array of coordinate values:

```
type
    coords = array[0..maxvert] of real;
    points = record
                    x,y : coord    {the individual vertices}
             end;

var
    vertex: points;    {record of polygon vertices}
```

Using this data structure, we can enter the 20 coordinates of the polygon with

```
with vertex do
    {loop through reading each (x, y) vertex}
    for i := 0 to maxvert do
        readln(x[i],y[i]);
```

The second representation creates an array of records. Each record corresponds to an (*x*, *y*) coordinate pair:

```
type
    points = record
                    x,y : real
             end;
    coords = array[0..maxvert] of points;    {vertices}

var
    vertex: coords;    {array of polygon vertices}
```

Polygon Filling

Using this data structure, we can enter the 20 coordinates of the polygon with

```
for i := 0 to maxvert do
    {loop through reading each vertex}
    with vertex[i] do
        readln(x,y);
```

The choice between these two representations is more a matter of taste than substance. In this text, we shall use the first representation.

There is one final concern before describing the filling algorithms. In most cases, the polygon is defined by its vertices in world coordinates. Prior to filling, a polygon-clipping algorithm (Chapter 3) is invoked to obtain a closed polygon inside the window. Since several filling algorithms are based on scan-line order (that is, filling in a polygon one scan line at a time, incrementing or decrementing the y value by one unit at each step), the next step converts world coordinate vertices into screen coordinates using the window-to-viewport transformation, as described in Chapter 3. These screen coordinates are now used for the filling algorithms. Hence, the algorithms and procedures that follow assume that all vertices are in integer screen coordinates.

10–3 FRAME BUFFER FILLING

SCAN-LINE FILLING

A relatively easy method of filling a polygon is to first have the polygon boundary drawn in the frame buffer. In many cases the polygon has been entered interactively and is currently displayed on the screen. Thus, the only pixels in the frame buffer that are illuminated are those defining the polygon. The filling algorithm proceeds in scan-line order starting with the left-most pixel on each scan line. Scanning from left to right, the boolean function **screenbit**(x, y) (true if pixel (x, y) is illuminated) is used to determine if an edge has been encountered by testing whether a pixel is on. If it is, the subsequent pixels on that scan line are set (illuminated) until the next edge is encountered. This edge is found by locating the next pixel on the current scan line that has previously been set. In order to speed up the filling, the algorithm first determines the x values of both the left edge and right edge on the scan line and then draws a line between them, filling in that segment. This test is repeated until the last pixel on that scan line is reached. The outer **repeat** loop is used to locate multiple fill segments on one scan line (Figure 10-4 on page 224). The following procedure, Buffer_Fill, implements this algorithm.

FIGURE 10–4
Scan-line frame
buffer filling

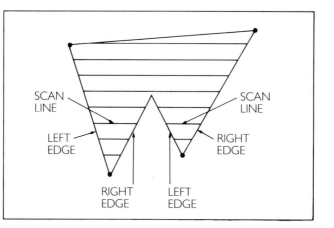

```
Procedure Buffer_Fill;
    {performs frame buffer polygon filling}

const
    ymax = 511;    {top scan line}
    xmax = 511;    {right-most pixel on scan line}

var
    x,y,                        {screen coordinates}
    xstart : integer;           {left edge of fill segment}

begin
    for y := 0 to ymax do
        {each scan line}
        begin    {for}
            x := 0;   {first pixel on scan line}
            repeat    {until last pixel on scan line}
                {find the left edge of a fill segment}
                while not screenbit(x,y) and (x<xmax) do
                    x := x + 1;   {keep searching for an on pixel}
                if x < xmax then
                    {found left edge}
                    begin    {if}
                        x := x + 1;   {next pixel after edge}
                        xstart := x;    {begin fill here}
                        {now find the corresponding right edge of the fill
                        segment}
                        while not screenbit(x,y) do
                        x := x + 1;   {perform the search}
                        {the x value now has the right edge value}
                        {fill in the segment between the edges}
                        moves(xstart,y);
                        draws(x,y);
                        {set up for next starting edge on same scan line}
                        x := x + 1
```

```
                    end    {if}
            until x >= xmax
        end    {for}
end;    {Buffer_Fill}
```

One problem with this algorithm is the repeated testing necessary to determine the inside of the polygon using the boolean **Screenbit** function. For large frame buffers having a small polygon, a lot of time is spent testing pixels that are not turned on. We could make the algorithm more efficient by limiting the x and y values to the maximum and minimum values that the polygon attains (called its **extent**). This limitation can significantly improve processing speed.

One problem with procedure Buffer_Fill is that it does not correctly fill all types of polygons. For example, as illustrated in Figure 10-5, the algorithm incorrectly draws the dotted line between the two bottom vertices A and B. There's also a problem with the scan line intersecting vertex C. Although these problems can be circumvented, there is a more efficient method of performing frame buffer filling.

FLOOD FILLING

To correctly fill the polygon residing in the frame buffer, using flood filling, any pixel inside the polygon is selected and sent to the recursive procedure Flood_Fill. Whenever an interior pixel is sent to Flood_Fill (**screenbit**(x, y) is false), that pixel is illuminated and, through calls to itself, the same test is performed on each of the four surrounding pixels. Since the boundary of the polygon resides in the frame buffer, all boundary pixels (x, y) have **screenbit**(x, y) equal to true.

While this procedure is easy to code, the depth of recursion often results in stack overflow for microcomputers with limited memory. One method of dealing with this problem is to create a global integer variable,

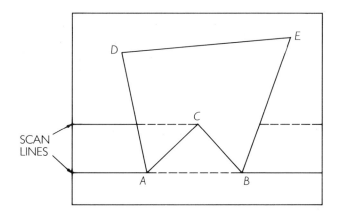

FIGURE 10–5
Incorrect polygon filling by pairing x intersection values

depth, with value equal to the number of times the recursive procedure is called. If depth becomes greater than the size of the stack, 500 in the procedure, the recursion is terminated before the system aborts the run. The interactive user must now choose a new unlit interior pixel and pass it to Flood_Fill. This process must be repeated until the entire polygon is filled. To reduce the number of times this might need to be done, the variable depth is decremented by one unit at the completion of a recursive call, since at this time the stack size is decreased by 1.

```
Procedure Flood_Fill(
        x,y : integer    {test pixel});

    begin
        if not screenbit(x,y) and depth < 500 then
            {(x, y) is an interior pixel and must be illuminated}
            begin    {if}
                depth := depth + 1;
                plotpoint(x,y)
                {test surrounding four pixels}
                Flood_Fill(x + 1,y);
                Flood_Fill(x − 1,y);
                Flood_Fill(x,y + 1);
                Flood_Fill(x,y − 1);
                depth := depth − 1
            end    {if}
    end;    {Flood_Fill}
```

10-4 CONVEX FILLING

A polygon is **convex** if for any two points that lie within the polygon, the line segment connecting them is also inside the polygon. A polygon is **horizontal convex** if for any two points in the polygon having the same y value, the horizontal line connecting them is also in the polygon. Certainly all convex polygons are also horizontal convex. Figure 10-6 illustrates polygons that are convex, horizontal convex, and neither. The following filling algorithm works only for convex and horizontal convex polygons.

FIGURE 10–6
Convex and non-convex polygons

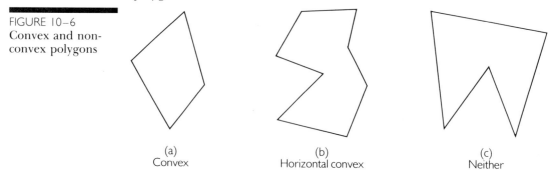

(a)
Convex

(b)
Horizontal convex

(c)
Neither

A polygon of the type we are currently considering has at most two edges on a scan line, according to our definition. For reasons to be explained later, all horizontal edges will be omitted from our discussion. We shall shortly see that this omission does not affect the filling.

A **scan-line table** is used to record the maximum and minimum x values for the edges on each scan line. The x value of the left edge is placed in the minimum value for that scan line, while the x value of the right edge is placed in the maximum value for that scan line. If the scan line intersects a vertex, two edges come together, and that x value is both the maximum and minimum x value. The table is initialized so that all minimum entries are set to screen maximum x, and all maximum entries are set to screen minimum x. See the polygon and accompanying scan-line table in Figure 10-7, where xmax = 10.

The first step in the fill algorithm draws the polygon. The next, and most complicated, step determines the minimum and maximum x values for each scan line. These extreme values are then entered in the scan-line table. Let's see how we can compute these values.

If there is a nonhorizontal edge from $(x1, y1)$ to $(x2, y2)$, the reciprocal of its slope is

$$\frac{1}{m} = \frac{(x2 - x1)}{(y2 - y1)}.$$

If $y1 < y2$, the y value is incremented by one unit as we move up one scan line at a time. We know the x value when y equals $y1$; that is, it is $x1$. To obtain the x value, denoted by **xnext**, of the edge on the next scan line, $y1 + 1$, we observe that

$$m = \frac{(y1 + 1 - y1)}{(xnext - x1)} = \frac{1}{(xnext - x1)}$$

or

$$xnext = x1 + \frac{1}{m}.$$

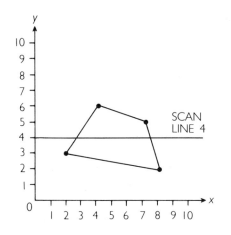

SCAN LINE	XMIN	XMAX
•		
•		
•		
6	4	4
5	3	7
4	3	7
3	2	8
2	8	8
1	10	0
0	10	0

FIGURE 10-7
Scan-line table filling

This equation presents some difficulty, however. The x values are integers while the inverse of the slope, $\frac{1}{m}$, is real valued. We might attempt to correct this by using the round function:

$$\text{xnext} = \textbf{round}(x1 + \tfrac{1}{m}).$$

Unfortunately, this is also incorrect. If $\frac{1}{m}$ is less than 0.5, the value of xnext is never incremented and always equals the initial value of x. Our method of addressing this problem is to maintain and update a real-valued x. By doing this, the values of $\frac{1}{m}$ are able to accumulate, and the round function is used only to plot the point.

Generalizing this discussion, we conclude that the x intersection of the edge with the next scan line is obtained from the previous scan line x intersection and the slope of the edge:

$$\text{xnext} = \text{xprevious} + \tfrac{1}{m}.$$

This process starts at $y1 + 1$ and continues until the top of the edge is reached, $y = y2$. If $y2 < y1$, a similar process is used while decrementing the y value by one unit.

Procedure Calculate_x determines the x intersection value of an edge with a scan line. Assume the following environment:

```
const
    ymax = 511;    {number of scan lines less one}

var
    xval : array[0..ymax] of integer;    {x edge intersection value on scan
                                           line}
    xreal: real;    {x value before being rounded up to an integer value}

Procedure Calculate_x(
    x1,y1,x2,y2 : integer    {endpoints of edge});

    var
        m_inverse : real;        {1/m = 1/slope}
        temp,                    {used to swap x and y values}
        y           : integer;   {current scan line}

    begin
        m_inverse := (x2 − x1)/(y2 − y1);
        {want y1 < y2}
        if y1 > y2 then
            {swap them}
            begin    {if}
                temp := y1;
                y1 := y2;
                y2 := temp;
                temp := x1;
                x1 := x2;
                x2 := temp
            end;    {if}
```

```
{starting and ending x values for loop}
    xval[y1] := x1;
    xval[y2] := x2;
    {initialize real-valued x}
    xreal := x1;
    {initialize y to next scan line}
    y := y1 + 1;
    while y < y2 do
        {get x value}
    begin
        {update x value}
        xreal := xreal + m_inverse;
        {convert to integer x value}
        xval[y] := round(xreal);
        {go to next scan line}
        y := y + 1
    end     {while}
end;    {Calculate_x}
```

As soon as an x edge value is calculated, it should be compared to the minimum and maximum values for that y entry in the scan-line table. If the x value is less than the minimum or greater than the maximum, this x edge value is inserted into the appropriate entry.

The scan-line table can be represented by the following data structure:

```
type
    table = record
                xmin,xmas : integer
            end;

var
    scan_table : array[0..ymax] of table;
```

Using the previously defined array xval, the following code segment performs the max-min test and insertion.

```
if xval[y] < scan_table[y].xmin then
    {update minimum value}
    scan_table[y].xmin := xval[y];
if xval[y] > scan_table[y].xmax then
    {update maximum value}
    scan_table[y].xmax := xval[y];
```

By incorporating the max-min test into procedure Calculate_x, the array xval can be eliminated. We leave this improvement as an exercise for the reader.

After each edge is processed and the appropriate values are entered into the scan-line table, the polygon is ready to be filled. This is accomplished by drawing line segments on a scan line from xmin to xmax whenever xmin < xmax. We observe that xmin > xmax only when that line is still initialized, and hence an edge of the polygon was never intersected on that scan line. Procedure Convex_Fill performs this final step.

```
Procedure Convex_Fill;
    {draws line segments between edges}

    var
        y : integer;      {current scan line}

    begin
        for y := 0 to ymax do
            with scan_table[y] do
                if xmin < xmax then
                    begin      {if}
                    {draw line segment}
                        moves(xmin,y);
                        draws(xmax,y)
                    end      {if}
    end;      {Convex_Fill}
```

If we want to fill the polygon by drawing lines every other scan line, we replace the **for** loop with a **while** loop and increment the y value by 2. To control the density of the fill, we can input the increment as a variable. This algorithm was used to shade the exploded pie chart in Figure 10-8a. Each sector of the pie is a horizontal convex polygon, and each such polygon was sent one at a time through this algorithm. Observe that the pie chart in Figure 10-8b cannot be shaded using this algorithm since the largest slice does not satisfy the convex criterion.

FIGURE 10–8
Filling exploded pie charts

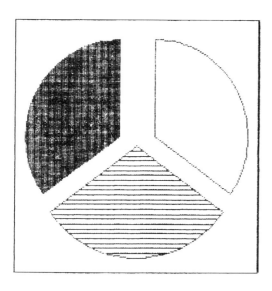

(a)   (b)

Polygon Filling

10–5 GENERAL POLYGON FILLING

The convex filling technique works well for polygons that have at most two edges on a scan line. Figure 10-9a illustrates the incorrect results when this algorithm is applied to an arbitrary polygon. The major problem is that the filled line segment continues across the boundaries of the polygon while drawing to the maximum x value; compare this with the correct fill in Figure 10-9b.

Examination of Figure 10-9b shows that we should fill in the pixels on a scan line between pairs of edges that are intersected by the scan line. An algorithm to accomplish this will have the following steps:

1. Compute the x coordinate values of the intersections of the current scan line with all edges.
2. Sort these edge intersections by increasing x value.
3. Group the edge intersections by pairs.
4. Fill in the pixels on the scan line between pairs of x values.

Although this algorithm is relatively simple to describe, its implementation is somewhat complicated. In particular, we want an efficient method of computing the edge intersections on each scan line. In addition, certain vertices must be counted twice, others only once. We shall examine these and other details as we go through the steps of the algorithm. Do not be discouraged if you must study this algorithm several times before you understand all of it.

EDGE INTERSECTION TABLE

A straightfoward way of computing the x values of the intersection points of a scan line and an edge is to substitute the current y value into the equation of the line segment representing the edge and then solve for x. An initial concern here is to determine first which edges actually do intersect the current scan line. We shall postpone this problem for a

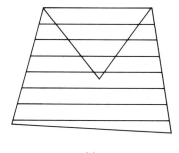

(a)

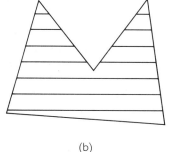

(b)

FIGURE 10–9
(a) Incorrect and (b) correct polygon filling

while. A second concern is that the calculation of the equation of the line segment defining an edge can be time-intensive. For polygons with many edges, this calculation can slow down the filling considerably. Fortunately, there is an efficient way of performing the edge intersections that is similar to our technique of obtaining the xmin and xmax edge values for convex polygons.

Recall that if m is the slope of an edge (line segment), then if xprevious is the (real-valued) x intersection value of scan line y with the edge, then

(10–1) $xnext = xprevious + \frac{1}{m}$

is the x intersection of the next scan line $y + 1$ with that edge (Figure 10-10). Therefore, if we know the bottom-most scan line an edge intersects, we can use equation 10-1 to compute the edge intersections of those scan lines above it. This suggests that we fill the polygon from bottom to top, moving up one scan line at a time.

We still need an efficient means to determine which edges a scan line intersects. (We do not want to spend time testing each scan line with each edge.) To do this we create a table of all edges in the polygon. The data structure for this table is an **array of buckets**, one bucket for each scan line. Each bucket contains those edges whose lower y value starts at the scan line represented by that bucket. A bucket is actually a pointer that points to a list of edges. The Pascal **nil** pointer is used for buckets that have no associated edge list. The creation of this data structure is called a bucket or radix sort. Figure 10-12 illustrates this edge table data structure for the polygon in Figure 10-11.

Once this table is constructed, the filling algorithm uses it to determine which edges the current scan line intersects and what is the x coordinate of each intersection. The y coordinate of an edge intersection is, of course, the value of the current scan line. To facilitate this process, each edge entry in the edge table is represented by a record. The first

FIGURE 10–10
Calculation of
XNEXT using the
slope and previous
x value

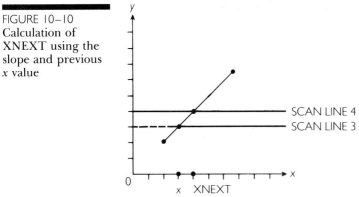

field contains the top-most y value of that edge—that is, the y value of the last scan line this edge intersects. Denote this by **ytop**. The second field of the record contains the x coordinate value of the smallest y value for that edge, denoted by **xmin**. The next field is the reciprocal of the

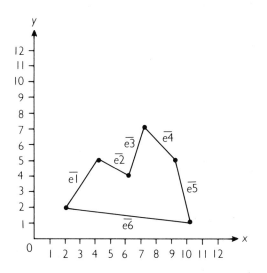

FIGURE 10–11
Polygon edges

FIGURE 10–12
An edge table data structure

BUCKET

FIGURE 10–13
An edge table entry

YTOP	XMIN	M_INVERSE	NEXT

slope of the edge, **m_inverse**. The final field, next, is a pointer to the next edge in the same y bucket. The edges within a bucket are sorted in increasing order based on the xmin field (Figure 10-13). The variable xmin is of real data type since it changes value according to equation 10-1.

This edge table is represented in Pascal as follows:

const
        ymax = 511;   *{number of scan lines less one}*

type
        ptr = ^edge_info;   *{bucket pointer}*

        edge_info = **record**
                    ytop : **integer**;   *{top scan line of edge}*
                    xmin,   *{x value of bottom of edge}*
                    m_inverse :**real**;   *{1/slope of edge}*
                    next : ptr   *{next edge in bucket}*
              end;

var
        edge_table : **array**[0..ymax] **of** ptr;

VERTEX CONSIDERATIONS

The edge table we just built is adequate for scan lines that do not intersect a vertex. Vertex intersections must be treated separately, and we modify the edge table accordingly. Figure 10-14 illustrates this problem. Scan line $y = 2$ intersects the polygon at edges $\overline{e1}$, $\overline{e2}$, and $\overline{e4}$ with corresponding x intersection values 2, 2, and 4. Grouping these pixels in pairs incorrectly results in the illumination of pixel (2, 2) and those pixels on scan line 2 from $x = 4$ to the end of the display screen. However, scan line $y = 4$ intersects the polygon at edges $\overline{e2}$ and $\overline{e3}$ with x intersection values 4 and 4. Grouping into pairs, only one pixel (4, 4) is correctly illuminated.

To obtain the correct results we examine Figure 10-15, with the current scan line intersecting the vertices 1, 2, 3, and 4. This represents the distinct cases we must now examine.

Vertex 1 connects an edge of increasing slope $(\overline{e1})$ to an edge of decreasing slope $(\overline{e2})$. A vertex with this property is called an extrema. Edges that meet an extrema can be inserted into the edge table without any additional processing. That is, both edges are counted, resulting in two intersections with the scan line.

Vertices 2 and 3 are the endpoints of the horizontal edge $\overline{e4}$ having

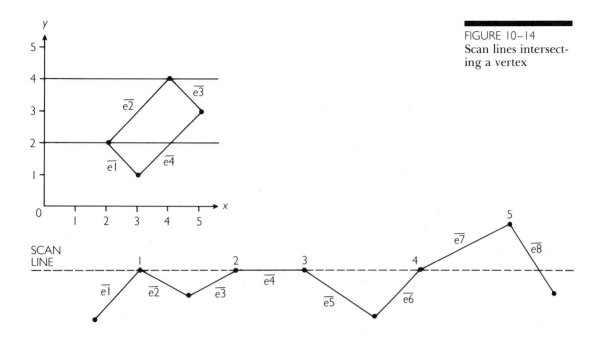

FIGURE 10–14
Scan lines intersect-
ing a vertex

FIGURE 10–15
Vertex considera-
tions for a scan line

zero slope. The current scan line intersects edge $\overline{e4}$ for many different
x values. Our policy, as for convex polygons, is not to include in the
edge table those edges with zero slope. Although edge $\overline{e4}$ is removed
from further processing, vertices 2 and 3 are still used for edges $\overline{e3}$ and
$\overline{e5}$. Observe that horizontal edges reappear when the boundary of the
polygon is drawn.

Vertex 4 is not a local extrema, and that vertex must be counted
only once in the edge table for the current scan line. (That is, vertex 4
should not be included in both edges $\overline{e6}$ and $\overline{e7}$.) If we counted it twice,
there would be no x coordinate pair to fill pixels between vertex 4 and
edge $\overline{e8}$. To ensure that vertex 4 is counted only once, edge $\overline{e7}$ is shortened by one unit (pixel) in the y direction. The x coordinate value of
the new vertex 4' is calculated using equation 10-1. Thus, whenever we
encounter a vertex that is not an extrema, the lower end of the upper
edge is shortened (Figure 10-16 on page 236). Vertices shall be represented as described in Section 10-1:

var
  vertex: points;

THE CURRENT SCAN LINE

As we progress through the algorithm, it is necessary to know the
value of the current scan line. This value is tested against the top-most

FIGURE 10–16
Shortening of the
edge $e\overline{7}$

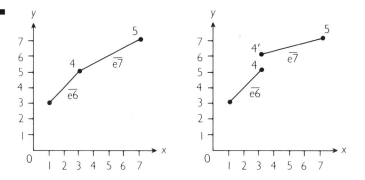

scan line the polygon intersects. If the current scan line has y value greater than this top-most scan line, the processing stops.

In addition, a scan-line bucket is needed to hold a sorted list of edges that the current scan line intersects. This current scan line is a variable of type ptr.

var
    scan_line : ptr;

THE ALGORITHM

After the edge table is built, the algorithm proceeds as follows:

1. Start with the smallest y value in the edge table having a nonempty bucket.
2. Initialize the scan-line bucket to **nil**.
3. While the current scan-line y value is not greater than the top-most scan line of the polygon, do
   a. For the current y value, merge the edge table with the scan-line list, maintaining the sort on increasing xmin values.
   b. Fill the pixels between pairs of rounded xmin values in the scan-line list.
   c. Remove edges from the scan-line list whose maximum y value, ytop, equals the current scan-line value.
   d. Increment the xmin value by m_inverse for those remaining edges in the scan-line list.
   e. Resort the scan-line list on increasing xmin values.
   f. Increment the current scan-line y value by 1 to give the next scan line.

Before describing the procedures to implement this algorithm, let's go through these steps for the polygon in Figure 10-17. This is illustrated in Figure 10-18a–10-18f on page 238.

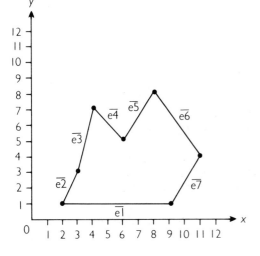

FIGURE 10–17
A polygon-filling
example

First build the edge table in Figure 10-18a. Using this edge table, the algorithm starts with scan line 1 and edges $\overline{e2}$ and $\overline{e7}$ (Figure 10-18b). The first fill segment drawn is the horizontal line on scan line 1 from xmin = 2 of edge $\overline{e2}$ to xmin = 9 of edge $\overline{e7}$. Observe that this is the horizontal edge $\overline{e1}$.

Since neither of the edges $\overline{e1}$ nor $\overline{e7}$ have ytop = 1, the current scan line, no edges are removed. Incrementing the xmin fields of $\overline{e1}$ and $\overline{e7}$ by their respective m_inverse, we obtain for scan line 2 (resorting is not necessary) Figure 10-18c. A horizontal fill segment is drawn on scan line 2 from $x =$ **round**(2.5) = 3 to $x =$ **round**(9.67) = 10. Once again no edges are removed, and the xmin fields are incremented and the horizontal line on scan line 3 is drawn between $x = 3$ and $x =$ **round**(10.3) = 10 (Figure 10-18d).

Edge $\overline{e2}$ is now removed from the scan-line list since its ytop = 3, the current scan line. The xmin field of $\overline{e7}$ is incremented and edge $\overline{e3}$, starting on scan line 4, is now merged into the scan-line list for scan line 4. A horizontal line is drawn on scan line 4 from $x = 3$ to $x =$ **round**(10.67) = 11 (Figure 10-18e).

Edge $\overline{e7}$ is now removed since its ytop = 4, and the xmin value of $\overline{e3}$ is incremented to 3.3. Edges $\overline{e4}$, $\overline{e5}$, and $\overline{e6}$ are merged with $\overline{e3}$ giving the list in scan line 5 in Figure 10-18f. Two horizontal fill segments are now drawn between the two edge pairs. One from $x =$ **round**(3.3) = 3 to $x = 6$, and the other from $x = 6$ to $x =$ **round**(10.25) = 10.[†]

[†]The reader is encouraged to go through the remaining steps of the algorithm for this polygon (it stops after scan line 8).

FIGURE 10–18
The formation of
an edge table and
scan-line lists

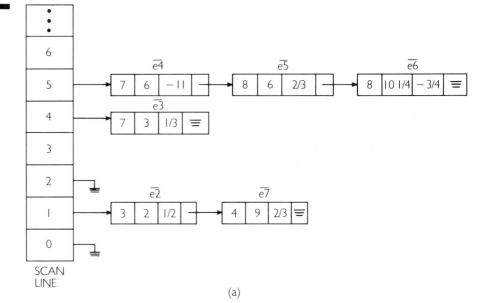

SCAN
LINE

(a)

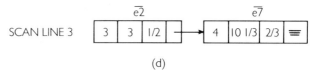

SCAN LINE 1

(b)

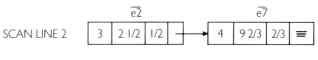

SCAN LINE 2

(c)

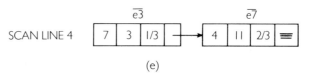

SCAN LINE 3

(d)

SCAN LINE 4

(e)

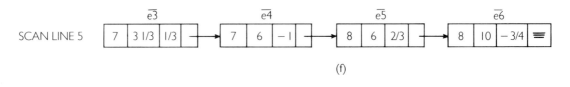

SCAN LINE 5

(f)

The filling algorithm requires the use of procedures to sort, merge, insert, and remove a node from a linked list. Although these operations are encountered in a data structure course, they are presented here for completeness. We use the previously defined data structures.

```
Procedure Insert(var node,list:ptr);
    {inserts a new edge (node) in a list of edges sorted on the xmin field}

    var
        trav,               {current node}
        trl: ptr;           {previous node}

    begin
        if list = nil then
            {empty list}
            list := node
        else {node belongs at start of list}
            if node^.xmin <= list^.xmin then
                begin {if}
                {insert at front of list}
                    node^.next := list;
                    list := node
                end {if}
        else {find correct location of node}
            begin {else}
                {initialize to start of list}
                    trav := list;
                {start search}
                    while (trav^.next <> nil) and
                            (trav^.xmin < node^.xmin) do
                        begin {while}
                            {point to previous node}
                            trl := trav;
                            {point to current node}
                            trav := trav^.next
                        end; {while}
                    {found correct location}
                    if (trav^.next = nil) and
                        (trav^.xmin < node^.xmin) then
                        {node goes at end of list}
                        trav^.next := node
                    else {node goes between current and previous node}
                        begin {else}
                            node^.nest := trav;
                            trl^.next := node
                        end {else}
            end {else − find}
    end; {Insert}
```

Procedure Create_Table builds the edge table by examining non-horizontal edges. If the lower end of a nonhorizontal edge is not a minimum extrema, it is shortened by one unit; otherwise, the edge is

FIGURE 10–19
Possible vertex
combinations

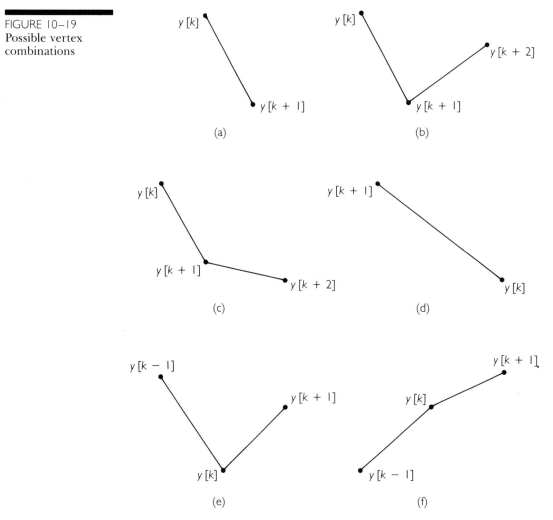

inserted as is. The identifier "numvertices" is the number of vertices in the polygon. Since the last edge joins the last vertex to the first vertex, the mod function is used whenever we increment vertices. Figure 10-19 explains the various cases, as described in the comments in this procedure.

Create_Table invokes the function Inverse, which returns the inverse of the slope of the *i*th edge of the polygon. If the line is horizontal, it returns a dummy value of zero, which is not used.

```
Function Inverse(i:integer):real;
    {computes inverse slope of ith edge}

    begin
        with vertex do
            if y[i] = y[i+1] then
```

Polygon Filling

```
                {horizontal edge}
                Inverse := 0
        else
                Inverse := (x[i] − x[i + 1])/(y[i] − y[i + 1])
    end; {Inverse}

Procedure Create_Table;
    {builds the edge table}

    var
        yval,                   {scan line}
        k       : integer;      {vertex}
        node    : ptr;          {edge}

    begin
        {initialize edge table buckets to nil}

    for yval := 0 to ymax do
        edge_table[y] := nil;

    {place the edge information into the nodes and
    put the nodes into the edge table}

    with vertex do
        for k := 0 to numvertices − 1 do
            begin {for}
                new(node); {create node}
                node^.m_inverse:= Inverse(k);
                node^.ptr:= nil;

                {if y[k] is higher up than y[k + 1] then set ytop
                 to y[k]—Figure 10-19a}
                if y[k] > y[(k + 1) mod numvertices] then
                    begin {if}
                        node^.ytop := y[k];
                        {if (k + 1) vertex is an extreme minimum don't
                         shorten the edge—Figure 10-19b}
                            if y[(k + 1) mod numvertices] <
                                                y[(k + 2) mod numvertices] then
                                begin {if}
                                    node^.xmin := x[(k + 1) mod numvertices]
                                        Insert(node,
                                                edge_table[y[(k + 1) mod numvertices]])
                                end {if}
                            else
                            {if (k + 1) vertex is not an extrema, shorten the lower end—
                             Figure 10-19c}
                            begin {else}
                                node^.xmin := x[(k + 1) mod numvertices] +
                                                node^.m_inverse;
                                Insert(node,
                                        edge_table[y[(k + 1) mod numvertices] + 1])
                            end {else}
```

```
                        end {if—y[k] is higher than y[k + 1]}
                  else
                        {if y[k + 1] is higher than y[k], set ytop to y[k + 1]
                          —Figure 10-19d}
                        if y[k] < y[(k + 1) mod numvertices] then
                              begin {if}
                                    node^.ytop : = y[(k + 1) mod numvertices];
                                    {if not extreme minimum, don't shorten line
                                      —Figure 10-19e}
                                    if y[k] < y[(k-1) mod numvertices] then
                                          begin {if}
                                                node^.xmin : = x[k];
                                                Insert(node,edge_table[y[k]])
                                          end {if}
                                    else
                                          {kth vertex is not extrema; shorten lower
                                            end of edge—Figure 10-19f}
                                                begin {else}
                                                      node^.xmin : = x[k] + node^.m_inverse;
                                                      Insert(node,edge_table[y[k] + 1])
                                                end {else}
                        end {if—y[k + 1] is higher}
            end {for}
end; {Create_Table}
```

Once the edge table is built, the scan-line list is created by merging it with the correct edge table bucket. Both lists are ordered in increasing order on the xmin value. Procedure Merge performs this task.

```
Procedure Merge(var newlist,oldlist : ptr);
      {newlist is the edge_table bucket; oldlist is scan_line}

      var
            temp, newptr: ptr; {used for traversal of newlist}

      begin
            if oldlist = nil then
                  {empty scan line}
                  oldlist : = newlist
            else
                  {merge both lists}
                  begin {if}
                        {initialize pointer}
                        newptr : = newlist;
                        while newptr <> nil do
                              {place edge into scan_line}
                              begin {while}
                                    temp : = newptr^.next;
                                    Insert(newptr,oldlist);
                                    {get next edge}
                                    newptr : = temp
```

                                  end {*while*}
        end {*else*}
end; {*Merge*}

Procedure Remove deletes from scan_line those edges that end at the current scan line.

Procedure Remove:

    var
        trav,trl : ptr; {*used for traversal*}

    begin
        {*initialize to front of scan line*}
        trav := scan_line;
        while trav <> **nil do**
            begin {*while*}
                {*test to remove the first edge*}
                if trav = scan_line **then**
                      if trav^.ytop = yval **then**
                          {*remove first edge*}
                          begin {*if*}
                              scan_line := scan_line^.next;
                              {*advance traversal pointers*}
                              trav := scan_line;
                              trl := trav
                          end {*if*}
                      else
                        {*first edge is not removed*}
                        begin {*else*}
                          {*advance traversal pointers*}
                          trl := trav;
                          trav := trav^.next
                        end {*else*}
                else {*first if—not the first edge*}
                      begin {*else*}
                        if trav^.ytop = yval **then**
                          {*remove edge*}
                          trl^.next := trav^.next
                      else
                        {*advance pointer*}
                        trl := trav;
                    {*in either case advance pointer*}
                    trav := trav^.next
            end {*else*}
        end {*while*}
    end {*Remove*}

The scan_line list must now have its xmin values incremented by m_inverse. Scan_line is then resorted on this updated xmin field.

Procedure Resort does this by rebuilding scan_line using Insert.

```
Procedure Resort;

    var
        sortptr, sortnext: ptr; {used for traversal}

    begin
        {increment xmin field of first edge}
        scan_line^.xmin := scan_line^.xmin +
                            scan_line^.m_inverse;
        {point to remainder of original list}
        sortptr := scan_line^.next;
        scan_line^.next := nil;
        {scan_line now has only first edge}
        while sortptr <> nil do
            begin {while}
                {increment xmin}
                sortptr^.xmin := sortptr^.xmin + sortptr^.m_inverse;
                {save next edge}
                sortnext := sortptr^.next;
                {need only one edge for Insert}
                sortptr^.next := nil;
                {rebuild scan_line}
                Insert(sortptr,scan_line);
                {advance pointer}
                sortprt := sortnext
            end {while}
    end; {Resort}
```

The final procedure, Fill_Scan, fills in the line segment between pairs of xmin values on scan_line. It does this by alternating between moves and draws. The parameter yval contains the y coordinate value of the current scan line.

```
Procedure Fill_Scan(yval:integer);
    {draws line segments on scan line yval}

    var
        k : integer; {0 = draw, 1 = move}
        trav : ptr; {used for traversal}

    begin
        k := 0;
        if scan_line <> nil then
            {something to fill}
            begin {if}
                {initialize pointer}
                trav := scan_line;
                while trav <> nil do
                {draw line segments}
                begin {while}
```

```
            k := k+1;
            if k mod 2 = 1 then
                moves(round(trav^.xmin),yval)
            else
                draws(round(trav^.xmin),yval);
            {end of if-then-else}
            {advance pointer}
            trav := trav^.next
        end {while}
    end {if}
        end; {Fill_Scan}
```

Figures 10-20a–10-20c illustrate several polygons that were filled using this algorithm. The figures that are composed of several polygons use multiple invocations of the filling algorithm.

Scan line filling, as described here, can illuminate extra pixels. Figure 10-21 illustrates this potential problem. Ignoring horizontal edges, scan lines 3 to 5 intersect the polygon (Figure 10-21a on page 246) at $x = 1$ and 4, causing the fill algorithm to illuminate pixels $x = 1$ to 4 on scan lines 3 to 5. This incorrect result is shown in Figure 10-21b on page 247. The correctly filled polygon should illuminate only the pixels $x = 1$ to 3 and only on scan lines 3 and 4. To correct this error, the testing scan lines are centered in the middle of the pixels. Figure 10-21c illustrates that only scan lines $y = 3.5$ and 4.5 intersect the polygon at x values 1 and 4. Using these results, we illuminate only those pixels on scan lines $y = 3$ and $y = 4$, with x values satisfying

$$1 <\, = x + \frac{1}{2} <\, = 4,$$

namely, those x values 1, 2, and 3. This result gives the correctly filled polygon. The implementation of this modification is left as an exercise.

10–6 **PATTERN FILLING**

In the previous sections we illuminated all pixels within the boundaries of a polygon. Some applications, however, require that only those pixels that correspond to a pattern are to be illuminated, a technique

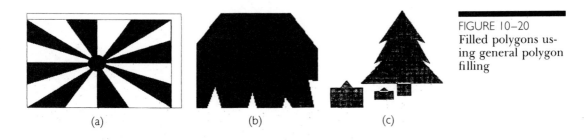

(a)   (b)   (c)

FIGURE 10–20
Filled polygons using general polygon filling

FIGURE 10–21 (a)
Scan lines centered
on and between in-
tegral values

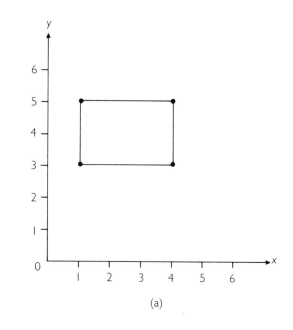

(a)

called **pattern filling** (Figure 10-22). This extension of polygon filling can also be used to give a textured appearance to polygons.

A pattern is defined as a two-dimensional boolean array of size 10 in each dimension:

var
    pattern : **array**[0..9,0..9] **of boolean;**

FIGURE 10–22
Pattern-filled
polygons

Figure 10-23a illustrates the pattern used to fill the polygon in Figure 10-23b. Filled-in pixels correspond to true values in the array. Observe that the lower-left corner is the entry pattern[9, 0].

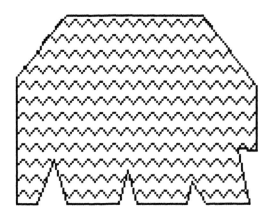

(a)

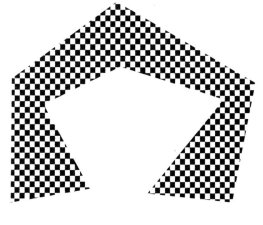

(b)

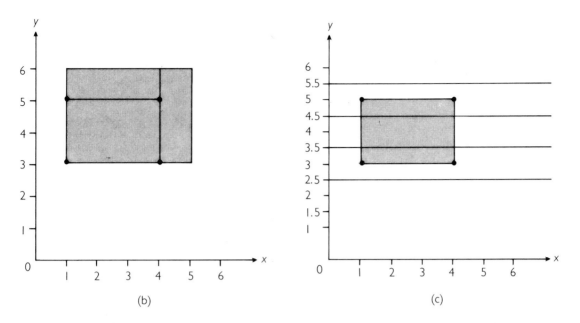

(b)   (c)

FIGURE 10–21 (b–c)

Conceptually these small patterns are placed end to end to give the repeating pattern effect in Figure 10-23b. Each pixel within the polygon is tested against its corresponding entry in the repeated pattern. A pixel is illuminated only if its associated pattern entry has boolean value true. Let's see how this can be programmed.

The variable starty is the first scan line that intersects the polygon; startx is the minimum x value of the polygon on that scan line. Thus (startx, starty) is the coordinate value of the lower-left vertex of the polygon. Each time we reference a pixel (currentx, currenty) in the polygon, we want to determine the offset (distance) from this starting vertex. The offset is given by the equations

    xoffset = currentx − startx
    yoffset = currenty − starty.

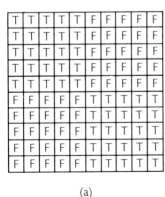

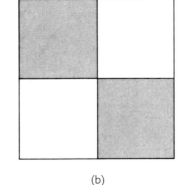

FIGURE 10–23
A pattern array

(a)   (b)

These offsets are used in the following way. The pixel (startx, starty) corresponds to the lower-left entry of the pattern, pattern[0, 9]. Our goal is to determine which pattern entry (currentx, currenty) corresponds to. It turns out that this is just the offset from array entry pattern[0, 9] (Figure 10-24). Since the pattern covers only a 10 × 10 pixel grid, modular 10 arithmetic is used to replicate the pattern over the entire polygon. Thus, if (x, y) is the entry in the pattern array we are seeking, then

$$x = (currentx - startx) \bmod 10$$
$$y = (9 - (currenty - starty)) \bmod 10.$$

As an example, suppose that (5, 12) are the screen coordinates of the lower-left vertex of the polygon, and we want to determine if the point (21, 18), lying inside the polygon, should be illuminated. Substituting these values into the preceding equations we get

$$x = (21 - 5) \bmod 10 = 6$$
$$y = (9 - (18 - 12)) \bmod 10 = 3.$$

Thus, the point (21, 18) is illuminated only if the entry pattern[6, 3] is true.

Procedure Pattern_Fill is invoked instead of the **moves, draws** sequence in Procedure Fill_Scan. Its parameters are the beginning and end x values of the fill segment and the current scan line y value. Assume the following Pascal environment:

var
       startx,starty : **integer**; *{lower-left vertex of the*
                             polygon obtained from the
                             polygon-filling routine}

Procedure Pattern_Fill(xbegin,xend,currenty: **integer**);
        {parameters are the beginning and end x values of a fill
        segment on the current scan line}

FIGURE 10–24
Calculation of a pattern entry value

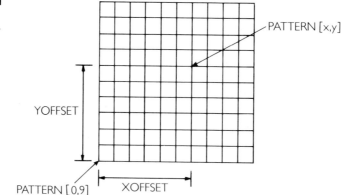

PATTERN [x,y]

YOFFSET

PATTERN [0,9]   XOFFSET

```
var
    currentx,                    {x value of pixel on scan line}
    xi,yj          :  integer; {pattern index}
begin
    {compute y offset}
    yj := (9 − (currenty − starty)) mod 10;
    for currentx := xbegin to xend do
        begin {for}
            {compute x offset}
            xi := (currentx − startx) mod 10;
            if pattern[yi,xi] then
                {set corresponding pixel}
                plotpoint(currentx,currenty)
        end {for}
end; {Pattern_Fill}
```

10-7 CONCLUSION

This chapter has examined several techniques for filling polygons. Procedures Flood_Fill and Buffer_Fill are perhaps the most general since each can be used to fill any connected region whose boundary resides in the frame buffer. Although many graphics systems have polygon-filling procedures, be aware of the restrictions placed on the type of polygons involved. For example, the polygon may have to be convex or horizontal convex.

EXERCISES

1. Why doesn't it make sense to fix Buffer_Fill so that it works for all types of polygons? Think of how this would compare with the general polygon-filling algorithm.
2. Modify the general scan-line filling so that the scan lines are centered between integral values of *y*.
3. Show that Flood_Fill correctly fills polygons having one or more holes.
4. Create interesting patterns and use them to fill polygons.

Detail of Figure 11–3

11

THREE-DIMENSIONAL GRAPHICS

11–1 **INTRODUCTION**

Our world is composed of three-dimensional images. Objects not only have height and width but also depth. Displaying three-dimensional objects on a two-dimensional display screen seems to be an impossible task. If height and width are represented by x, y coordinates, how can the third dimension, depth, be displayed? The techniques used in computer graphics to display this three-dimensional world are based on the same principles an artist or a photographer employs in producing a realistic image on paper or film. The difference is that the computer uses a mathematical model instead of a paint brush or lens to create the image.

As we increase the realism of our computer-generated image, we also increase the complexity of the mathematics used in its production. Realistic scenes require a knowledge of sophisticated mathematics and physics. The laws of physics describe, for example, how light is absorbed, transmitted, or reflected from an object.[†]

In this text, we shall try to keep the mathematics at a reasonable level. However, a minimum degree of "mathematical maturity" is needed to understand some of the advanced concepts. If three-dimensional coordinate geometry and vectors are new to you, some of the material in this and subsequent chapters may be difficult to grasp the first time around. Don't let this discourage you from trying. We will try to explain in understandable terms those specific mathematical concepts used in the text.

11–2 **COORDINATE SYSTEMS**

An image in three dimensions is often defined in terms of points, lines, and planes. In order to specify these primitive building blocks, a coordinate system is needed. A three-dimensional coordinate system can be viewed as an extension of the two-dimensional coordinate system. The third dimension, depth, is represented by the z-axis, which is at right angles to the x, y coordinate plane (Figure 11-1).

Any point in this rectangular coordinate system can be described by an ordered triple (x, y, z) of coordinate values. Each coordinate represents a directed distance—that is, a positive or negative direction along its corresponding coordinate axis (Figure 11-1).

[†]A thorough discussion of these topics is beyond the scope of this text. The interested reader should refer to Foley/Van Dam, *Fundamentals of Interactive Computer Graphics*, 1982.

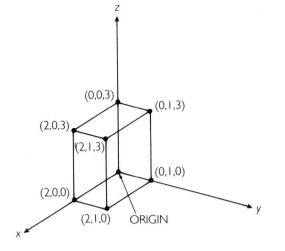

FIGURE 11–1
A right-handed
three-dimensional
coordinate system

The coordinate system we have illustrated is called a **right-handed** system. If we curl the fingers of our right hand from the positive x-axis into the positive y-axis, the thumb points in the direction of the positive z-axis. The choice of a right-handed system is arbitrary and is used primarily because mathematicians are familiar and comfortable with it. We often refer to this as the **world coordinate system**.

Another three-dimensional coordinate system is used to display computer-generated images. The display screen is a two-dimensional plane with the origin at the lower-left corner, the positive y-axis moving up and the positive x-axis moving to the right. We view the z-axis starting at the origin and pointing into the screen. This coordinate system has the property that, as we view the display screen, objects that are further away have larger positive z values (Figure 11-2). This is a **left-handed** system since if we curl the fingers of our left hand from x into y, our

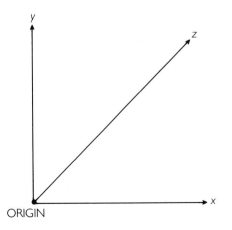

FIGURE 11–2
A left-handed
three-dimensional
coordinate system

thumb points in the z direction. This coordinate system can be defined independently of the display screen and is called the **eye**, or **viewing**, **coordinate system** since the viewer's eye is placed at the origin.

A major undertaking in this chapter is the transformation of an image described in the right-handed world coordinate system into the left-handed eye coordinate system. This may seem puzzling: If we have to go through a lot of effort to change coordinate systems, why not use the eye coordinate system in the first place? After all, mathematicians should be able to adjust to a different coordinate system. It turns out that if we did it this way, we would place severe restrictions on users of our three-dimensional viewing system. However, before examining this issue further, we must discuss three-dimensional transformations.

11–3 TRANSFORMATIONS

Transformations in three dimensions are simply extensions of the two-dimensional transformations discussed in Chapter 5. In fact, all two-dimensional transformations can be described using three-dimensional transformations.

Recall that all two-dimensional geometric modeling transformations can be expressed as 3×3 matrices. To generalize this to three dimensions, a three-dimensional point (x, y, z) will be associated with a homogeneous row vector $[x, y, z, 1]$. By doing this, we can represent all three-dimensional linear transformations by multiplication of 4×4 matrices. These transformations can be combined by multiplying their associated matrices. As in the two-dimensional case, the order in which the matrices are multiplied affects the resulting transformation.

TRANSLATION

The transformation that **translates** a point (x, y, z) Tx units in the x direction, Ty units in the y direction, and Tz units in the z direction to the new point (x', y', z') is represented by the matrix

$$Tr(Tx, Ty, Tz) = \begin{bmatrix} 1 & 0 & 0 & 0 \\ 0 & 1 & 0 & 0 \\ 0 & 0 & 1 & 0 \\ Tx & Ty & Tz & 1 \end{bmatrix}.$$

The translated homogeneous point is

$$[x', y', z', 1] = [x, y, z, 1] \times Tr(Tx, Ty, Tz)$$

where

$$x' = x + Tx$$
$$y' = y + Ty$$
$$z' = z + Tz.$$

The inverse translation matrix is obtained by negating the Tx, Ty, and Tz values. Thus, to translate the point (x', y', z') back to (x, y, z), multiply the homogeneous point $[x', y', z', 1]$ by the matrix $Tr(-Tx, -Ty, -Tz)$.

ROTATION

A three-dimensional **rotation** is performed about an axis. For now, we shall only consider the cases when the axis of rotation is one of the three coordinate axes: x, y, or z. The angle of rotation will be positive when looking from a positive rotation axis toward the origin, and a counterclockwise rotation is performed (Figure 11-3).

A two-dimensional rotation about the origin is equivalent to a three-dimensional rotation in the x, y plane about the z-axis. In general, the rotation of a point about an axis takes place in a plane perpendicular to that axis; that is, the point remains in this plane.

A rotation of angle θ about the z-axis is represented by the matrix

$$Rz(\theta) = \begin{bmatrix} \cos(\theta) & \sin(\theta) & 0 & 0 \\ -\sin(\theta) & \cos(\theta) & 0 & 0 \\ 0 & 0 & 1 & 0 \\ 0 & 0 & 0 & 1 \end{bmatrix}.$$

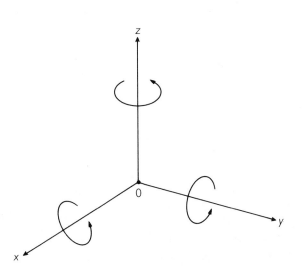

FIGURE 11–3
Directions of the positive three-dimensional rotations

Observe the similarity between this 4×4 matrix and the 3×3 rotation matrix in Chapter 4. Applying $Rz(\theta)$ to a homogeneous point $[x, y, z, 1]$, we obtain the transformed point

$$[x', y', z', 1] = [x, y, z, 1] \times Rz(\theta)$$

where

$$x' = x\cos(\theta) - y\sin(\theta)$$
$$y' = x\sin(\theta) + y\cos(\theta)$$
$$z' = z.$$

Notice that the z coordinate value did not change. This is because a rotation about the z-axis is performed in a plane parallel to the x, y plane.

A rotation of a point about the y-axis is performed in a plane parallel to the x, z plane. The y coordinate value does not change. The rotation matrix is

$$Ry(\theta) = \begin{bmatrix} \cos(\theta) & 0 & -\sin(\theta) & 0 \\ 0 & 1 & 0 & 0 \\ \sin(\theta) & 0 & \cos(\theta) & 0 \\ 0 & 0 & 0 & 1 \end{bmatrix}.$$

The homogeneous point $[x, y, z, 1]$ is transformed to the homogeneous point $[x'\ y'\ z'\ 1]$, where

$$x' = x\cos(\theta) + z\sin(\theta)$$
$$y' = y$$
$$z' = -x\sin(\theta) + \cos(\theta).$$

A rotation of a point about the x-axis takes place in a plane parallel to the y, z plane. The x coordinate value does not change. Its rotation matrix is

$$Rx(\theta) = \begin{bmatrix} 1 & 0 & 0 & 0 \\ 0 & \cos(\theta) & \sin(\theta) & 0 \\ 0 & -\sin(\theta) & \cos(\theta) & 0 \\ 0 & 0 & 0 & 1 \end{bmatrix}.$$

The homogeneous point $[x, y, z, 1]$ is transformed to the homogeneous point $[x', y', z', 1]$ where

$$x' = x$$
$$y' = y\cos(\theta) - z\sin(\theta)$$
$$z' = y\sin(\theta) + z\cos(\theta).$$

The derivation of these three rotation matrices is similar to that of the two-dimensional rotation matrix, as described in Chapter 5. Just use the corresponding coordinate planes to perform the computations. As an aid in visualizing the three-dimensional geometry, let the axis of

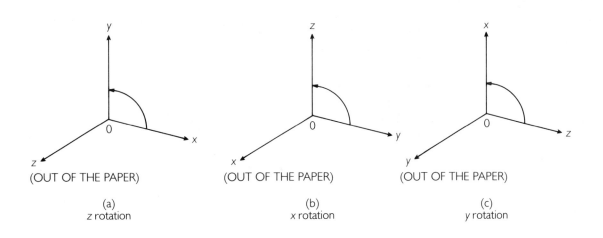

| (a) | (b) | (c) |
| z rotation | x rotation | y rotation |

rotation be perpendicular to the paper (Figure 11-4).

The inverse of a rotation θ degrees is simply a rotation of $-\theta$ degrees (θ degrees in the clockwise direction). The inverse matrices are obtained by replacing θ by $-\theta$ in the corresponding matrix. Since $\cos(-\theta) = \cos(\theta)$ and $\sin(-\theta) = -\sin(\theta)$, it is necessary to switch the signs only on the sine terms.

FIGURE 11–4
The rotation axis perpendicular to the paper

SCALING

A three-dimensional **scaling** allows for a contraction or stretching in any of the x, y or z directions. As in the two-dimensional case, we describe scaling when the fixed point is at the origin. To obtain a scaling with an arbitrary fixed point, translate the fixed point to the origin, scale the object, then perform the inverse of the original translation. The scaling matrix with scale factors Sx, Sy, Sz in the x, y, z directions, respectively, is given by the matrix

$$Sc(Sx, Sy, Sz) = \begin{bmatrix} Sx & 0 & 0 & 0 \\ 0 & Sy & 0 & 0 \\ 0 & 0 & Sz & 0 \\ 0 & 0 & 0 & 1 \end{bmatrix}.$$

The homogeneous point $[x, y, z, 1]$ is transformed to the homogeneous point $[x', y', z', 1]$, where

$x' = x \times Sx$
$y' = y \times Sy$
$z' = z \times Sz.$

The inverse of a scaling is obtained by using the reciprocals of the scale factors: $1/Sx$, $1/Sy$, $1/Sz$.

SHEARING

For the two-dimensional case, we described the *x*-shear and the *y*-shear transformations. We shall now describe the three-dimensional **z-shear**.

Suppose we want to transform the line $y = -bz$ in the *y, z* plane to the *z*-axis so that all *z* values remain fixed (Figure 11-5a). Since the *z*-axis has a *y* value equal to zero, we must subtract the *y* value of each point on the line, $-bz$, from each of the *y* coordinates. Therefore, this transformation sends (y, z) to (y', z'), where

$$y' = y - (-bz) = y + bz$$
$$z' = z.$$

We similarly transform the line $x = -az$ lying in the *x, z* plane to the *z*-axis (Figure 11-5b) by the equations

$$x' = x - (-az) = x + az$$
$$z' = z.$$

The combined three-dimensional transformation is a *z*-shear that takes an arbitrary line, not lying in the *x, y* plane, passing through the origin, and moves it to the *z*-axis so that the *z* values remain fixed. Its matrix representation is given by

$$Sh(a, b) = \begin{bmatrix} 1 & 0 & 0 & 0 \\ 0 & 1 & 0 & 0 \\ a & b & 1 & 0 \\ 0 & 0 & 0 & 1 \end{bmatrix}.$$

The values of *a* and *b* in the third row are obtained from the line equation. To compute these values, let $P:(x1, y1, z1) \neq 0$ be any point lying on the line through the origin:

$$x = -a \times z$$
$$y = -b \times z.$$

Substituting the point *P* into these equations gives

$$a = -\frac{x1}{z1} \quad \text{and} \quad b = -\frac{y1}{z1}.$$

From this result we see why the original line cannot lie in the *x, y* plane: We would be dividing by $z1 = 0$.

ROTATION ABOUT AN ARBITRARY AXIS

We have described the transformations for a rotation about any of the three coordinate axes. There are situations, however, when the axis of rotation is not one of these. For example, the moon revolves about

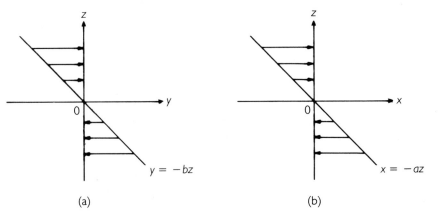

FIGURE 11–5
A z-shear
transformation

(a) $y = -bz$

(b) $x = -az$

the earth's north–south axis, which has the sun as the center of the coordinate system. Determining this kind of arbitrary rotation is similar to, but more complicated than, determining the two-dimensional rotation about an arbitrary point. Before we examine this transformation, let's agree on a representation of the rotation axis, which is a straight line.

Two points, $P1:(x1, y1, z1)$ and $P2:(x2, y2, z2)$, define a line (Figure 11-6 on page 260). The parametric equations for the line passing through these points are

$$x = (x2 - x1)t + x1$$
$$y = (y2 - y1)t + y1$$
$$z = (z2 - z1)t + z1$$

where t assumes real values. If $t = 0$, we get the point $P1$, while $t = 1$ gives the point $P2$. The line segment from $P1$ to $P2$ has t values restricted between 0 and 1.

The preceding three equations for a line can be viewed in a slightly different way that is more convenient for our present discussion. Let

$$a = (x2 - x1)$$
$$b = (y2 - y1)$$
$$c = (z2 - z1).$$

The equations of the line now have the form

$$x = at + x1$$
$$y = bt + y1$$
$$z = ct + z1.$$

Observe that $P1$ and $P2$ can be considered as vectors, and the difference $P2 - P1 = (x2 - x1, y2 - y1, z2 - z1) = (a, b, c)$ is the (direction) vector from $P1$ to $P2$ along the line through $P1$ and $P2$ (Figure 11-6). Therefore, three values—a, b, c—describe the **direction** of the line through the point $(x1, y1, z1)$ toward the point $(x2, y2, z2)$.

FIGURE 11–6
A vector represen-
tation of a line

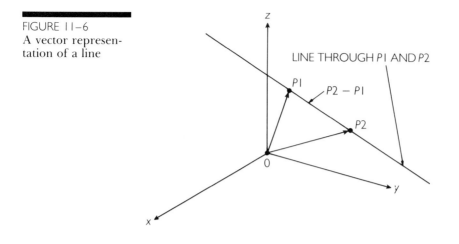

Hence, a line can be defined by a point on it, $(x1, y1, z1)$ and by a direction, (a, b, c).

Returning to the axis of rotation, let $(x1, y1, z1)$ be a point through which the rotation axis passes, having direction vector (a, b, c). A rotation of angle θ about this axis can be described by the following seven steps:

1. Translate the point $(x1, y1, z1)$ to the origin.
2. Rotate about the x-axis until the rotation axis is in the x, z plane.
3. Rotate about the y-axis until the rotation axis corresponds to the z-axis.
4. Rotate about the z-axis angle θ.
5. Perform the inverse rotation of step 3.
6. Perform the inverse rotation of step 2.
7. Perform the inverse translation of step 1.

These steps transform the rotation axis to the z-axis, perform the rotation of angle θ, and then transform the rotation axis back to its original position. Let's go through these seven steps.

The initial translation is represented by the matrix

$$Tr(-x1, -y1, -z1) = \begin{bmatrix} 1 & 0 & 0 & 0 \\ 0 & 1 & 0 & 0 \\ 0 & 0 & 1 & 0 \\ -x1 & -y1 & -z1 & 1 \end{bmatrix}.$$

After this translation the direction vector (a, b, c) defining the rotation axis is in the position illustrated in Figure 11-7a.

Since step 2 rotates this line about the x-axis, we can use its projection in the y, z plane and consider this to be a rotation about the origin, with the x-axis coming out of the paper (Figure 11-7b). When the rotation axis is projected onto the y, z plane, any point on it has x coordinate equal to zero. In particular, $a = 0$.

FIGURE 11-7
Rotation about an
arbitrary axis

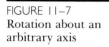

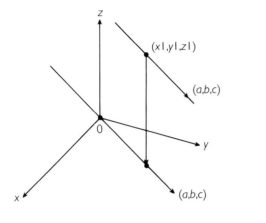

(a)

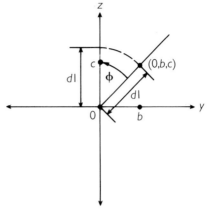

(b)

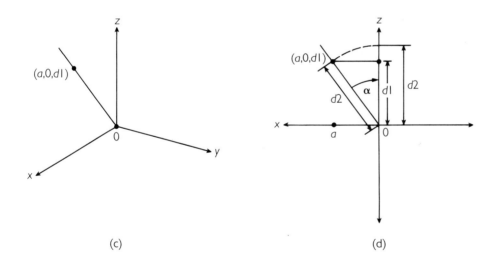

(c)   (d)

This projected line, or, equivalently, the point $(0, b, c)$, is rotated ϕ degrees until the line corresponds to the z-axis. We actually do not have to find the angle ϕ but rather the sine and cosine of the angle since these trigonometric functions define the rotation matrix. From Figure 11-7, we find that the distance from the origin to $(0, b, c)$ is $\sqrt{b^2 + c^2} = d1$. Hence

$$\sin \phi = b/d1$$
$$\cos \phi = c/d1.$$

Substituting these values into the x-axis rotation matrix, we have

$$Rx(\phi) = \begin{bmatrix} 1 & 0 & 0 & 0 \\ 0 & c/d1 & b/d1 & 0 \\ 0 & -b/d1 & c/d1 & 0 \\ 0 & 0 & 0 & 1 \end{bmatrix}.$$

After this step the rotation axis is in the x, z plane and the point $(0, b, c)$ has been transformed to the point $(0, 0, d1)$. Since rotation about the x-axis does not change the x coordinate values, the point (a, b, c) is now at location $(a, 0, d1)$ (Figure 11-7c).

The next step is a rotation about the y-axis until the point $(a, 0, d1)$ lies on the z-axis. Since $(a, 0, d1)$ lies in the x, z plane, we can visualize this as a rotation about the origin, with the y-axis coming out of the paper (Figure 11-7d). A rotation of angle α in the clockwise direction performs this task. Since the counterclockwise direction is positive, we must perform a rotation of angle $-\alpha$. As before, we need only compute the sine and cosine of angle α. From Figure 11-7d, we see that the hypotenuse

$$d2 = \sqrt{a^2 + d1^2} = \sqrt{a^2 + b^2 + c^2}.$$

Thus

$$\sin \alpha = a/d2$$
$$\cos \alpha = d1/d2$$

and

$$\sin(-\alpha) = -a/d2$$
$$\cos(-\alpha) = d1/d2.$$

Substituting these values into the y rotation matrix gives

$$Ry(-\alpha) = \begin{bmatrix} d1/d2 & 0 & a/d2 & 0 \\ 0 & 1 & 0 & 0 \\ -a/d2 & 0 & d1/d2 & 0 \\ 0 & 0 & 0 & 1 \end{bmatrix}.$$

Step 4 simply requires the rotation matrix $Rz(\theta)$. The final three steps use the inverse matrices of the first three transformations. The inverse rotation matrices of $Rx(\phi)$ and $Ry(-\alpha)$ are $Rx(-\phi)$ and $Ry(\alpha)$, respectively. The inverse of the translation matrix $Tr(-x1, -y1, -z1)$ is $Tr(x1, y1, z1)$.

The composite transformation representing these seven steps is given by the product

$$Tr(-x1, -y1, -z1) \times Rx(\phi)Ry(-\alpha) \times$$
$$Rz(\theta)Ry(\alpha)Rx(-\phi)Tr(x1, y1, z1).$$

11–4 **THREE-DIMENSIONAL GRAPHICS PACKAGE**

Graphics display systems offer an assortment of three-dimensional graphics capabilities. The absolute and relative line-drawing commands are:

move3(x,y,z)
draw3(x,y,z)
rmove3(dx,dy,dz)
rdraw3(dx,dy,dz).

All parameters are in world coordinates. The three-dimensional graphics commands are analogous to the two-dimensional drawing commands (Chapter 3) except that they accept three coordinate parameters. The actual drawing is a two-dimensional orthogonal projection; that is, the z coordinate is dropped and is not used for drawing. However, the z coordinate is needed when geometric transformations are performed.

The translation, the three rotations, and the scaling transformations are provided in all graphics systems with three-dimensional capabilities. Usually, the application programmer must write his or her own shear procedure, if it is needed. A three-dimensional transformation behaves as its two-dimensional counterpart does. After one or more transformations are invoked, all subsequent points drawn, using the move or draw commands, are transformed accordingly.

11–5 **TRANSFORMING COORDINATE SYSTEMS**

Objects that are defined in one coordinate system may have to be expressed in terms of another coordinate system. As an example, suppose your home represents the origin in a two-dimensional coordinate system. To get to the market from home, you have to travel five blocks north (positive y-axis direction) and three blocks east (positive x-axis direction). However, if you are at school and are going to the market, the school is the new origin and the directions are: Go two blocks north (positive y-axis direction) and four blocks west (negative x-axis direction) (Figure 11-8 on page 264). Hence, the market in the home coordinate system has coordinates (3, 5), while in the school coordinate system it has coordinates $(-4, 2)$.

The school can, of course, be represented in terms of the home coordinate system. In this case, its coordinates are (7, 3). If we transform the school coordinate system to the home's, we must translate the school's origin (7, 3) to the origin of the home (0, 0). This is a translation of -7 units in the x direction and -3 units in the y direction. If this

FIGURE 11–8
The market relative
to the home and
school coordinate
systems

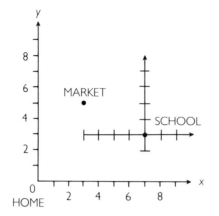

FIGURE 11–9
A second coordi-
nate system
(a) rotated and (b)
translated and ro-
tated from the ini-
tial coordinate
system

same translation is applied to the market's coordinates as represented in the home system, (3, 5), the market's new coordinates are (3 − 7, 5 − 3) = (−4, 2), which are the market's coordinates in the school system. This did not happen accidentally.

In general, if an object is defined in terms of coordinate system 1, it can be defined in terms of another coordinate system 2 by transforming the axis of coordinate system 2 into the axis of coordinate system 1. This transformation, when applied to the representation of the object in coordinate system 1, gives the object's representation in coordinate system 2.

The previous example for the market was simplified by the fact that the two coordinate systems differed by only a translation. Let's examine the situation in Figure 11-9a, where the second coordinate system, de-

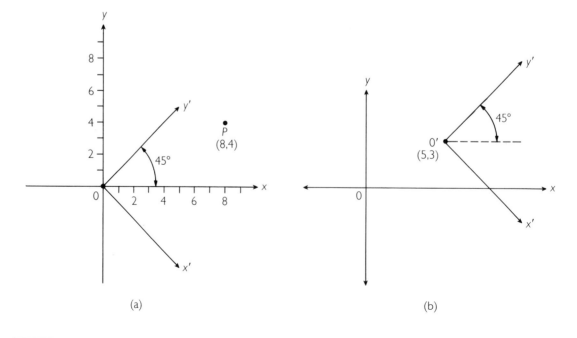

Three-Dimensional Graphics

noted by x' y', is at a clockwise angle of 45 degrees with the original x, y coordinate system. According to this transformation rule, the required two-dimensional transformation sending the second coordinate system, x', y', to the first coordinate system, x, y, is a counterclockwise rotation of 45 degrees.

$$Rotate(\pi/4) = \begin{bmatrix} \cos \pi/4 & \sin \pi/4 & 0 \\ -\sin \pi/4 & \cos \pi/4 & 0 \\ 0 & 0 & 1 \end{bmatrix}.$$

or

$$(11-1) \quad Rotate(\pi/4) = \begin{bmatrix} 1/\sqrt{2} & 1/\sqrt{2} & 0 \\ -1/\sqrt{2} & 1/\sqrt{2} & 0 \\ 0 & 0 & 1 \end{bmatrix}.$$

Therefore, the point $P = (8, 4)$ in the x, y coordinate system is represented as $P' = (2\sqrt{2}, 6\sqrt{2})$ in the x', y' coordinate system where

$$[2\sqrt{2}, 6\sqrt{2}, 1] = [8, 4, 1] \times Rotate(\pi/4).$$

If the rotated x', y' coordinate system has its origin at $(5, 3)$ with respect to the x, y coordinate system (Figure 11-9b), the coordinate transformation is formed by premultiplying the preceding rotation matrix by the two-dimensional translation matrix

$$Translate(-5, -3) = \begin{bmatrix} 1 & 0 & 0 \\ 0 & 1 & 0 \\ -5 & -3 & 1 \end{bmatrix}.$$

This technique works well as long as the angle of rotation is given or easily computed. However, in most cases these angles are not known and their calculation requires considerable effort. In particular, we shall examine situations where the new coordinate system is defined by its origin and the directions of its three perpendicular axes with respect to the standard coordinate system. As we saw in the previous section, these directions are vectors along the three axes.

A two-dimensional direction vector, (a, b), defining an axis has a certain length: $l = \sqrt{a^2 + b^2}$. If each component of the vector is divided by the length, l, the resulting vector, u, has unit length. This process is referred to as normalizing a vector, and the resulting vector has norm (length) equal to 1:

$u = (a/l, b/l);$

$\text{length of } u = \sqrt{(a/l)^2 + (b/l)^2} = \dfrac{\sqrt{(a^2 + b^2)}}{(a^2 + b^2)} = 1.$

Returning to Figure 11-9b, the x', y' coordinate system has x' axis defined by the unit direction vector $(1/\sqrt{2}, -1/\sqrt{2})$, and the y'-axis is defined by the unit direction vector $(1/\sqrt{2}, 1/\sqrt{2})$. We form the 3×3

matrix whose first column is the u vector, second column the v vector, and third column the vector $[0, 0, 1]$:

$$R = \begin{bmatrix} 1/\sqrt{2} & 1/\sqrt{2} & 0 \\ -1/\sqrt{2} & 1/\sqrt{2} & 0 \\ 0 & 0 & 1 \end{bmatrix}.$$

Observe that this is the rotation matrix equation 11-1. This also is no accident. From this observation we can conclude that the desired coordinate transformation rotation matrix is obtained from the normalized direction vectors of the new coordinate system.

Everything we have discussed up till now can be extended to three dimensions, which is our present concern. The general result we want is this. Let a coordinate system x', y', z' be defined in terms of the standard x, y, z coordinate by the perpendicular unit vectors

$$u = (ux, uy, uz)$$
$$v = (vx, vy, vz)$$
$$w = (wx, wy, wz).$$

Furthermore, assume the origin of the x', y', z' coordinate system is at $(x1, y1, z1)$ with respect to the x, y, z coordinate system (Figure 11-10). The transformation sending the x', y', z' coordinate system to the x, y, z system, with u going to x, v going to y, and w going to z is given by the product of a translation followed by a rotation:

$$Tr \times R = \begin{bmatrix} 1 & 0 & 0 & 0 \\ 0 & 1 & 0 & 0 \\ 0 & 0 & 1 & 0 \\ -x1 & -y1 & -z1 & 1 \end{bmatrix} \begin{bmatrix} ux & vx & wx & 0 \\ uy & vy & wy & 0 \\ uz & vz & wz & 0 \\ 0 & 0 & 0 & 1 \end{bmatrix}.$$

FIGURE 11–10
A three-dimensional
coordinate system
transformation

It is interesting to note that the rotation matrix, R, is actually the product of an x, y, and z rotation matrix. A point P defined in the x, y,

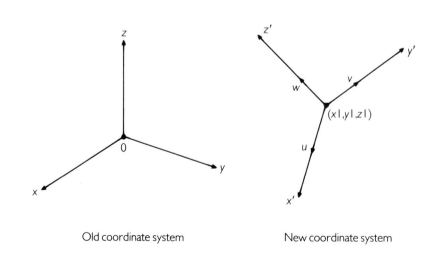

Old coordinate system   New coordinate system

Three-Dimensional Graphics

z coordinate system has representation P' in the x', y', z' coordinate system given by $P' = P \times Tr \times R$.[†]

11–6 **PROJECTIONS**

In computer graphics, a three-dimensional object is viewed on a two-dimensional display. A **projection** is a transformation that performs this conversion from a three-dimensional representation to a two-dimensional representation. This process is not unique to the field of computer graphics, however. Artists use a perspective projection to create realistic pictures; architects use several parallel projections to depict different views of a building; cartographers use Mercator and conical projections to draw maps of the world. These are just a few examples of different types of projections and their uses. In this section we describe two of these projections: parallel and perspective.

PARALLEL PROJECTION

The simplest method of projecting a three-dimensional image into two dimensions is to discard one of the coordinates. This is referred to as a **parallel** or **orthogonal projection**. We consider only the case of dropping the z coordinate, which projects the x, y, z coordinate system into the x, y plane (Figure 11-11 on page 268).

The projection of a point Q:(x, y, z) lying on the cube is that point Q':(xp, yp) in the x, y plane, where a line passing through Q and parallel to the z-axis intersects the x, y plane. These parallel lines are called **projectors**. The mathematics describing this is very simple:

$$xp = x$$
$$yp = y.$$

Parallel projections have the property that straight lines are transformed into straight lines. Therefore, it is only necessary to project the endpoints of a line in three dimensions and then draw a two-dimensional line between these projected points. This speeds the transformation process up considerably.

The major disadvantage of a parallel projection is its lack of depth information. A viewer looking at the projection of the cube—namely,

---

[†]For readers with a knowledge of linear algebra who are looking for a justification of what we have just done, observe that the vectors u, v, and w form an orthonormal basis. When the orthogonal matrix R is applied to each of these vectors, we obtain the standard basis vectors i, j, k. Thus the matrix R transforms the x', y', z' coordinate system into the direction of the x, y, z coordinate system.

FIGURE 11–11
A parallel
projection

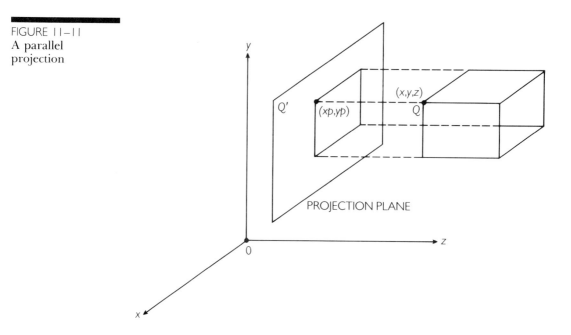

the square—has no idea that the original three-dimensional object is the cube. Realistic two-dimensional displays must convey to the viewer a more accurate representation of the three-dimensional image.

PERSPECTIVE PROJECTION

Perspective projection enhances the realism of a displayed image by providing the viewer with depth cues. Portions of the image that are further away from the viewer are drawn smaller than those portions in the foreground. This reflects the real world, where objects closer to an observer look larger than those in the background.

In a perspective projection, the lines of projection, the projectors, connect the eye with a point on the object. The point of intersection of the projector with a plane, called the **projection plane**, is the projected point (Figure 11-12). Unlike parallel projections, all the projectors are not parallel but, by definition, converge at the eye.

To examine the mathematics of perspective projection, let us assume that the projection plane is parallel to the x, y plane at a distance D from the eye. The eye is called the center of projection. We shall use a left-handed coordinate system in our illustrations.

Let $Q = (x1, y1, z1)$ be a point that projects to the point $Q' = (xp, yp, D)$, as in Figure 11-12. There are two standard methods used to derive the coordinates of projection xp, yp. It is instructive to examine both.

In the first derivation, the line joining the center of projection,

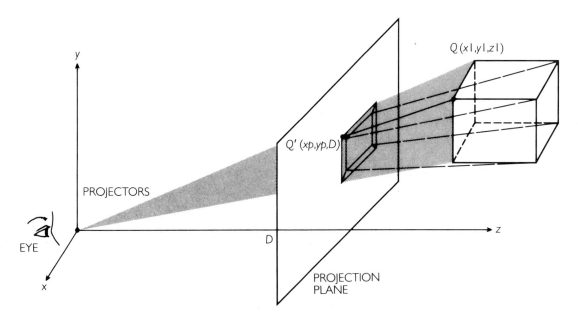

FIGURE 11–12
A perspective
projection

$(0, 0, 0)$, and the point Q has parametric equations

$$x = x1 \times t$$
$$y = y1 \times t \qquad t \text{ a real number.}$$
$$z = z1 \times t.$$

The projected point (xp, yp, D) lies on this line and has $z = D$. Hence

$$D = z1 \times t \qquad \text{or} \qquad t = \frac{z1}{D}.$$

Substituting this value of t into the preceding equations we obtain the values of the projected point:

$$xp = D \times x\frac{1}{z1}$$

$$yp = D \times \frac{y1}{z1}.$$

The second derivation uses similar triangles. Figure 11-13 on page 270 illustrates a top view and a side view of Figure 11-12. From the proportionality property of similar triangles we obtain the ratios:

$$xp/D = x1/z1, \quad yp/D = y1/z1$$

or

$$xp = D \times \frac{x1}{z1}$$

$$yp = D \times \frac{y1}{z1}.$$

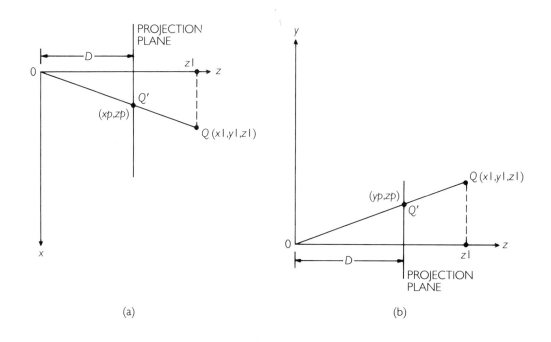

(a)   (b)

FIGURE 11–13
Top and side views
of the perspective
projection in Figure
11–12

Since the z value represents the distance of a point from the eye, depth information is included in these projection equations. Objects that are farther away have their x and y coordinates divided by larger z values than those closer, causing these distant objects to be drawn smaller.

An object can be at any distance from the eye. This includes cases where the object intersects the projection plane or lies behind the eye (negative z-axis). However, since the perspective projection equations involve division by the z coordinate of the point, the object cannot have z value equal to zero—that is, have it intersect the x, y plane.

What happens to a perspective drawing when the projection plane is moved? If the plane is moved farther away from the eye, the objects appear larger and hence the viewer can see less of the entire scene. If the plane is moved closer to the eye, the objects appear smaller and more of the scene is displayed.

The perspective projection can be described using a matrix. However, a simple matrix multiplication of a three-dimensional point by this transformation matrix is not enough; we must also divide by the fourth term of the homogeneous coordinate.

If D is the distance from the eye to the projection plane, the perspective transformation matrix, Per, is

$$Per \; = \; \begin{bmatrix} 1 & 0 & 0 & 0 \\ 0 & 1 & 0 & 0 \\ 0 & 0 & 1 & 1/D \\ 0 & 0 & 0 & 0 \end{bmatrix}.$$

Multiplying the homogeneous point $Q = [x, y, z, 1]$ by the matrix *Per* gives

$$[x, y, z, 1] \, Per = [x, y, z, \frac{z}{D}] = Q'.$$

To obtain the projected point (xp, yp), it is necessary to divide the first and second components of Q' by its fourth component:

$$xp = D \times \frac{x}{z}$$

$$yp = D \times \frac{x}{z}.$$

This agrees with the previous results.

It can be shown that the perspective projection sends lines in three dimensions to lines on the two-dimensional projected plane. Thus, to project an image made of objects that are defined by straight lines, we need only project the endpoints of these lines and connect the projected endpoints with straight lines.

Figure 11-14a on page 272 illustrates this perspective effect. The three-dimensional rectangle *ABCD* with coordinates $A = (4, -2, 6)$, $B = (4, 2, 6)$, $C = (-4, 2, 12)$, and $D = (-4, -2, 12)$ is projected onto a projection plane that is at a distance of three units away from the x, y plane. The resulting figure, Figure 11-14b, is the trapezoid $A'B'C'D'$ in the xp, yp plane. The coordinates of this projected trapezoid are:

$$A': xp = 3 \times \frac{4}{6} = 2$$

$$yp = 3 \times \frac{(-2)}{6} = -1$$

$$B': xp = 3 \times \frac{4}{6} = 2$$

$$yp = 3 \times \frac{2}{6} = 1$$

$$C': xp = 3 \times \frac{(-4)}{12} = -1$$

$$yp = 3 \times \frac{2}{12} = \frac{1}{2}$$

$$D': xp = 3 \times \frac{(-4)}{12} = -1$$

$$yp = 3 \times \frac{(-2)}{12} = -\frac{1}{2}.$$

FIGURE 11–14
A perspective pro-
jection of a
rectangle

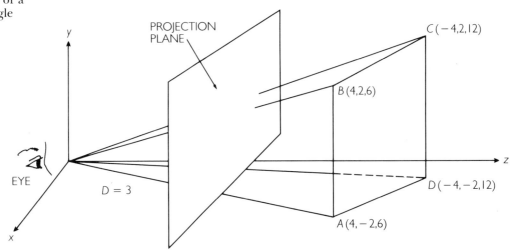

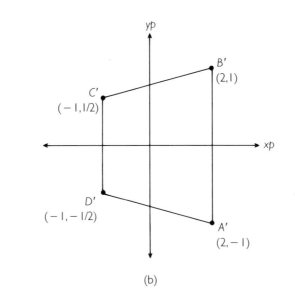

(b)

11–7 **VIEWING TRANSFORMATION**

In the previous section we saw how to project a three-dimensional
image into a two-dimensional plane. To do this, we assumed that the
eye was at the origin of a left-handed system and the projection plane

was parallel to the *x, y* plane (Figure 11-12). Unfortunately, this simplified point of view does not mirror the real world.

An image consisting of buildings, streets, cars, and other objects is constructed using a three-dimensional world coordinate system. This is usually a right-handed system. If the viewer of this scene is in an airplane, the eye can be anywhere above the ground, looking in any direction, and the projection plane (airplane window) can also be facing in any direction (Figure 11-15). This general viewing situation is much too complex to be displayed using the previous methods.

Recall that objects comprising an image are defined in their own natural coordinate system. Each object is placed in its proper position in the image world coordinate system by an appropriate geometric modeling transformation. The viewing transformation is the process of changing this right-handed world coordinate image into left-handed eye coordinates. This process gives a specific view of the scene as seen from the eye through a rectangular window. (In Section 11-5, we observed that the steps involved in this process are equivalent to transforming the eye coordinate system into the world coordinate system.) The final step in displaying the image is the projection transformation, which converts the three-dimensional eye coordinate system to the two-dimensional screen coordinate system. We shall study only the case for a perspective projection.† This section describes the viewing and projection transformations in detail.

FIGURE 11–15
Arbitrary three-dimensional viewing

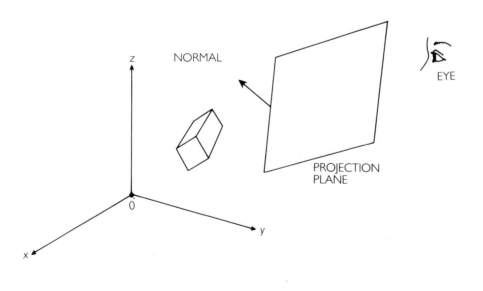

†The transformation for a parallel projection is similar and is left as an exercise for the interested reader.

VIEWING PARAMETERS

We will describe the viewing parameters in terms of the CORE system. These specifications are general and may appear unnecessarily complicated at first. However, this approach gives an unrestricted view of the scene—one that can be used in any reasonable situation. All parameters are specified in right-handed world coordinates.

The projection plane, now called the **view plane,** is defined by a point on the plane and a normal (perpendicular vector) to the plane. This point, called the **view reference point (VRP),** plays a central role in the viewing transformation. The other viewing parameters are defined relative to this point. The **view plane normal (VPN)** gives the orientation of the view plane. Together with the view reference point, it completely defines the view plane (Figure 11-16).

We want to use the view plane's normal to define a new left-handed coordinate system. To do this, we need another direction (vector) perpendicular to the VPN and lying on the view plane. The **view up (VUP)** vector defines any direction not parallel to the view plane's normal. This view up vector need not be perpendicular to the view plane normal (that is, it need not lie on the view plane), but we can project the VUP vector onto the view plane, giving a direction vector perpendicular to VPN. This projected vector defines the *v*-axis on the view plane (Figure 11-16). The third axis, the *u*-axis, also lies on the view plane and is perpendicular to both the *v*-axis and the view plane's normal. The di-

FIGURE 11–16
Viewing parameters

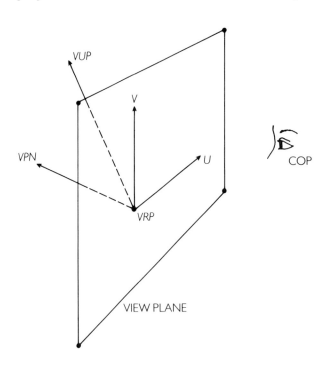

rection of the *u*-axis is chosen so that u, v, and VPN form a left-handed system.

The view reference point (VRP) is the origin of the two-dimensional u, v coordinate system. However, the VRP is not the origin of the three-dimensional eye coordinate system we are defining. The location of the eye, the **center of projection (COP),** is the origin of this left-handed coordinate system. The coordinates of the center of projection are defined relative to the VRP, using world coordinates. The VUP vector can now be interpreted as the up direction of the viewer's head (Figure 11-16).

We now have the parameters necessary to form the perspective transformation projecting the scene onto the view plane. However, in most cases, the entire scene cannot be seen by the viewer. A rectangular window on the view plane clips part of the image. This two-dimensional window has sides parallel to the u, v-axis, and the location and size of this window is defined in terms of distances from the VRP. The window and the COP define a **view volume** pyramid that defines in three dimensions those parts of the image that the viewer can see (Figure 11-17). The line from the COP through the center of the window specifies the **view direction.** All objects outside this view volume are clipped and not projected onto the view plane.

If an object in the view volume is close to the eye (COP), it will block out all objects further away. Similarly, an object far away may appear as only a few indistinguishable pixels on the display screen, while the com-

FIGURE 11–17
The center of a
projection and a
window defining
the view volume

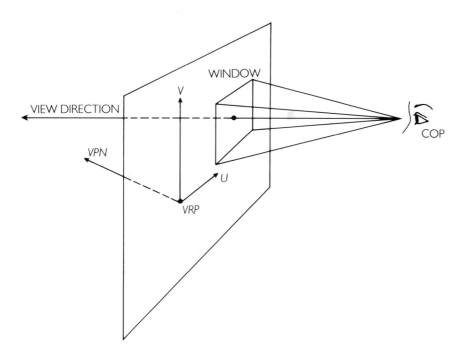

putation involved in projecting this object can be quite expensive in terms of time. Therefore, it is useful to eliminate objects very close or distant from the COP. This is done by specifying front and back clipping planes, which are perpendicular to the view plane normal (Figure 11-18). The view volume is now finite, and is called a truncated view volume.

PRELIMINARY MATHEMATICS

Let **v1** = $(x1, y1, z1)$ and **v2** = $(x2, y2, z2)$ be two three-dimensional vectors. The **dot product** of these two vectors is defined as

$$\mathbf{v1} \cdot \mathbf{v2} = x1x2 + y1y2 + z1z2.$$

For example, if **v1** = (1, 2, 3) and **v2** = $(-2, 1, -4)$ then

$$\mathbf{v1} \cdot \mathbf{v2} = 1(-2) + 2(1) + 3(-4) = -12.$$

Observe that the dot product of two vectors is not a vector but a real number (scalar).

The cosine of the acute angle θ between two vectors **v1** and **v2** is defined as

$$\cos \theta = \frac{\mathbf{v1} \cdot \mathbf{v2}}{(|\mathbf{v1}| \, |\mathbf{v2}|)}$$

where $|\mathbf{v1}|$ is the length of the vector **v1** and $|\mathbf{v2}|$ is the length of **v2** (Figure 11-19). Rearranging this equation, the dot product can be expressed as

$$\mathbf{v1} \cdot \mathbf{v2} = |\mathbf{v1}| \, |\mathbf{v2}| \times \cos \theta.$$

FIGURE 11-18
A truncated view volume

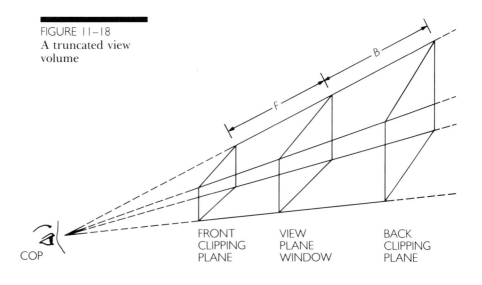

FRONT CLIPPING PLANE

VIEW PLANE WINDOW

BACK CLIPPING PLANE

COP

Three-Dimensional Graphics

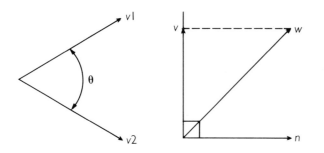

FIGURE 11–19
An acute angle be-
tween vectors **v1**
and **v2**

FIGURE 11–20
An orthogonal pro-
jection of a vector

An important consequence of this equation is that if **v1** and **v2** are at right angles to each other, $\theta = 90$ and $\cos \theta = 0$. Hence, the dot product of perpendicular vectors equals zero, and, conversely, if two vectors have a dot product of zero, they are perpendicular.

The **length** of a vector $\mathbf{v} = (x, y, z)$ is defined as $\sqrt{x^2 + y^2 + z^2}$. Taking the dot product of **v** with itself

$$\mathbf{v}\cdot\mathbf{v} = x^2 + y^2 + z^2,$$

the square of its length. Using the previous notation, we write this as $\mathbf{v}\cdot\mathbf{v} = |\mathbf{v}|^2$. If $|\mathbf{v}| = 1$, a vector has length or **norm** equal to 1.

The dot product has a distributive property similar to real numbers. If **u**, **v**, and **w** are vectors and r is a real number, then

$$\mathbf{u}\cdot(\mathbf{v} + r \times \mathbf{w}) = \mathbf{u}\cdot\mathbf{v} + r \times (\mathbf{u}\cdot\mathbf{w}).$$

Our present application of the dot product is to solve the following problem. Given a vector **n** with length equal to 1 and another vector **w** not parallel to **n**, how can we project **w** to a vector **v**, which lies on a plane perpendicular to **n** (Figure 11-20)? Let's define the vector **v** by

(11–2) $\mathbf{v} = \mathbf{w} - (\mathbf{n}\cdot\mathbf{w}) \times \mathbf{n}.$

Then

$$\begin{aligned}
\mathbf{n}\cdot\mathbf{v} &= \mathbf{n}\cdot[\mathbf{w} - (\mathbf{n}\cdot\mathbf{w}) \times \mathbf{n}] \\
&= \mathbf{n}\cdot\mathbf{w} - (\mathbf{n}\cdot\mathbf{w}) \times (\mathbf{n}\cdot\mathbf{n}).
\end{aligned}$$

Since **n** has length equal to 1, $\mathbf{n}\cdot\mathbf{n} = 1$. Substituting this into the equation gives $\mathbf{n}\cdot\mathbf{v} = 0$. This implies that **n** and **v** are at right angles to each other. Therefore, **v** is a vector that lies on a plane perpendicular to **n**.

The **cross product** of the two vectors **v1** and **v2** is another vector:

$$\mathbf{v1} \times \mathbf{v2} = (y1z2 - z1y2, z1x2 - x1z2, x1y2 - y1x2).$$

The cross product of two nonparallel vectors is a vector perpendicular to both vectors. Thus the dot product of one of these vectors with the perpendicular cross product equals zero:

$$\mathbf{v1}\cdot(\mathbf{v1} \times \mathbf{v2}) = \mathbf{v2}\cdot(\mathbf{v1} \times \mathbf{v2}) = 0.$$

The direction of the vector $\mathbf{v1} \times \mathbf{v2}$ is such that if the fingers in your right hand are curled around $\mathbf{v1}$ in the direction of $\mathbf{v2}$, then $\mathbf{v1} \times \mathbf{v2}$ is pointing in the direction of your thumb. The cross product is not commutative: $\mathbf{v1} \times \mathbf{v2} = -\mathbf{v2} \times \mathbf{v1}$. Thus the direction of $\mathbf{v2} \times \mathbf{v1}$ is the opposite of $\mathbf{v1} \times \mathbf{v2}$; use your left hand to determine its orientation.

UTILITY ROUTINES

Implementation of the viewing transformation requires several procedures and functions involving matrices and vectors. Since these routines can be applied to a wide variety of problems, we describe them here independently of the details of viewing. When the viewing transformation is constructed, we invoke these routines with the appropriate parameters.

Assume the following Pascal environment:

```
type
    xyzw        = (x,y,z,w); {user-defined coordinate type}
    point       = array[xyzw] of real; {homogeneous point or vector}
    matrix      = array[1..4,1..4] of real; {transformation matrix}

var
    VPN,VUP,COP,              {viewing parameters}
    u,v,                      {viewplane coordinate system}
    CENT,                     {center of window}
    P,Pprime,                 {original and transformed point}
    VRPprime,                 {transformed VRP}
    tempvect    : point;      {temporary vector}
    T,Rot,                    {translation, rotation}
    Sh,Sc,                    {shear, scale}
    Viewmat     : matrix;     {combined viewing transform matrix}
    scalar      : real;
    index       : integer;
    i           : xyzw;       {loop index}

Function Dot_Prod (v1,v2:point): real;
    {returns the dot product of v1 and v2. The fourth component has value 1
    and is omitted}

    begin
        Dot_Prod := v1[x]*v2[x] + v1[y]*v2[y] + v1[z]*v2[z]

    end;    {Dot_Prod}

Procedure Cross_Prod(v1,v2:point; var result : point);
    {obtains the cross product of v1 and v2. The fourth component is omitted
    and has value 1}
```

```
        begin
            result[x] := v1[y]*v2[z] - v1[z]*v2[y];
            result[y] := v1[z]*v2[x] - v1[x]*v2[z];
            result[z] := v1[x]*v2[y] - v1[y]*v2[x]

        end; {Cross_Prod}

Procedure Normalize (var v1 : point);
        {the resulting vector v1 has length 1}

        var
            length : real;

        begin
            length := sqrt(Dot_Prod(v1,v1));
            for index := x to z do
                {divide by length}
                v1[index] := v1[index]/length

        end; {Normalize}

Procedure Multiply_Mat (A,B: matrix; var C: matrix);
        {C is the product of A and B}

var
    i,j,k : integer;

        begin
            for i := 1 to 4 do
                for j := 1 to 4 do
                    begin {for}
                        C[i,j] := 0; {initialize}
                        for k := 1 to 4 do
                            C[i,j] := C[i,j] + A[i,k]*B[k,j]
                    end {for}

        end; {Multiply_Mat}

Procedure Multiply_Vec (A : matrix; v1 : point; var v2 : point);
        {v2 is the product v1 × A}

        var
            i : xyzw;
            j : integer;

begin
    for i := x to w do
        begin {for}
            j := ord(i) + 1; {ord(x) = 0, . . . , ord(w) = 3}
            v2[i] := v1[x]*A[1,j] + v1[y]*A[2,j] +
                     v1[z]*A[3,j] + v1[w]*A[4,j]
        end {for}
end; {Multiply_Vec}
```

Procedure Subtract_Vec (v1,v2 : point; **var** result : point);
{*result* = **v1** - **v2**}

begin
    result[x] := v1[x] − v2[x];
    result[y] := v1[y] − v2[y];
    result[z] := v1[z] − v2[z];
    result[w] := 1

end; {*Subtract_Vec*}

BUILDING THE VIEWING MATRIX

We are now ready to construct the viewing transformation that changes the image described in right-handed world coordinates into left-handed eye coordinates. Figure 11-21 illustrates this process from the modeling transformation to the projection transformation.

The first step in the process is to obtain from user input the four viewing parameters: view reference point (VRP), view plane normal (VPN), view up direction (VUP), and center of projection (COP). In addition the window on the view plane is also user-specified at this time. Using the VRP as the origin of the view plane, the coordinates of the lower-left corner and top-right corner of the window are input. Denote this pair of coordinates by (umin, vmin), (umax, vmax). (Technically, we are using the u, v coordinate system, which has not yet been defined. This does not cause any difficulties since these window points represent displacements from the origin on the view plane. The u, v coordinate system defines the direction of these displacements.)

The front and back clipping planes are also entered at this time. The back clipping plane is defined by a B value, which is a positive distance from the view plane. The front clipping plane is defined by an F value, which can be positive or negative as long as the front clipping

FIGURE 11-21
The three-dimensional viewing process

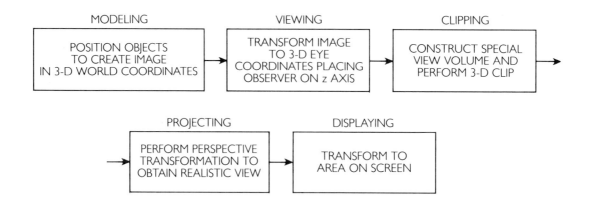

Three-Dimensional Graphics

plane is between the COP and the back clipping plane (Figure 11-22).

The next step produces the u, v coordinate system. The vector v is the projection of VUP onto the view plane. In order to use equation 11-2, VPN must be normalized to length 1. Using this normalized vector, the projected v vector has the form

$$v = \text{VUP} - (\text{VPN} \cdot \text{VUP})\text{VPN} .$$

In Pascal this is implemented by the code segment:

```
begin
    Normalize(VPN)
    {VPN now has length 1}
    {obtain the dot product term}
    scalar := Dot_Prod(VPN,VUP);
    for i := x to z do
        {multiplication of scalar and vector}
        tempvect[i] := scalar*VPN[i];
    {assign 1 to fourth homogeneous component}
    tempvect[w] := 1;
    {calculate the v vector}
    Subtract_Vec(VUP,tempvect,v)

end;
```

The vector u is calculated so that u, v, and VPN form a left-handed eye coordinate system:

$$u = \text{VPN} \times v .$$

In Pascal

```
Cross_Prod(VPN,v,u);
```

The next step is to transform the left-handed eye coordinate system

FIGURE 11–22
Positions of front and back clipping planes

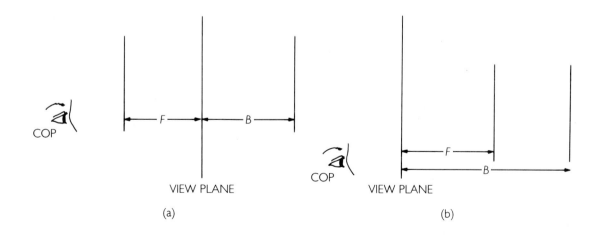

VIEW PLANE	VIEW PLANE
(a)	(b)

defined by u, v, and VPN into the right-handed world coordinate system. This is accomplished by three steps:

1. The origin of the eye coordinate system, the COP, is translated to the origin, $(0, 0, 0)$, of the world coordinate system.
2. Rotate so that
   a. The axis in the u direction is parallel to the world coordinate x-axis,
   b. The axis in the v direction is parallel to the world coordinate y-axis,
   c. The VPN is parallel to the negative z-axis—that is, going into the display screen.
3. Make the negative z-axis the positive direction so that the positive z direction goes into the screen.

Let's examine the matrices required to perform this transformation. Since the center of projection (COP) is defined relative to the VRP, the translation matrix is

$$T = \begin{bmatrix} 1 & 0 & 0 & 0 \\ 0 & 1 & 0 & 0 \\ 0 & 0 & 1 & 0 \\ -(\text{VRP}[x]+\text{COP}[x]) & -(\text{VRP}[y]+\text{COP}[y]) & -(\text{VRP}[z]+\text{COP}[z]) & 1 \end{bmatrix}.$$

The rotation matrix is

$$R = \begin{bmatrix} u[x] & v[x] & -\text{VPN}[x] & 0 \\ u[y] & v[y] & -\text{VPN}[y] & 0 \\ u[z] & v[z] & -\text{VPN}[z] & 0 \\ 0 & 0 & 0 & 1 \end{bmatrix}.$$

The matrix to change the sign (direction) of the z-axis is a reflection about the z-axis

$$Ch = \begin{bmatrix} 1 & 0 & 0 & 0 \\ 0 & 1 & 0 & 0 \\ 0 & 0 & -1 & 0 \\ 0 & 0 & 0 & 1 \end{bmatrix}.$$

Multiplying the matrices R and Ch, we obtain the matrix $Rot = R \times Ch$, whose entries are the same as R except that the third column has positive signs. We shall henceforth use this matrix, Rot.

Figure 11-23 illustrates the transformation of the view volume by these three steps. Observe that the right-handed world coordinate system has been transformed to the left-handed eye coordinate system. The view reference point (VRP) has been transformed to the point VRPprime on the view plane, where

VRPprime $= \text{VRP} \times T \times Rot$.

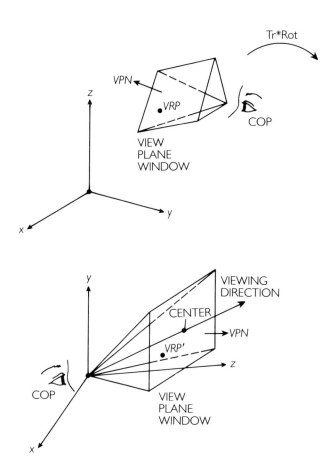

FIGURE 11–23
Transformations of
the view plane

In Pascal

```
{form combined matrix T × Rot}
Multiply_Mat(T,Rot,Viewmat);
{multiply VRP by Viewmat}
Multiply_Vec(Viewmat,VRP,VRPprime);
```

Notice in Figure 11-23 that the viewing direction—that is, the line through the COP and the center of the window—is not along the z-axis. The next step is a z-shear that transforms this line to the z-axis. This centers the window, and the view volume, about the z-axis (and makes the subsequent clipping process easier).

To compute the z-shear, we first calculate the coordinates of the center of the window. Since the COP is now at the origin and the z-axis is perpendicular to the view plane (Figure 11-23), the z value of any point on the view plane is VRPprime[z]. Thus the center has z coordinate Cent[z] = VRPprime[z].

FIGURE 11–24
A window position
in the *u, v* plane

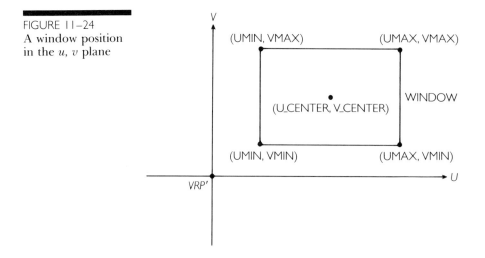

To evaluate the center's *x* and *y* coordinate, examine Figure 11-24. (Recall that the *u, v*-axis is now parallel to the *x, y*-axis.) The *v* value of the center is halfway between vmin and vmax. Thus

$$v\_center = vmin + \tfrac{1}{2}(vmax - vmin)$$
$$= \tfrac{1}{2}(vmax + vmin).$$

Similarly, the *u* value of the center is halfway between umin and umax:

$$u\_center = \tfrac{1}{2}(umax + umin).$$

Since these coordinate values are displacements from VRPprime, the center's *x, y* coordinates are:

$$Cent[x] = VRPprime[x] + \tfrac{1}{2}(umax + umin)$$
$$Cent[y] = VRPprime[y] + \tfrac{1}{2}(vmax + vmin).$$

Having calculated the coordinates of a point on this line passing through the origin, the third row entries of the *z*-shear matrix are the negative quotients of the *x* and *y* coordinates of this point divided by the *z* coordinate.

$$Sh = \begin{bmatrix} 1 & 0 & 0 & 0 \\ 0 & 1 & 0 & 0 \\ -Cent[x]/Cent[z] & -Cent[y]/Cent[z] & 1 & 0 \\ 0 & 0 & 0 & 1 \end{bmatrix}.$$

The *z*-shear sends the center of the window to the *z*-axis and the *x, y* coordinates of the upper-right corner of the window are:

$$(11–3) \quad x = \tfrac{1}{2}(umax - umin)$$
$$y = \tfrac{1}{2}(vmax - vmin).$$

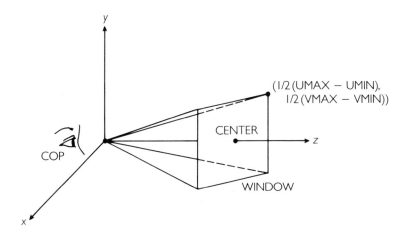

FIGURE 11–25
A viewing pyramid
with the center line
coincident with the
z-axis

Figure 11-25 illustrates the position of the view volume after the combined transformation $T \times Rot \times Sh$ is performed. This transformation correctly reorients both the image and our eye in a corresponding manner so that the image is not distorted as viewed from the COP (origin).

CLIPPING

Before projecting the image onto the view plane, it is necessary to clip against the truncated view volume (Figure 11-18). To do this, we must first calculate the equations of the six planes defining this volume and then, for all lines that define the image, calculate their intersections with each of these planes. Only those portions of lines lying inside the view volume are projected onto the view plane.

While there are several techniques available to obtain these points of intersection (for example, binary search subdivision and brute force substitution), we would like one that is not time-consuming, and we describe one such method here.

The basic idea is to transform the truncated view volume pyramid into another volume that makes the intersection calculations easier. This special volume is defined by the planes:

right plane: $x = z$,   left plane: $x = -z$,

top plane: $y = z$,   bottom plane: $y = -z$,

front plane: $z = $ mindist,   back plane: $z = 1$.

Figure 11-26 on page 286 illustrates a two-dimensional y, z view of the original and the special truncated view volumes. The z distance of

FIGURE 11–26
A scaling transfor-
mation of view vol-
ume to special view
volume

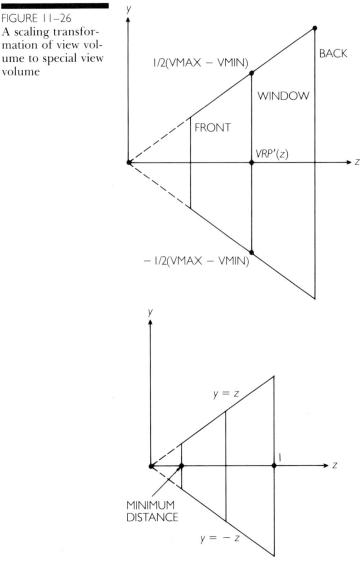

the front clipping plane, mindist, cannot be specified in advance, but rather is a consequence of the specifications of the other boundary planes.

The transformation required to create this new volume is a scaling in all three directions. Let's carefully examine how the scale factors are determined.

To send the back clipping plane $z = \text{VRPprime}[z] + B$ to $z = 1$, we use the z scale factor:

$$Sz = \frac{1}{(\text{VRPprime}[z] + B)} .$$

This z scale factor transforms the view plane $z = \text{VRPprime}[z]$ to $z = \text{VRPprime}[z]/(\text{VRPprime}[z] + B)$.

The z value of the upper-right corner of the view plane, after the z scale, is $\text{VRPprime}[z]/(\text{VRPprime}[z] + B)$. The x and y coordinate values are not affected by the z scale. Their values are still given by equation 11-3. To transform the x and y coordinate values so that $x = y = z$, we multiply x by $z/x = Sx$, and multiply y by $z/y = Sy$:

$$Sx = 2 \times \frac{\text{VRPprime}[z]}{[(\text{umax} - \text{umin})(\text{VRPprime}[z] + B)]} ,$$

$$Sy = 2 \times \frac{\text{VRPprime}[z]}{[(\text{vmax} - \text{vmin})(\text{VRPprime}[z] + B)]} .$$

To obtain the scale matrix, we substitute the value of the scale factors into

$$Sc = \begin{bmatrix} Sx & 0 & 0 & 0 \\ 0 & Sy & 0 & 0 \\ 0 & 0 & Sz & 0 \\ 0 & 0 & 0 & 1 \end{bmatrix} .$$

This scaling transforms the front clipping plane of the original view volume

$$z = \text{VRPprime}[z] + F$$

to

$$z = \frac{(\text{VRPprime}[z] + F)}{(\text{VRPprime}[z] + B)} = \text{MinDist}.$$

Unless the window is specified as square, scaling distorts the image. This may not be a significant problem. In any case, we shall soon see how to correct it.

Prior to clipping, each point P in the image is transformed to a new point P' by the transformation equation

$$P' = P \times T \times Rot \times Sh \times Sc.$$

In Pascal we have the following invocations:

```
{Viewmat = T × Rot}
Multiply_Mat(T,Rot,Viewmat);
{Viewmat = Viewmat × Sh}
Multiply_Mat(Viewmat,Sh,Viewmat);
{Viewmat = Viewmat × Sc}
Multiply_Mat(Viewmat,Sc,Viewmat);
{P' = P × Viewmat}
Multiply_Vec(Viewmat,P,Pprime);
```

A line segment is clipped against this view volume by extending the

Cohen–Sutherland algorithm of Chapter 3. The procedure Region must be modified as follows:

```
type
        direction = set of (left,right,bottom,top,front,back);

Procedure Region (p: point; var endpoint : direction);

    begin
        endpoint := [ ];
        if p[x] < − p[z] then endpoint := [left]
            else
                if p[x] > p[z] then endpoint := [right];
        if p[y] < − p[z] then endpoint := endpoint + [bottom]
            else
                if p[y] > p[z] then endpoint := endpoint + [top];
        if p[z] < MinDist then endpoint := endpoint + [front]
            else
                if p[z] > 1 then endpoint := endpoint + [back]
    end; {Region}
```

The calculation of the point of intersection of a line and one of the clipping planes is straightfoward. As an illustration, we'll compute the case where the line segment from $(x1, y1, z1)$ to $(x2, y2, z2)$ intersects the right clipping plane $x = z$.

The equation of the line segment is

$$x = (x2 − x1)t + x1$$
$$y = (y2 − y1)t + y1 \qquad 0 <= t <= 1$$
$$z = (z2 − z1)t + z1.$$

Setting $x = z$ we get

$$(x2 − x1)t + x1 = (z2 − z1)t + z1$$

or

$$t = \frac{(z1 − x1)}{[(x2 − x1) − (z2 − z1)]}.$$

The denominator cannot equal zero since the line segment does not lie on the clipping plane $x = z$. This computed value of t is substituted into the line equations to obtain the three coordinate values of the point of intersection.

If the line segment intersects the back plane, $z = 1$, or the front plane, $z = $ MinDist, the corresponding t values are

$$t = \frac{(1 − z1)}{(z2 − z1)}$$
$$t = \frac{(\text{MinDist} − z1)}{(z2 − z1)}.$$

PERSPECTIVE PROJECTION

The clipping algorithm returns the endpoints of the line segments that are within the view volume. If the scaling matrix, used for clipping, significantly distorts the image, these clipped endpoints should now be multiplied by the inverse of the scale matrix.

The final step of the viewing transformation is to project the image onto the two-dimensional view plane. The perspective projection of Section 11-5 performs this, where D is the z value of the view plane. Thus

$$D = \frac{\text{VRPprime}[z]}{(\text{VRPprime}[z] + B)}$$

if the inverse scale matrix is not used. Otherwise, $D = \text{VRPprime}[z]$.

11-8 DISPLAYING THE IMAGE

After the endpoints of the lines that define the image have been transformed to two-dimensional points on the view plane, we still have to determine which lines connect these points. This determination depends on the format of the data structure used to store the original image.

As an example, suppose that the image consists of two triangles sharing an edge (Figure 11-27). These two triangles are described (inefficiently) in consecutive entries in a display file table as follows:

(i)   **move3**(a[x], a[y], a[z]);

(ii)   **draw3**(b[x], b[y], b[z]);

(iii)   **draw3**(d[x], d[y], d[z]);

(iv)   **draw3**(a[x], a[y], a[z]);

(v)   **move3**(c[x], c[y], c[z]);

(vi)   **draw3**(b[x], b[y], b[z]);

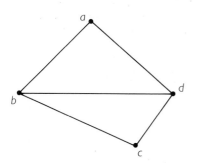

FIGURE 11–27
An image composed of two triangles sharing a common edge

(vii)   **draw3**(d[x], d[y], d[z]);

(viii)   **draw3**(c[x], c[y], c[z]);

Our rule is as follows. If the current command is a *move*, save its endpoints and advance to the next command. If the current command is a *draw*, send that point and the previous point through the viewing transformation and draw the line segment between these projected points.

For this display file, we have the following sequence:

1. Transform point a and save it.
2. Transform point b and draw the line segment using the previous point a.
3. Transform points b and d and draw the line segment.
4. Transform points d and a and draw the line segment.
5. Transform point c and save it.
6. Transform point b and draw the line segment using the previous point c.
7. Transform points b and d and draw the line segment.
8. Transform points d and c and draw the line segment.

It's not necessary to send the same point through the entire viewing transformation twice. However, we must send a pair of preclipped points through the clipping algorithm.

Prior to displaying the image, the window in the graphics package must be set. Its parameters are the values of the window boundary in the view plane. Hence, if the special view volume is used, invoke the command

window$(-D,D,-D,D)$

where $D = $ VRPprime[z]/(VRPprime[z] $+ B$).

Figure 11-28 illustrates in world coordinates several views of a rectangular box centered at the origin and a pyramid with its base on the z-axis. (For clarity, hidden lines are removed. See Chapter 13 for details.) A fish-eye view is obtained by making the line through the COP and the center of the window (viewing direction) intersect the VPN with an angle greater than 80 degrees.

11–9 EFFICIENCY CONSIDERATIONS

The complete viewing transformation has five matrices that must be multiplied: T, Rot, Sh, Sc, and Per. A significant amount of processing time can be saved by combining and even eliminating some of these matrices. For example, T and Rot can be combined into one matrix that

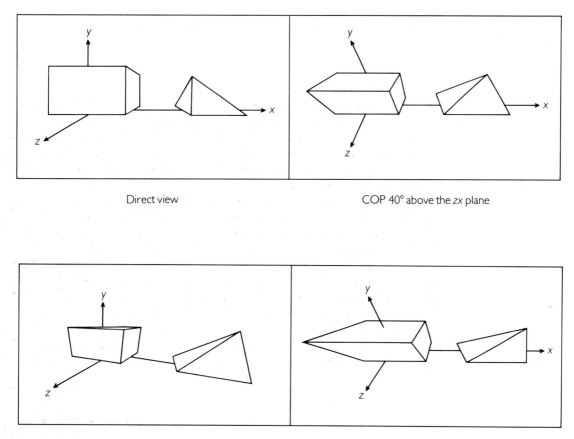

Direct view

COP 40° above the zx plane

Right face clip

COP 45° above the zx plane with a fisheye lens

has the first three rows identical to *Rot*. The last row of this combined matrix has the zero entries replaced by the product of the three translation terms and the 3×3 rotation submatrix—that is, by

$$[Tx \ Ty \ Tz] \begin{bmatrix} ux & vx & wx \\ uy & vy & wy \\ uz & vz & wz \end{bmatrix}.$$

Thus, we have replaced a product of two 4×4 matrices with a much quicker copy of a 3×3 submatrix and a product of a translation vector with this 3×3 matrix.

Similarly the z-shear and the scale matrices can be combined into one matrix, with diagonal entries the same as the scale matrix and zeros everywhere else except for the two shear terms in the third row. The first term is multiplied by *Sx* and the second by *Sy*.

FIGURE 11–28
Several views of a box and a pyramid

Finally, there's no need to use the perspective matrix *Per*. After the clipping is performed, just multiply the *x* and *y* coordinates by *D/z*.

11–10 **CONCLUSION**

In this chapter we described the three-dimensional viewing process that transforms an image as viewed from an arbitrary position to a location on the display screen. Because of the amount of processing time required for matrix multiplication and real-valued arithmetic, most microcomputer graphics display systems restrict the viewing by offering a limited selection of viewing parameters. More sophisticated graphics workstations use special-purpose hardware to perform the complete viewing transformation. In fact, some expensive display systems have a separate special-purpose processor for each step of the viewing process.

EXERCISES

1. Derive the equations for the rotations about the three coordinate axes.
2. Determine the equation of the line passing through the point $(4, -6, 3)$ and having direction $(-9, 7, 1)$.
3. Determine the rotation matrix for a 30-degree counterclockwise rotation about the axis (line) in exercise 2.
4. Suppose that a second two-dimensional coordinate system has its origin at location $(-3, 8)$ and its *y*-coordinate axis is at an angle of 60 degrees in the clockwise direction from the vertical. Find the transformation matrix that converts the second coordinate system to the standard two-dimensional coordinate system.
5. Suppose that a second three-dimensional coordinate system is defined in terms of the standard *x*, *y*, *z* coordinate system by the perpendicular vectors

$$u = \left(\frac{2}{3}, \frac{1}{3}, \frac{2}{3} \right)$$

$$v = \left(\frac{-2}{3}, \frac{2}{3}, \frac{1}{3} \right)$$

$$w = \left(\frac{-1}{2}, \frac{-2}{3}, \frac{2}{3} \right)$$

   Normalize these three vectors and determine the transformation sending *u* to *x*, *v* to *y*, and *w* to *z*.
6. Determine the perspective matrix that has the eye located at $(0, 0, 2)$ and the projection plane parallel to the *x*, *y*-axis passing through the point $(0, 0, 16)$.

7. If the eye is at infinity on the positive z-axis, with view direction looking toward the origin, show that the view direction vector can be represented in homogeneous coordinates by $[0, 0, -1, 0]$.

8. Determine the viewing transformation matrix for a parallel orthogonal projection.

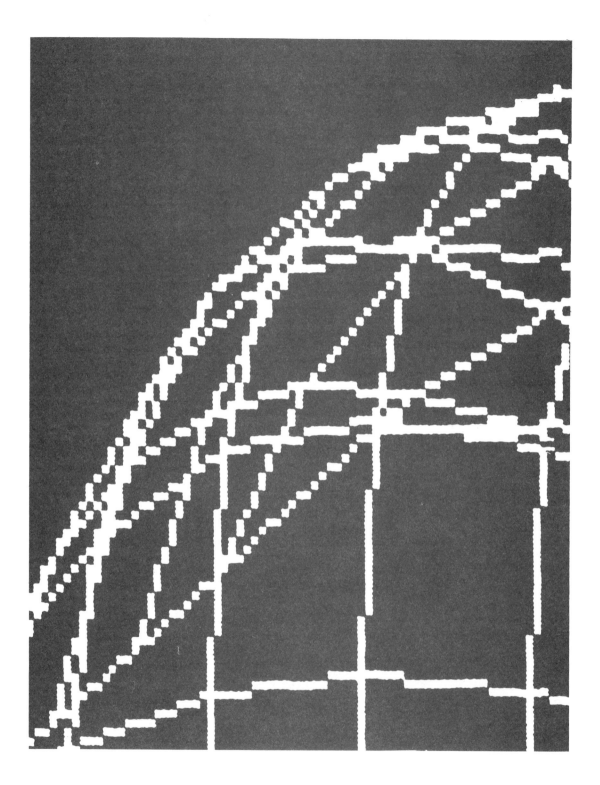

Detail of Figure 12−14

12
CURVES
AND
SURFACES

12–1 **INTRODUCTION**

Our three-dimensional world has many interesting objects of varying shapes and sizes. A cola bottle has a pleasing symmetry that makes it both attractive and useful; a sports car body has a sleek appearance that, at the same time, is aerodynamically efficient. In the 1970s automobile manufacturers and other engineering design groups started using the computer to aid in the design of their products. This chapter is an introduction to some of these design methods.

Two approaches are used to model complex objects. The first technique uses many polygons to approximate a curved surface. By increasing the number of polygons, and decreasing the size of each polygon, any object can be represented with exacting detail. The cola bottle may require several hundred polygons for its representation. Complex objects such as saxophones have been realistically displayed using tens of thousands of polygons. One difficulty with this polygon representation is the amount of space required to store the data structure defining the surface. An even more pressing concern is the amount of time consumed in generating and changing the shape or orientation of a surface. In fact, a simple alteration may require an update of thousands of coordinate values.

A second representation divides the surface into subsurfaces, called **patches,** each of which can be defined mathematically. The boundaries of these patches are mathematically defined curves. The generation of curves and surface patches requires more sophisticated algorithms than are needed to generate polygon approximations. However, a surface can be represented by many fewer patches than polygons. Therefore less space is needed to store the surface description, and modifications to the surface require fewer changes. However, in defense of polygon approximation, we must say that some complex objects (for example, the saxophone) do not have a convenient surface patch representation. This chapter begins with a mathematical description of three-dimensional curves. These techniques are later extended to three-dimensional surfaces[†]. Figure 12-1 illustrates two images created with cubic curves.

12–2 **MATHEMATICS PRELIMINARIES**

Before jumping into the task of generating curves that satisfy specific conditions, let's examine some elementary properties of functions.

[†]For a more comprehensive exposition, the reader is referred to Rogers/Adams, *Mathematical Elements for Computer Graphics*, 1976.

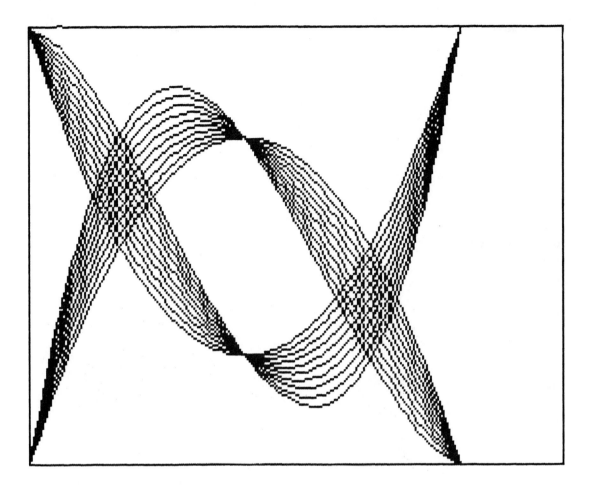

Suppose we are given a finite set of two-dimensional data points:

$$\{(x_0, y_0), (x_1, y_1), \ldots ,(x_N, y_N)\}$$

We want to find a function f, called an **interpolant**, whose curve passes through these $N + 1$ data points. The solution of this problem depends on the specified properties of the interpolating function. For example, if no additional restrictions are placed on the interpolant, a trivial solution is:

$$f(x) = y_i \quad \text{if } x = x_i, \quad i = 0, \ldots , N.$$
$$\quad\;\; = 0 \quad \text{otherwise.}$$

The graph of this function consists of a horizontal line along the x-axis with holes at those points where $y_i \neq 0$ (Figure 12-2 on page 298). One obvious problem with this solution is the curve's lack of continuity. This can easily be corrected by creating a function that consists

FIGURE 12–1
Images produced
using cubic curves

FIGURE 12–2
A graph of a hori-
zontal line with
holes at data points

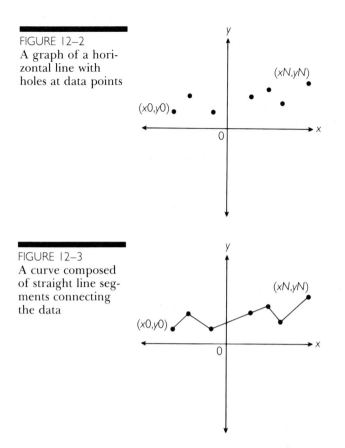

FIGURE 12–3
A curve composed
of straight line seg-
ments connecting
the data

of straight-line segments between adjacent data point (Figure 12-3). Al-though an improvement, this curve is not "smooth" but has corners at the points where the line segments connect.

A polynomial function is continuous and smooth everywhere. It would seem that if we can construct a polynomial whose curve passes through the $N + 1$ data points, our problem may be solved. For ex-ample, the **Lagrange polynomial** is the unique polynomial of degree N passing through these $N + 1$ points. This polynomial interpolant can be thought of as an approximation of some other function passing through these $N + 1$ points. Therefore, the more data points we use, the better our approximation to the original function should be. Un-fortunately, this is not the case.

Since the degree of the Lagrange polynomial is one less than the number of data points, increasing the number of points simply increases the degree of the polynomial. The problem with this is that while the polynomial of degree N passes through these data points, between these points it can oscillate (Figure 12-4). Another problem with high-degree

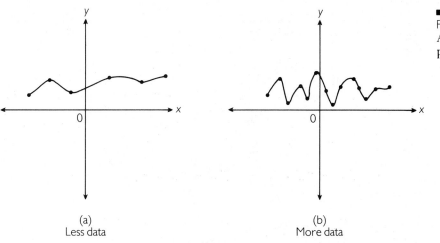

FIGURE 12–4
An oscillation
problem

(a)
Less data

(b)
More data

polynomials is the amount of computations required to evaluate them. Straightforward calculations require N additions and $2 \times N - 1$ multiplications for N degree polynomials. Nested multiplication (Horner's method) reduces this to N additions and N multiplications. In either case, though, these calculations must be performed for each x in the interval where the polynomial is defined. These and other reasons make the Lagrange polynomial unattractive for our use.

Another approach is to look for a polynomial of fewer degrees than N passing through these $N + 1$ data points. In general, this is not possible. However, we can combine polynomials of lesser degree passing through several consecutive data points, as we did with straight-line segments (Figure 12-5). The problem with this method is that the overall

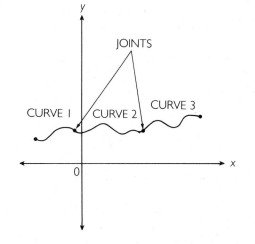

FIGURE 12–5
Polynomials joined
at the data points

JOINTS

CURVE 1   CURVE 2   CURVE 3

curve is not smooth at the joints. This is not an insurmountable problem, though, since it is possible to describe "smoothness" conditions at the data points and obtain a polynomial having these properties. This technique of smoothly piecing curves together is called **blending**. It is a process we shall use throughout the chapter.

The three-dimensional curves that we'll be examining have their functions expressed in parametric form:

$x = x(t)$
$y = y(t)$ t is a real number.
$z = z(t)$.

For a given real-value t, each point, $p = p(t)$, on the curve has coordinates $(x(t), y(t), z(t))$.

Recall that we used this parametric representation in Chapter 11 to define a straight line. There are several reasons for using parametric equations. For our use, their main advantage is in describing curves that have vertical tangents. For example, a circle with radius r centered at the origin has parametric equations

$x = r \times \cos(t)$
$y = r \times \sin(t)$ $0 <= t <= 2\pi$
$z = 0$.

This circle has vertical tangents where it crosses the x-axis (Figure 12-6). The slope of the tangent line is the first derivative of the function, and vertical tangents have derivatives equal to infinity. However, this derivative can be expressed as a ratio of two finite slopes:

$$dy/dx = \frac{(dy/dt)}{(dx/dt)}$$

FIGURE 12–6
A circle with infinite slope when $y = 0$

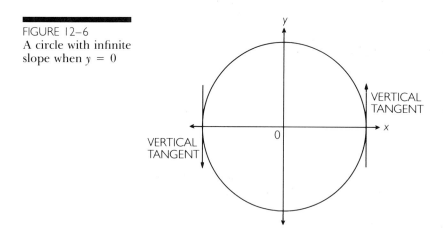

Curves and Surfaces

For the circle

$$dy/dt = r \times \cos(t), \qquad dx \cdot dt = -r \times \sin(t).$$

There is a vertical tangent when $t = 0$: $x = 1$ and $y = 0$. At this point,

$$dy/dt = 1 \qquad \text{and} \qquad dx/dt = 0.$$

One additional observation: In computer graphics, as opposed to numerical analysis, we are not totally concerned with generating a polynomial function that accurately approximates another function. Our objective is to obtain a curve that has a certain appearance while satisfying some properties. This attractiveness criterion can be completely subjective and dependent on the application.

We are now ready to describe some three-dimensional curves.

12-3 **CUBIC SPLINES**

A **cubic spline** has the property that the three coordinate functions, $x(t)$, $y(t)$, and $z(t)$, are each cubic polynomials in the variable t:

$$x(t) = at^3 + bt^2 + ct + d$$
$$y(t) = et^3 + ft^2 + gt + h$$
$$z(t) = jt^3 + kt^2 + lt + m.$$

Since our concern is with curve segments, the domain of t is finite and we shall assume that $0 <= t <= 1$.

A spline passes through two points and satisfies a differentiability condition at each of these endpoints. These four conditions require a polynomial degree of at least 3. That's why cubic splines are so popular. If $N + 1$ data points are given, we must blend together N cubic splines. Equal derivatives at the endpoints of each spline ensure smoothness at these joints (Figure 12-7).

The derivations of the cubic polynomials for x, y, and z are similar. The only difference is the assigned values for the endpoint data and derivatives. For this reason, we describe only the equation for $x(t)$. Given $N + 1$ data points

$$(x_0, y_0, z_0), (x_1, y_1, z_1), (x_2, y_2, z_2), \ldots, (x_N, y_N, z_N),$$

we want to obtain the cubic spline joining two consecutive points. Recall

FIGURE 12-7
Four cubic splines blended with equal derivatives at endpoints

that the values of the parameter t range from 0 to 1 for each spline. For each pair of points x_i, x_{i+1} our assumptions are:

1. The spline curve passes through these two endpoints:

    $x(0) = x_i$
    $x(1) = x_{i+1}$

2. The spline satisfies a differentiability condition at these points. Thus
    $x'(0)$ and $x'(1)$
    are known, where the prime represents differentiation with respect to t.

Since $x(t) = at^3 + bt^2 + ct + d$, differentiating with respect to t gives

$x'(t) = 3at^2 + 2bt + c.$

Substituting the values $t = 0$ and $t = 1$ into these equations gives

12–1 $x(0) = d$
       $x(1) = a + b + c + \mathrm{d}$
       $x'(0) = c$
       $x'(1) = 3a + 2b + c.$

This is a linear system of four equations having four unknowns: a, b, c, and d. Solving for the unique solution gives

$a = 2x(0) - 2x(1) + x'(0) + x'(1)$
$b = -3x(0) + 3x(1) - 2x'(0) - x'(1)$
$c = x'(0)$
$d = x(0).$

In terms of matrices:

$$(12\text{–}2) \quad \begin{bmatrix} a \\ b \\ c \\ d \end{bmatrix} = \begin{bmatrix} 2 & -2 & 1 & 1 \\ -3 & 3 & -2 & -1 \\ 0 & 0 & 1 & 0 \\ 1 & 0 & 0 & 0 \end{bmatrix} \begin{bmatrix} x(0) \\ x(1) \\ x'(0) \\ x'(1) \end{bmatrix}.$$

The coefficients of the cubic spline polynomials $y(t)$ and $z(t)$ are similarly obtained by replacing the x data and derivative values by the y and z data and derivative values, respectively.

To draw a cubic spline between two consecutive data points, we compute several values of $x(t)$, $y(t)$, and $z(t)$ where t assumes values between 0 and 1. Line segments connect the computed values. The following procedure, Compute_x_Spline, evaluates $x(t)$ between two data points $x0$ and $x1$ having derivatives $x0$prime, $x1$prime.

Assume the following Pascal environment.

```
var
    x, y, z : array[1..21] of real;     {21 data points}

Procedure Compute_x_Spline (x0,x1,     {endpoints}
        x0prime,x1prime     {derivatives}: real);

    var
        t,incr,                             {parameter increment values}
        a,b,c,d : real;                     {spline coefficients}
        step : integer;                     {array index}
    begin
        {solve for coefficients}
        a := 2*x0 − 2*x1 + x0prime + x1prime;
        b := −3*x0 + 3*x1 − 2*x0prime − x1prime;
        c := x1prime;
        d := x0;
        {initialize array index}
        step := 1;
        incr := 0.05;     {20 increments of t}
        t := 0;
        while t <= 1 do
            begin     {while}
                x[step] := a*t*t*t + b*t*t + c*t + d;
                step := step + 1;
                t := t + incr
            end     {while}
    end;     {Compute_x_Spline}
```

Twenty-one values are similarly computed for $y(t)$ and $z(t)$. The spline curve is drawn using the three-dimensional drawing commands:

```
move3(x[1],y[1],z[1]);
for i := 2 to 21 do
    draw3(x[i],y[i],z[i]);
```

The display screen cannot actually draw in three dimensions and these three-dimensional drawing commands are in reality two-dimensional draws of the orthogonal projection; that is, the z coordinate is eliminated. (See Section 12-6 for additional discussion of three-dimensional drawing.) If we want to have a realistic image, the coordinates of the curve must be sent through the entire perspective transformation procedure. Figure 12-8 on page 304 illustrates three blended cubic spline curves.

There are several other formulations of cubic splines. Some of them allow the specification of second-order differentiability at the joints. The problem with these, as with the one described earlier, is that the spline

FIGURE 12–8
Cubic splines

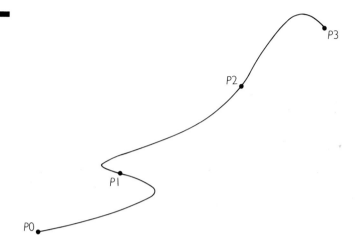

curves are often created in an interactive environment, and the user has no idea as to the values at the joints of the three derivatives: $x'(t)$, $y'(t)$, $z'(t)$. The next section illustrates a class of curves that allows the user to describe these "smoothness" conditions easily.

12–4 **BEZIER CURVES**

P. Bezier developed these curves while working for the Renault automobile company in France. We shall examine here only the Bezier cubic polynomial. As with cubic splines, Bezier curves are blended at the joints.

A (cubic) **Bezier curve** is completely determined by four consecutive points: (x_0, y_0, z_0), (x_1, y_1, z_1), (x_2, y_2, z_2), (x_3, y_3, z_3). The curve follows the polygonal line segment through these four **control points** but only passes through the first and fourth data points (Figure 12-9). The two intermediate points are used to define the slope of the curve at the endpoints. We shall derive only the equations for the x variable — y and z are similar. Let

$$x(t) = at^3 + bt^2 + ct + d \qquad 0 <= t <= 1$$

Our assumptions are

1. The curve passes through the endpoints:

$$x(0) = x_0$$
$$x(1) = x_3$$

2. The slope at the endpoints is determined by the endpoint and the

Curves and Surfaces

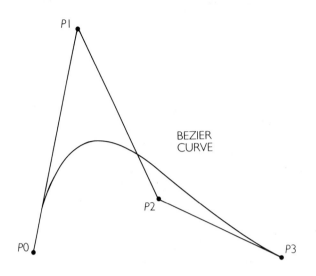

P1

BEZIER
CURVE

P2

P0

P3

FIGURE 12–9
A Bezier curve and
its four control
points

adjacent point. The coefficient 3 is a result of the fact that the derivative of x^3 is $3x^2$:

$$x'(0) = 3(x_1 - x_0)$$
$$x'(1) = 3(x_3 - x_2)$$

Substituting these values into the left-hand side of equation 12-1 and
simplifying, we get

$$a = -x_0 + 3x_1 - 3x_2 + x_3$$
$$b = 3x_0 - 6x_1 + 3x_2$$
$$c = -3x_0 + 3x_1$$
$$d = x_0.$$

In terms of matrices, this can be expressed as:

$$\begin{bmatrix} a \\ b \\ c \\ d \end{bmatrix} = \begin{bmatrix} -1 & 3 & -3 & 1 \\ 3 & -6 & 3 & 0 \\ -3 & 3 & 0 & 0 \\ 1 & 0 & 0 & 0 \end{bmatrix} \begin{bmatrix} x_0 \\ x_1 \\ x_2 \\ x_3 \end{bmatrix}.$$

Letting M represent this 4×4 matrix, the cubic polynomial $x(t)$ can be
compactly represented as

$$(12\text{--}3) \quad x(t) = [t^3 \; t^2 \; t \; 1] \times M \times \begin{bmatrix} x_0 \\ x_1 \\ x_2 \\ x_3 \end{bmatrix}.$$

FIGURE 12–10
A circle composed
of four Bezier
curves

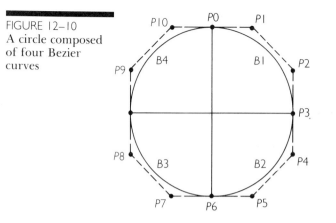

If the coefficients are substituted into the equation for $x(t)$ and those terms are rearranged, we get an equivalent and more popular representation

$$x(t) = (1 - t)^3 x_0 + 3t(1 - t)^2 x_1 + 3t^2(1 - t)x_2 + t^3 x_3.$$

The Pascal procedure to compute $x(t)$ is similar to Compute_x_ Spline except for the different values of the coefficients a, b, c, and d.

Observe that if B_1 is a Bezier curve corresponding to the points P_0, P_1, P_2, and P_3, and B_2 is the Bezier curve corresponding to the points P_3, P_4, P_5, and P_6, then the combined curve is differentiable at the joint

FIGURE 12–11
Snoopy, specified by
a series of Bezier
curves

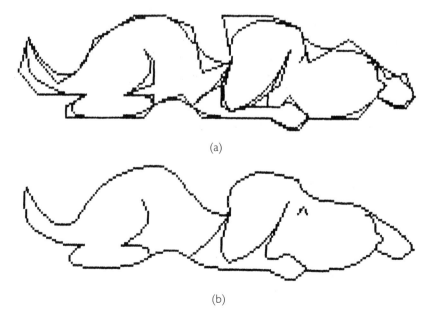

(a)

(b)

P_3 only if the points P_2, P_3, and P_4 are collinear (lie on a straight line). This is a consequence of the fact that the slope is determined by the endpoints and the adjacent points. Figure 12-10 illustrates this by constructing a circle using four piece-wise Bezier curves.

The advantage of Bezier over cubic splines should now be clear. The direction of the curve (the derivatives) at the joints can be defined and changed simply by specifying the second (initial slope) and third (final slope) data points.

It is important to observe that a Bezier curve does not pass through all four data points. The two intermediary control points are used to control the shape of the curve passing through the first and fourth points. If the Bezier curve is to pass through all $N + 1$ data points, it is necessary to specify two intermediary control points between each pair of data points. Figure 12-11 illustrates a Bezier curve construction of Charles Schultz's "Snoopy."

Changing a control point not only affects the shape of the curve near that control point, but also has an influence throughout the entire span of the curve. This lack of local control is one of the weaknesses of Bezier curves. B-spline curves are a class of curves having this local shape property. In fact, Bezier curves are a special class of B-spline curves.[†]

12-5 **BICUBIC BEZIER SURFACES**

A three-dimensional point P on a surface can be described in parametric form by the equation

$$P(s, t) = [x(s, t), y(s, t), z(s, t)],$$

where each of the x, y, z coordinates are functions of the real-valued numbers s and t. By restricting the two parameters s and t to some rectangular subset between 0 and 1, a finite surface patch is described (Figure 12-12 on page 308). **Bicubic patches** have the property that each of the functions $x(s, t)$, $y(s, t)$, and $z(s, t)$ is a cubic polynomial in the variables s and t. As with curves, we shall describe only the equation for $x(s, t)$. Let

$$x(s,t) = \begin{matrix} a_{11}s^3t^3 & + a_{12}s^3 t^2 & + a_{13}s^3t & + a_{14}s^3 \\ a_{21}s^2t^3 & + a_{22}s^2t^2 & + a_{23}s^2t & + a_{24}s^2 \\ a_{31}st^3 & + a_{32}st^2 & + a_{33}st & + a_{34}s \\ a_{41}t^3 & + a_{42}t^2 & + a_{43}t & + a_{44} \end{matrix}.$$

[†]The interested reader should see Rogers/Adams, *Mathematical Elements for Computer Graphics*, 1976, for additional information on B-splines.

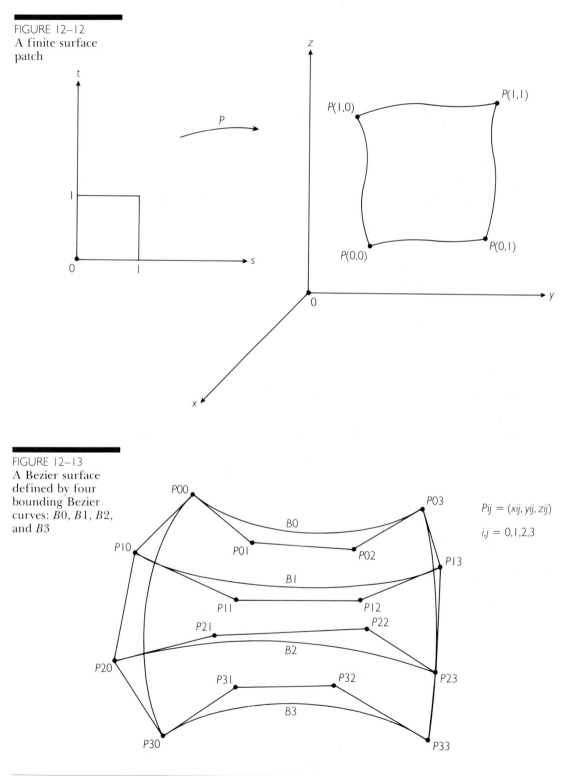

This equation has 16 unknown coefficients a_{ij}. Given 16 pairs of points s, t, we can solve this linear system of 16 equations for the 16 unknowns. The matrix of this system has 16 rows and 16 columns—a "monster" to solve. Instead of attacking this generalized surface problem, we shall assume that the bicubic surface patch has four Bezier curves as its boundaries. This has the combined effect of reducing the computations required to obtain the surface equation while making the user specification and manipulation of the surface patch easier.

We defined a Bezier curve by the parametric equation:

$$x(s) = [s^3 \ s^2 \ s \ 1] \times M \times \begin{bmatrix} x_0 \\ x_1 \\ x_2 \\ x_3 \end{bmatrix} \qquad 0 <= s <= 1.$$

Suppose that these four points, $x_0 = x_{00}$, $x_1 = x_{10}$, $x_2 = x_{20}$, and $x_3 = x_{30}$ are (the x coordinates of) the initial points of four distinct Bezier curves defined by the t parameter (Figure 12-13). This can be interpreted as saying that

$$(12\text{–}4) \quad x(s, t) = [s^3 \ s^2 \ s \ 1] \times M \times \begin{bmatrix} x_0(t) \\ x_1(t) \\ x_2(t) \\ x_3(t) \end{bmatrix} \qquad \begin{array}{l} 0 <= t <= 1 \\ 0 <= s <= 1. \end{array}$$

is a bicubic Bezier surface, where

$x_0(0) = x_{00}$, $x_1(0) = x_{10}$, $x_2(0) = x_{20}$, and $x_3(0) = x_{30}$.
$x_0(1) = x_{03}$, $x_1(1) = x_{13}$, $x_2(1) = x_{23}$, and $x_3(1) = x_{33}$.

Since the $x_i(t)$, $i = 0$ to 3, are Bezier curves, each can be expressed as

$$x_i(t) = [t^3 \ t^2 \ t \ 1] \times M \times \begin{bmatrix} x_{i0} \\ x_{i1} \\ x_{i2} \\ x_{i3} \end{bmatrix} \qquad 0 <= t <= 1.$$

These four $x_i(t)$ Bezier curves can be represented in matrix notation:

$$[x_0(t) \ x_1(t) \ x_2(t) \ x_3(t)] = [t^3 \ t^2 \ t \ 1] \times M \times \begin{bmatrix} x_{00} & x_{10} & x_{20} & x_{30} \\ x_{01} & x_{11} & x_{21} & x_{31} \\ x_{02} & x_{12} & x_{22} & x_{32} \\ x_{03} & x_{13} & x_{23} & x_{33} \end{bmatrix}.$$

Taking the transpose of both sides using the identity $(abc)^T = c^T \ b^T \ a^T$, we get

$$\begin{bmatrix} x_0(t) \\ x_1(t) \\ x_2(t) \\ x_3(t) \end{bmatrix} = \begin{bmatrix} x_{00} & x_{01} & x_{02} & x_{03} \\ x_{10} & x_{11} & x_{12} & x_{13} \\ x_{20} & x_{21} & x_{22} & x_{23} \\ x_{30} & x_{31} & x_{32} & x_{33} \end{bmatrix} \times M^T \times \begin{bmatrix} t^3 \\ t^2 \\ t \\ 1 \end{bmatrix} \qquad 0 <= t <= 1.$$

Designating the 4×4 data matrix by B and substituting into equation 12-4 gives

$$(12\text{–}5) \quad x(s,t) = [s^3 \; s^2 \; s \; 1] \times M \times B \times M^T \times \begin{bmatrix} t^3 \\ t^2 \\ t \\ 1 \end{bmatrix} \qquad \begin{array}{l} 0 <= s <= 1 \\ 0 <= t <= 1. \end{array}$$

This is the surface equation we want. It expresses the x coordinates of a Bezier bicubic surface patch in terms of 16 defining data points given in the B matrix. Similar equations exist for the y and z coordinates. Figures 12-14 and 12-15 illustrate two Bezier surfaces created using the 16 indicated points. An orthogonal projection was used, thereby eliminating the need for the z component. Observe that only the four corner points (x_{00}, y_{00}), (x_{03}, y_{03}), (x_{30}, y_{30}), and (x_{33}, y_{33}) must lie on the surface.

Since the matrix M is independent of the data points, changing a patch requires only a modification of the 4×4 B matrix. Of course, the three matrices must be remultiplied. Notice also that the matrix M equals its transpose M^T.

Figure 12.16 on page 312 illustrates two Bezier surface patches joined along a common edge. To guarantee smoothness across this edge, the following conditions must be satisfied:

FIGURE 12–14
Bezier surface and control points

1. The four points defining the common edge are equal:
    $P_{i3} = Q_{i0}$, $i = 0, 1, 2, 3$.

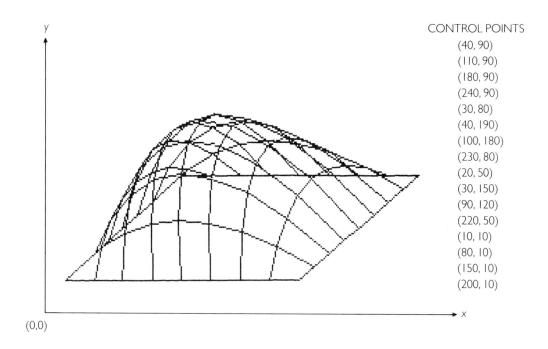

y

(0,0)

x

CONTROL POINTS
(40, 90)
(110, 90)
(180, 90)
(240, 90)
(30, 80)
(40, 190)
(100, 180)
(230, 80)
(20, 50)
(30, 150)
(90, 120)
(220, 50)
(10, 10)
(80, 10)
(150, 10)
(200, 10)

Curves and Surfaces

2. The following four sets of triples are collinear: (P_{02}, P_{03}, Q_{01}), (P_{12}, P_{13}, Q_{11}), (P_{22}, P_{23}, Q_{21}), and (P_{32}, P_{33}, Q_{31}).

3. The length of the four line segments defined by these triples is equal, up to a fixed constant multiple:

$$\text{length } (P_{i2}, Q_{i1}) = \text{const} \times \text{length } (P_{j2}, Q_{j1}) \qquad \begin{array}{l} i, j = 0, 1, 2, 3 \\ \text{and} \quad i \neq j. \end{array}$$

We could derive the equations for a bicubic spline surface patch in much the same way as we have just done for the Bezier patch. The matrix M is replaced by the corresponding 4×4 matrix in equation 12-2. The problem is with the corresponding B matrix. For splines, this matrix has four mixed partial derivatives. In most situations, the values

FIGURE 12–15
Bezier surface and
control points

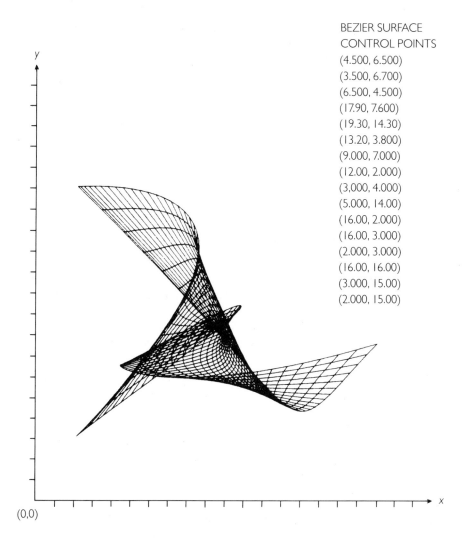

BEZIER SURFACE
CONTROL POINTS
(4.500, 6.500)
(3.500, 6.700)
(6.500, 4.500)
(17.90, 7.600)
(19.30, 14.30)
(13.20, 3.800)
(9.000, 7.000)
(12.00, 2.000)
(3,000, 4.000)
(5.000, 14.00)
(16.00, 2.000)
(16.00, 3.000)
(2.000, 3.000)
(16.00, 16.00)
(3.000, 15.00)
(2.000, 15.00)

(0,0)

FIGURE 12–16
Bezier surface
patches

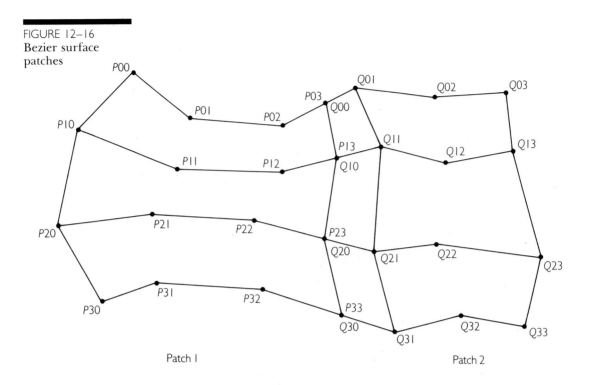

Patch 1   Patch 2

of these derivatives are totally unknown, making it difficult to have the
necessary control over the creation and modification of the patch. For
our needs, the Bezier surface should be an adequate design tool.

12–6 **DISPLAY ALGORITHM**

Surface patches are displayed by drawing curves on the surface that
are defined by constant s and constant t values. If the variable incr is
the increment between successive s and t values, there are **trunc**$(1/\text{incr})$
+ 1 values of s and t from 0 to 1. The following procedures generate
and display a parallel projection of a Bezier surface. An increment of
0.2 is chosen; thus the s and t parameters assume six values from 0 to
1, resulting in 36 points and 12 curves.

Assume the following Pascal environment:

```
type
    matrix = array[1..4,1..4] of real;
    point = array[1..4] of real;
    plot = array[1..6,1..6] of real;
```

var

M,	{*matrix M, which is also its transpose*}	
xB,yB,	{*B matrices for x and y data*}	
xresult,	{*M × xB × Mtrans*}	
yresult	{*M × yB × Mtrans*}	: matrix;
x,y	{*x and y values for curves*}	: plot;
s,	{*s vector*}	
t,temp	{*t vector and a temporary one*}	: point;
i,j	{*loop counters*}	: **integer**;
svalue,	{*s parameter values*}	
tvalue	{*t parameter values*}	: **real**;

We assume the existence of the procedures Multiply_Mat and Multiply_Vec. The first multiplies two matrices; the second multiplies a vector and a matrix (see Chapter 11 for their implementation). The following function Vector_Mult multiplies a 1 × 4 row vector by a 4 × 1 row vector. It returns a scalar (real number).

Function Vector_Mult(v1,v2 : point):**real;**
      {**v1** *is a 1 × 4 vector,* **v2** *is a 4 × 1 vector*}

   begin
      Vector_Mult: =
      v1[1]*v2[1] + v1[2]*v2[2] + v1[3]*v2[3] + v1[4]*v2[4]
   end; {*Vector_Mult*}

The next procedure sets the values of the 1 × 4 s vector and the 4 × 1 t vector depending on the value of the parameters s and t.

Procedure set_s_t (svalue,tvalue: **real**);

   begin
      t[1] := tvalue*tvalue*tvalue;
      t[2] := tvalue*tvalue;
      t[3] := tvalue;
      t[4] := 1;
      s[1] := svalue*svalue*svalue;
      s[2] := svalue*svalue;
      s[3] := svalue;
      s[4] := 1
   end;

Procedure Compute_Points evaluates equation 12-5 to determine the 36 points that define the 12 curves on the Bezier surface. Recall that M equals its transpose.

Procedure Compute_Points;

   begin
      {*enter 16 x and y data points of xB and yB matrices in row order*}
      for i := 1 **to** 4 **do**

```
            for j := 1 to 4 do
                readln(xB[i.j],yB[i,j]);
        {build the M matrix}
        M[1,1] := −1; M[1,2] :=    3; M[1,3] := −3; M[1,4] := 1;
        M[2,1] :=    3; M[2,2] := −6; M[2,3] :=    3; M[2,4] := 0;
        M[3,1] := −3; M[3,2] :=    3; M[3,3] :=    0; M[3,4] := 0;
        M[4,1] :=    1; M[4,2] :=    0; M[4,3] :=    0; M[4,4] := 0;
        {M × xB}
        Multiply_Mat(M,xB,xresult);
        {M × xB × Mtranspose}
        Multiply_Mat(xresult,M,xresult);
        {M × yB}
        Multiply_Mat(M,yB,yresult);
        {M × yB × Mtranspose}
        Multiply_Mat(yresult,M,yresult);
        {initialization}
        tvalue := 0;
        j := 1; {t parameter}
    {compute x(s, t) and y(s, t)}
    while tvalue <= 1 do
        begin {while}
            svalue := 0;
            i := 1; {s parameter}
            while svalue <= 1 do
                begin {while}
                    set_s_t(svalue,tvalue);
                    {s vector times M × xE × Mtranspose}
                    Multiply_Vec(xresult,s,temp);
                    {above result times column vector t}
                    x[i,j] := Vector_Mult(temp,t);
                    {same two steps for yB matrix}
                    Multiply_Vec(yresult,s,temp);
                    y[i,j] := Vector_Mult(temp,t);
                    {increment s parameter and corresponding i index}
                    i := i+1;
                    svalue := svalue + 0.2
                end; {while}
            {increment t parameter and corresponding j index}
            j := j+1;
            tvalue := tvalue + 0.2;
        end {while};
    end; {Compute_Points}
```

The final procedure, Display_Surface, displays 12 curves of the parallel projection of the Bezier surface using the two data arrays x and y.

```
Procedure Display_Surface;
    begin
        for i := 1 to 6 do
```

```
        begin {for}
            {draw curves of constant s by varying t}
            move2(x[i,1],y[i,1]);
            for j := 2 to 6 do
                draw2(x[i,j],y[i,j])
        end; {for}
    for j := 1 to 6 do
        begin {for}
            {draw curves of constant t by varying s}
            move2(x[1,j],y[1,j]);
            for i := 2 to 6 do
                draw2(x[i,j],y[i,j])
        end {for}
end {Display_Surface}
```

12–7 SURFACE OF REVOLUTION

A **surface of revolution** is produced by revolving a two-dimensional region about an axis. We restrict our discussion here to the specialized situation of revolving a Bezier curve about the y-axis. This technique has been used to create several interesting and striking images (Figure 12-17 on page 316).

A Bezier curve is rotated in equal increments for 360 degrees about the y-axis. To be more precise, those points on the curve generated by the Bezier equations are rotated. At each step, a new curve is drawn using the rotated points. The circular cross sections are formed by drawing line segments from points on the original curve to the rotated points.

If the surface of revolution created this way is drawn using a parallel projection (dropping the z coordinate), it has a flat two-dimensional appearance. We could enhance the realism of the image by sending it through the perspective transformation. However, there is an easier way to produce this realistic effect—that is, rotate the surface a small amount about the x-axis. This method produced both images in Figure 12-17.

Procedure Revolve_Surface accomplishes this task. Three two-dimensional arrays are used to store the x, y, and z coordinate values of the rotated curves. The first dimension represents the rotated curve number and the second dimension represents the points on the curve. Those points lying on the first, original curve have already been obtained from a Bezier curve-generating procedure. We perform the rotation about the y-axis by using the transformation equations instead of the slower matrix multiplication. Before issuing three-dimensional move and draw commands, we invoke the graphics command Rx(angle); this rotates the surface about the x-axis, tilting it in the direction of the viewer. Three-dimensional drawing commands are used since Rx(angle) needs the z (and y) coordinate to perform rotation about the x-axis.

```
Procedure Revolve_Surface(
                    angle:real {x-axis rotation});

    const
            pi = 3.14159;
            numb_of_curves = 10; {number of curves}
            numb_of_points = 15; {number of points on each curve}

    var
        curve,                      {rotated curve number}
        point :integer;            {point on the curve}
        inside : boolean;          {inside boundary of surface}
        theta : real;              {y rotation angle}

    begin
        {generate rotated points}
        theta := 2*pi/numb_of_curves;
        for curve := 2 to numb_of_curves do
            for point := 1 to numb_of_points do
                begin {for}
                    {equations for y rotation: the new point on
                    next curve is obtained from previous curve}
                    x[curve,point] := x[curve − 1,point]*cos(theta) +
                                        z[curve − 1,point]*sin(theta);
                    y[curve,point] := y[curve − 1,point];
                    z[curve,point] := − x[curve − 1,point]*sin(theta) +
                                        z[curve − 1,point]*cos(theta)
                end; {for}
        {draw Bezier curves}
        Rx(angle);
        {the following points are rotated about x-axis}
        for curve := 1 to numb_of_curves do
            for point := 1 to numb_of_points do
                if point = 1 then {first point}
                    move3(x[1,point],y[1,point],z[1,point])
                else
                    draw3(x[curve,point],y[curve,point],z[curve,point]);
        {draw cross sections—the last draw is back to original curve}
        {not finished}
        inside := true;
        {first point}
        point := 1;
        while inside do
            begin {while}
                if point >= numb_of_points then
                    begin {if}
                        {draw last cross section}
                        point := numb_of_points;
                        {completed surface}
                        inside := false
                    end; {if}
```

FIGURE 12–17
Surfaces of
revolution

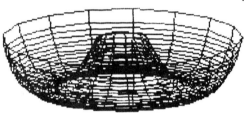

(a)

(b)

Curves and Surfaces

```
            for curve := 1 to numb_of_curves + 1 do
        begin {for}
                {go back to first curve}
                if curve = 1 then
                        {at first curve}
                        move3(x[1,point],y[1,point],z[1,point])
                else
                        if curve <> numb_of_curves + 1 then
                                {not back to first curve}
                                draw3(x[curve,point],y[curve,point],
                                        z[curve,point])
                        else
                                {complete circle by drawing back to first curve}
                                draw3(x[1,point],y[1,point],z[1,point])
                end; {for}
                {use every sixth computed point to draw cross-sectional curves}
                point := point + 5
        end {while}
    end; {Revolve_Surface}
```

12–8 **CONCLUSION**

This chapter examined several mathematically generated curves and surfaces. Each curve and surface was defined by a set of data points that controlled its shape. The control points are used to determine points on the curve or surface, each of which is displayed by connecting these points with line segments. Many fascinating and realistic objects have been produced using the techniques in this chapter. The reader is encouraged to let his or her imagination run wild when entering the defining control points. Some of the more interesting and bizarre objects have resulted from unplanned input. In the next chapter we will examine some techniques that make our images even more realistic.

EXERCISES

1. Horner's method rewrites the cubic polynomial $ax^3 + bx^2 + cx + d$ as $((ax + b)x + c)x + d$. The original representation requires three additions and five multiplications. How many additions and multiplications are there using Horner's representation?
2. Use Horner's method to reduce the computational time in all curve equations.
3. Construct an ellipse using Bezier curves.
4. Design an automobile body using Bezier surface patches.
5. Design a wine glass as a surface of revolution.

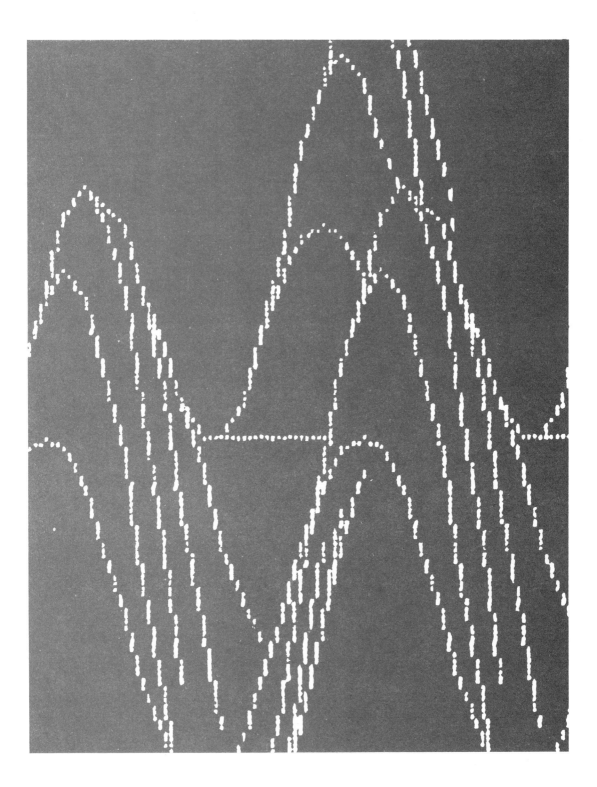

Detail of Figure 13–15

13
HIDDEN-SURFACE PROBLEM

13–1 **INTRODUCTION**

Realistic computer-generated images have the property that surfaces and edges that are not visible to the viewer are eliminated from the display. Those portions of the image that are visible and those that are hidden depend on the position and orientation of the center of projection (the eye). Images displayed without hidden surface removal look cluttered and make it difficult for the viewer to determine which object lies in front of another (Figure 13-1).

There are two approaches to solving the hidden-surface problem. The first describes objects in terms of polygonal surfaces. Each surface has a specific shade or color, and each pixel on the display screen is illuminated according to which surface is visible at that point. If no surface is visible at a pixel location, a background color is assigned to that pixel. Algorithms that attack the problem this way are called **image-space** algorithms.

The second approach considers the image to be made up of line segments; no shades or colors are used to describe the individual objects. An **object-space** algorithm displays only those line segments that are not obscured by any surface. Since most microcomputer systems have limited shading and color capabilities, object-space algorithms are often used to solve the hidden-surface problem, called the hidden-line problem, for these edge-defined objects. Our solution uses an object-space priority sort algorithm. We choose this approach since it incorporates

FIGURE 13–1
Hidden-line
removal

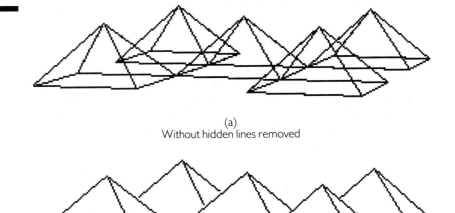

(a)
Without hidden lines removed

(b)
With hidden lines removed

Hidden-Surface Problem

some of the more sophisticated techniques while keeping the solution manageable. An image-space algorithm can be used to solve the hidden-line problem by illuminating only the edges of polygonal surfaces. We shall assume that all objects in the image are closed polyhedra, which are constructed using convex polygons.

13–2 **BACK FACE REMOVAL**

A polygon has two faces, an inside and an outside. We define the **outside face** to be the face that may be seen from some position outside the closed polyhedron. The **inside face**, on the other hand, cannot be seen when viewed from any position outside the object. Not all outside faces of a three-dimensional object are visible to the viewer. Some faces are on the back side of the object, facing away from the viewer, and are therefore hidden by other outside faces of the object. **Back face removal** is the process that eliminates these hidden faces. Figure 13-2 illustrates two objects, one with and one without back face removal.

FIGURE 13–2
Back face removal

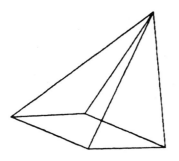
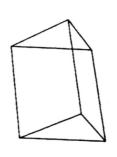

(a)
Without back face removal

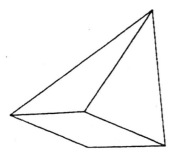
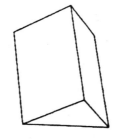

(b)
With back face removal

The first task of back face removal is to decide on a method of identifying the outside faces that are visible from a position outside the object. We choose the convention that a visible face is described by a clockwise listing of its vertices. The cube in Figure 13-3 has its top, outside facing surface (S), a square, defined by the listing

S: P1, P2, P3, P4.

If this face, as seen from the viewer (COP), is not obscured by any other faces of the cube, the face is deemed visible, and a clockwise listing of S starting with vertex P1 gives this ordered list. However, if the COP is below the cube, for example, S is not visible and a clockwise listing starting with P1 gives the order P1, P4, P3, P2. (To see this, number the four corners of a piece of paper as in Figure 13-3. Looking at the paper from any position where the numbers are visible gives the clockwise ordering P1, P2, P3, P4. Now lift the paper up and hold it toward the light so that you're looking underneath it but are still able to see the numbered vertices. Start at vertex P1 and go in a clockwise direction. Your ordering should be P1, P4, P3, P2.)

We are able to conclude from this discussion that an outside face is visible from the center of projection (COP) only if the viewed clockwise ordering of its vertices agrees with the original listing. If the outside face is visible, the polygon defining that face is displayed; otherwise, it is a back face and is not displayed. While this rule is easy for us to apply, it's difficult to construct an algorithm using it in its current form. We shall, however, use this ordering scheme to construct vectors, which make back face testing simpler.

Let $\mathbf{R} = P2 - P1$ be the vector (edge) from $P1$ to $P2$, and let $\mathbf{Q} = P3 - P2$ be the vector (edge) from $P2$ to $P3$ (Figure 13-4a). Observe that these vectors follow the clockwise description of the polygon S. In Chapter 11, we saw that the cross product of two noncollinear vectors is a vector perpendicular to these two vectors. Thus

$$\mathbf{N} = \mathbf{R} \times \mathbf{Q}$$

is a vector perpendicular to the S polygon having $\mathbf{R}$ and $\mathbf{Q}$ as edges. In the left-hand eye coordinate system, the vector $\mathbf{N}$ points in the direction of the outside face (Figure 13-4a and 13-4b).

Since $\mathbf{N}$ gives the direction of the outside face, an outside face is visible from the COP if $\mathbf{N}$ points toward the COP. Our next task is to determine in what direction $\mathbf{N}$ is pointing.

Let $\mathbf{P}$ be a vector from the COP to the polygon S. From Figure 13-4a–13-4d we see that an outside face is visible if the angle between $\mathbf{P}$ and $\mathbf{N}$ is between 90 and 180 degrees. If the angle is between 0 and 90 degrees, the face is not visible and should not be displayed. How can we determine this angle between $\mathbf{P}$ and $\mathbf{N}$?

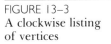

FIGURE 13–3
A clockwise listing of vertices

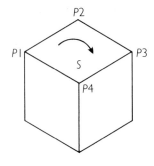

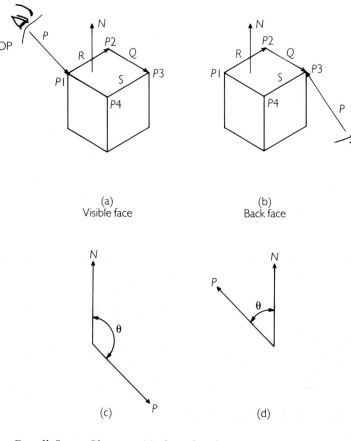

FIGURE 13–4
Determining visible
and back faces

(a)
Visible face

(b)
Back face

(c)

(d)

Recall from Chapter 11 that the dot product of two vectors is the product of the length of the vectors times the cosine of the angle between them:

$$\mathbf{P} \cdot \mathbf{N} = |\mathbf{P}|\, |\mathbf{N}|\, \cos(\theta).$$

The two lengths are always positive, and the cosine is either positive or negative. If θ is between 0 and 90 degrees, the cosine is positive. If θ is between 90 and 180 degrees, the cosine is negative. Hence, we are able to conclude that an outside face is visible to the viewer, the COP, if the dot product $\mathbf{P} \cdot \mathbf{N}$ is negative; a positive dot product indicates an invisible back face.

To obtain the vector $\mathbf{P}$, we recall that in the eye coordinate system the COP has been transformed to the origin. Therefore, any point on the transformed polygon S will serve as the vector $\mathbf{P}$. Simply choose $\mathbf{P}$ to be one of the vertices of the polygon.

Back face removal is usually the first step in hidden-surface removal routines. This relatively simple technique can eliminate more than half the number of surfaces in a complex image. For images that do not have any objects intersecting in the *x, y* plane, back face removal completely solves the hidden-surface problem. This simple technique has been called the "Poor Man's Hidden Surface Algorithm."

Let's examine how we can incorporate back face removal into the viewing transformation of Chapter 11. Assume that each polygon is defined separately in the display file. For example the display file command

    poly (5,0,0)

indicates that the following five display file commands describe a polygon. The two zeros are dummy values. In addition, we assume that the vertices are placed in the display file in the order of the previously discussed clockwise listing. Using the data structures defined in Chapter 11, the square face *S* in Figure 13-3 is defined in the display file as follows:

```
poly(5,0,0)
move3(P1[x],P1[y],P1[z])
draw3(P2[x],P2[y],P2[z])
draw3(P3[x],P3[y],P3[z])
draw3(P4[x],P4[y],P4[z])
draw3(P1[x],P1[y],P1[z]).
```

Back face removal is performed in the left-handed eye coordinate system prior to clipping. Three consecutive noncollinear vertices of the polygonal surface are initially transformed to the left-handed system. These vertices are used to form the two vectors **R** and **Q** (Figure 13-4) whose cross product is the normal vector **N**. A positive dot product of one of these transformed vertices (**P**) with the normal vector **N** indicates a back face. This back face is not displayed and is omitted from further processing. If the three vertices are collinear, the cross product gives the vector (0, 0, 0), and three other consecutive vertices must be chosen. To avoid this difficulty, we assume that the first three vertices defining a polygon are noncollinear.

Function Back_Face is a boolean function that returns a true value if the polygon is a back face. We assume the Pascal environment, the procedures Cross_Prod, Subtract_Vec, and the function Dot_Prod described in Section 11-6.

```
Function Back_Face (
        P1,P2,P3 : point          {three consecutive transformed vertices of the
                                   polygon}):boolean;

    var
        Normal,                    {visible normal}
        R,Q : point;               {Normal = R x Q}
```

```
begin
    {create the two vectors R and Q}
        Subtract_Vec(P2,P1,R);          {R = P2 – P1}
        Subtract_Vec(P3,P2,Q);          {Q = P3 – P2}
        Cross_Prod(R,Q,Normal);         {Normal = R × Q}
        {a positive dot product indicates a back face
        and Back_Face is assigned true}
        Back_Face := (Dot_Prod(P1,Normal) > 0)
end;    {Back_Face}
```

13–3 HIDDEN-LINE REMOVAL

Back face removal completely solves the hidden-line problem for scenes comprising a single object. For scenes having two or more objects, a visible face of one object can totally or partially hide a visible face (that is, not a back face) of another object. Which object obscures the other depends on the position of the viewer (COP). Figure 13-5 is used to examine different situations for a pyramid and a cube. In Figure 13-5a the pyramid is between the viewer and the cube, obscuring part of a visible face of the cube. Figure 13-5b has the viewing position moved so that the cube is between the pyramid and the viewer, obscuring parts of two visible faces of the pyramid. We shall later see that for complex images, back face removal is only the first step of the hidden-line algorithm.

Selecting a hidden-line or hidden-surface algorithm is not easy. There are hundreds of approaches, ranging from simple to complex. No one solution is best for all types of images and circumstances. The easiest ones to program require an exorbitant amount of computer time to generate a moderately complex image. Sophisticated programs that solve the problem in a reasonable time take advantage of the geometry

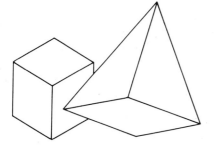

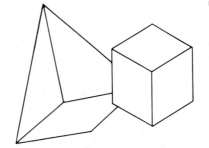

FIGURE 13–5 (a–b)
A pyramid and cube viewed from different directions

(a)   (b)

of the image to reduce the amount of calculations. While this is clearly the correct approach, the implementation relies heavily on geometric insight and clever logic. In addition, these programs tend to be very large.

The approach taken in this chapter is to give only a taste of the complexity of the hidden-line problem. While the solution presented solves the problem for a very special situation, the techniques used are found in some of the more sophisticated algorithms. By simplifying the problem, we hope to give some insight into the complexity and the solution of the problem.

PRIORITY SORTING

We shall assume that our scene consists of only two objects, each of which is a closed polyhedron. In addition, there is a plane, parallel to the view plane and dependent on the location of the viewer, that separates the two objects. A consequence of this is that it is obvious from any position which of the two objects is closer to the viewer. Let's assign a priority to each object. Priority 1 is given to the object lying on the same side of this plane as the viewer; the other object is assigned priority 2.

Since a priority 1 object is closer to the viewer, it cannot be obscured by a priority 2 object, and it can be displayed after its back faces are removed. Before drawing any lines of the priority 2 object, we must determine whether any part of the line segment is obscured by the priority 1 object. Figure 13-5c illustrates the situation where the pyramid has priority 1 and the dashed line segment of the cube is hidden by the pyramid. (This concept of separating planes is used with scenes consisting of many objects. Priority sorting, or geometric sorting in general, attempts to determine which objects can obscure other objects. Its use is a major factor in reducing the computational effort of hidden-line and hidden-surface algorithms.)

FIGURE 13–5 (c)

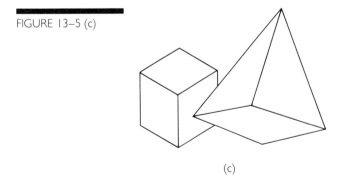

(c)

Hidden-Surface Problem

Recall that both objects are transformed by the viewing transformation, then clipping is performed, and the back faces are removed. Their priorities can now be determined. To do this we compare the z coordinate values of the objects. (The vertices defining the transformed objects are usually stored in a temporary data structure similar to the display file.) Since there is a plane separating the objects, any z value of a priority 1 object must be less than a z value of a priority 2 object (Figure 13-6).

Function Priority is invoked after clipping, and returns the integer value 1 or 2 corresponding to the object that has the smallest z value. Hence, function Priority determines which object has priority 1. The parameters, $z1,z2$, are the eye coordinate system z values of any vertex in object 1 and object 2, respectively.

```
Function Priority (z1,z2: real): integer;

    begin
        if z1 < z2 then Priority := 1
        else Priority := 2
    end; {Priority}
```

The priority 1 object, whose number has been assigned to Priority, can now be displayed (assuming back face removal has already been performed) by locating the correct segment, 1 or 2, in the segment table.

STORING PROJECTED POLYGONS

After assigning priorities to both objects, the priority 1 object is projected onto the two-dimensional window and can now be displayed. The priority 2 object also undergoes the perspective projection. However, before displaying any edges of this object, we must first determine if they are hidden by the closer priority 1 object. (For scenes having

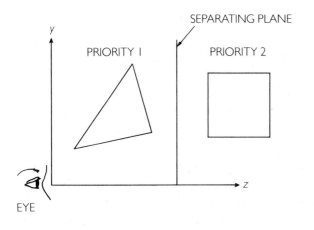

FIGURE 13–6
A plane separating
two objects

several objects, each object is assigned a priority. An object with priority N must be tested against all objects having priority less than N.) To do this, we compare each edge against all the projected visible polygons of the closer object. If an edge intersects a polygon, it is totally or partially obscured. Therefore, we need to store the projected polygons of the priority 1 object in some convenient data structure.

Assume the Pascal environment:

```
type
    edge = record {each edge has two endpoints}
                x,y : array [1..2] of real
            end;
    pointer = record {first and last edges defining a polygon}
                start,finish : integer
            end;
var
    side    : array [1..100] of edge; {100 possible edges}
    polygon : array [1..15] of pointer; {those edges defining up to 15
                                         polygons}
    k : 0..100; {the current edge}
    n : 0..15; {the current polygon}
    i : integer; {loop index}
```

Before describing several procedures that use this data structure, let's look at a simple example. Figure 13-7 illustrates a projected polygon P with its edges stored in the side array as follows:

side[1].x[1] := 1;	side[1].y[1] := 4;
side[1].x[2] := 5;	side[1].y[2] := 10;
side[2].x[1] := 5;	side[2].y[1] := 10;
side[2].x[2] := 8;	side[2].y[2] := 7;
side[3].x[1] := 8;	side[3].y[1] := 7;
side[3].x[2] := 1;	side[3].y[2] := 4;

FIGURE 13–7
A representation of
a projected triangle

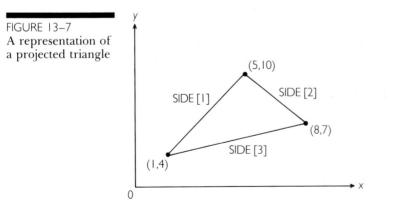

Hidden-Surface Problem

Polygon *P*'s first edge has index 1 and its last edge has index 3 in this side array. Therefore, the polygon-pointer array has for this first polygon:

```
polygon[1].start  := 1;
polygon[1].finish := 3;
```

The first procedure, Initialize, sets the start field of all polygon records to zero.

Procedure Initialize;
{initialize all polygon starting pointers to 0}

```
    begin
        for i := 1 to 15 do
            polygon[i].start := 0
    end; {Initialize}
```

In general, each time an edge of a priority 1 polygon is projected onto the view plane, the two endpoints defining the edge are placed in the side array. The array index of the first edge, side[k], of the *n*th polygon is assigned to the value of the start field of the polygon pointer:

```
polygon[n].start := k;
```

Each time another projected edge of polygon[n] is placed in the side array, a counter is incremented by 1. When the last edge of polygon[n] is entered into the side array, the value of the counter is added to the start field, and that result is the index in the side array of the last edge of this polygon:

```
polygon[n].finish := polygon[n].start + counter;
```

Procedure Enter_Poly uses these concepts to place a polygon into the side and polygon array. It is invoked each time a new polygon in the original display file survives clipping and back face removal. Still_more_edges is a global boolean variable that is true as long as the current polygon has an edge to be projected.

Procedure Enter_Poly;

```
    var
        counter:integer; {number of edges less one in polygon}
    begin
        counter := -1; {first edge assigns counter to 0}
        n := n + 1; {polygon number}
        while still_more_edges do
            begin {while}
                k := k + 1; {next index in side array}
                {first edge}
                polygon[n].start := k;
```

```
                counter := counter + 1;
            with side[k] do
                {place projected edge in array}
                Get_Edge(x[1],y[1],x[2],y[2])
        end; {while}
        {last edge}
        polygon[n].finish := polygon[n].start + counter
    end; {Enter_Poly}
```

Procedure Get_Edge assigns the projected coordinates of the end-points of an edge, that survived clipping and back face removal to an entry in the side array. We denote these endpoints by: x1proj, y1proj, x2proj, and y2proj.

```
    Procedure Get_Edge (

    var
        x1,y1,x2,y2 : real {endpoints of edge});

    begin
        x1 := x1proj;
        y1 := y1proj;
        x2 := x2proj;
        y2 := y2proj
    end; {Get_Edge}
```

EDGE-INTERSECTING POLYGONS

A convex polygon can obscure an edge in three different ways. (Recall that a priority 1 polygon is always in front of a priority 2 edge, so that only the edge can be hidden.) The first case has both endpoints of the edge lying within the polygon. If this happens, the entire edge is hidden and not displayed (Figure 13-8a). The second case has one end-point inside and the other endpoint outside the polygon (Figure 13-8b). In this case, we must find the point where the edge intersects the polygon. This point divides the edge into a visible and invisible part. The line segment inside the polygon is discarded and the segment out-

FIGURE 13–8
An edge-intersecting polygon

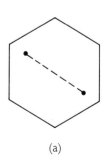

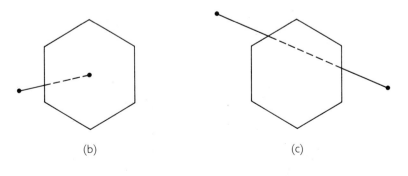

(a)   (b)   (c)

side must be tested against the remaining polygons making up the closer object.

The final case has both endpoints outside the polygon. The edge intersects two sides of the polygon, resulting in one invisible and two outside segments that must still be compared against all other polygons of the priority 1 object (Figure 13-8c).

From this discussion, it is clear that we need a procedure that locates the point of intersection of two line segments. Although this is not difficult to do, if we simply test each edge of a priority 2 object against the sides of all polygons of the closer priority 1 object, a large amount of computer time will be consumed. (Imagine the amount of computations required for a scene consisting of many objects described by thousands of small polygons.) Our approach is based instead on the observation that most edges do not intersect any polygons. Thus, if we can find efficient techniques for identifying these nonintersecting edges, we will reduce the number of intersection calculations.

BOUNDING-BOX TEST

A bounding-box test places boxes around the edge and the polygon. If the boxes do not intersect, the edge cannot intersect the polygon (Figure 13-9a). (For now we ignore the case of the edge lying completely inside the polygon.) These boxes should be chosen so that their sides are parallel to the x, y coordinate axis and as small as possible, while still containing the edge or polygon. Note that this test is not perfect since the two boxes can intersect even when there is not an intersection point (Figure 13-9b).

Our first task is to compute the bounding boxes. Observe in Figure 13-9 that the sides of a box are obtained from the minimum and maximum x, y values of the polygon (or edge). Thus we can state our test as follows. If the minimum x coordinate of the polygon is greater than

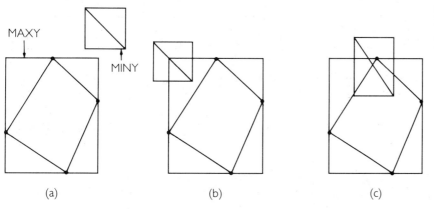

FIGURE 13–9
A bounding-box test

the maximum *x* coordinate of the edge, or vice versa, the two do not intersect. Similarly, if the minimum *y* coordinate of the polygon is greater than the maximum *y* coordinate of the edge, or vice versa, they do not intersect. In Figure 13-9a the edge and polygon cannot intersect since the minimum *y* value of the edge is greater than the maximum *y* value of the polygon. This is often called a **Minimax** test.

The following function Minimax returns true if the two bounding boxes do not intersect. It uses eight global variables to perform this test:

```
var
      xmaxedge,xminedge,ymaxedge,yminedge,
      xmaxpoly,xminpoly,ymaxpoly,yminpoly : real;
```

These minimum and maximum *x, y* values are obtained using the standard method to find a minimum and maximum of several values. We leave this part as an exercise for the reader.

```
Function Minimax: boolean;

    begin
        Minimax := (xminpoly > xmaxedge) or
                   (xminedge > xmaxpoly) or
                   (yminpoly > ymaxedge) or
                   (yminedge > ymaxpoly)
    end; {Minimax}
```

If the function Minimax returns false, the edge may or may not intersect the polygon (Figure 13-9b and 13-9c). Before locating the possible point(s) of intersection, a second Minimax test should be performed that tests the bounding box of the edge with bounding boxes surrounding each side of the polygon. Only those sides whose box intersects the edge's box need be tested for a point of intersection. A function that performs this test is similar to Minimax, where the polygon extrema are replaced by the extreme *x, y* values of the side that the edge is being tested against. This enhancement is left as an exercise for the reader.

INTERSECTION TEST

If the bounding boxes of an edge and the sides of a testing polygon intersect, we need a procedure to determine the intersection point of the two lines containing these edges, because even if these two lines intersect, the line segments representing the edge and side might not intersect (Figure 13-10). Thus, we need a procedure telling whether or not the point of intersection is interior to both line segments. We describe each of these in turn.

There are several methods available to find the point of intersection of two lines. Some solve the system of the two linear equations; others

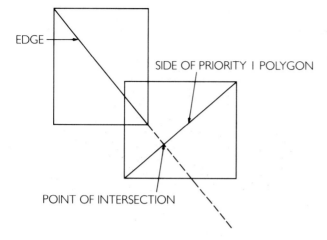

EDGE

SIDE OF PRIORITY I POLYGON

POINT OF INTERSECTION

FIGURE 13–10
An intersection test

perform a binary search for the point. The technique we present is easy both to code and explain—unfortunately, it's not the most efficient.

Both line segments are represented by their projected endpoints: $(x1, y1)$, $(x2, y2)$. The equation of a nonvertical line passing through these points is

$$\frac{(y - y1)}{(x - x1)} = \frac{(y2 - y1)}{(x2 - x1)}.$$

The right-hand side of the equation is the slope, denoted by m. Thus, rewriting this gives

$$y = m(x - x1) + y1.$$

The point of intersection of two nonparallel lines is found by equating the y values and solving for x. This computed x value is then substituted into either line equation to obtain the y intersection value. If one line is vertical, $x1 = x2$ and that common x value must be substituted into the nonvertical line equation. Precedure Find_Intersection performs this task.

```
Procedure Find_Intersection(
            x1edge,x2edge,y1edge,y2edge,
            x1side,x2side,y1side,y2side
            {endpoints of two line segments} : real;
            var xpt,ypt : real; {point of intersection});

    var
        xdiff_edge,xdiff_side,      {x differences}
        medge,mside : real;         {the slopes}
    begin
        xdiff_edge := x2edge − x1edge;
        xdiff_side := x2side − x1side;
        if xdiff_edge = 0 then
```

```
                    {vertical line}
                        begin {if}
                            xpt := x2edge;
                            ypt := (y2side − y1side)/xdiff_side *
                                    (xpt − x1side) + y1side;
                        end {if}
                    else
                        if xdiff_side = 0 then
                            {vertical line}
                            begin {if}
                                xpt := x2side;
                                ypt := (y2edge − y1side)/xdiff_edge *
                                        (xpt − x1edge) + y1edge;
                            end {if}
                        else
                            {neither line is vertical}
                            begin
                                medge := (y2edge − y1edge)/(x2edge −
                                            x1edge);
                                mside := (y2side − y1side)/(x2side − x2edge);
                                {set equations equal and solve for x}
                                xpt := (x1edge*medge − x1side * mside + yside
                                        − yedge)/(medge − mside);
                                {substitute xpt into either line equation}
                                ypt := m1edge(xpt − x1edge) + y1edge
                            end
        end; {Find_Intersection}
```

Function Valid_Intersection returns true if the computed point of intersection lies within both the edge of the priority 2 polygon and the side of the priority 1 polygon. It does this by first checking the x coordinate and then the y coordinate of the intersection point.

```
Function Valid_Intersection(x1edge,x2edge,y1edge,y2edge,
                            x1side,x2side,y1side,y2side,
                            xpt,ypt :real):boolean;

    var

        xresult: boolean;                {result of x test}
        temp : real;                     {for switching values}

    begin
        {want the x1 values less than x2 values}
        if x1edge > x2edge then
            {swap}
            begin {if}
                temp := x1edge;
                x1edge := x2edge;
                x2edge := temp
            end; {if}
```

```
        if x1side > x2side then
            {swap}
            begin {if}
                temp := x1side;
                x1side := x2side;
                x2side := temp
            end; {if}
        {check that xpt lies between both endpoints}
        xresult := (xpt >= x1edge) and (xpt <= x2edge) and
                   (xpt >= x1side) and (xpt <= x2side);
        if not xresult then
            {not in both line segments}
                Valid_Intersection := false
        else
        {perform similar test for y values}
        {want y1 values less than y2 values}
            begin {else}
                if y1edge > y2edge then
                    {swap}
                    begin {if}
                        temp := y1edge;
                        y1edge := y2edge;
                        y2edge := temp
                    end; {if}
                if y1side > y2side then
                    {swap}
                    begin {if}
                        temp := y1side;
                        y1side := y2side;
                        y2side := temp
                    end; {if}
                {check that ypt lies between both endpoints}
                Valid_Intersection := (ypt>=y1edge) and (ypt<=y2edge)
                                and (ypt>=y1side) and (ypt<=y2side)
            end {else}
    end; {Valid_Intersection}
```

POINT INSIDE POLYGON

Once a valid point of intersection is found, that part of the edge inside the polygon is discarded. This requires an algorithm that determines which endpoint is within the polygon. If both endpoints of an edge lie within the polygon, the entire edge is invisible and is discarded (Figure 13-8a).

A point is contained in a polygon if, for all edges of the polygon, that point is on the same side of the line containing the edge as a vertex of the polygon not on the edge (Figure 13-11 on page 336). (That is, both the point we're testing and a vertex off an edge lie either to the

FIGURE 13-11
A point inside a
polygon

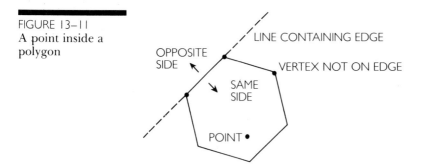

left or right of the edge.) Note that we assume that the polygon does not have three collinear vertices.

The equation of a line passing through points $(x1, y1)$ and $(x2, y2)$ can be expressed as

$$(13–1) \quad (x - x1)(y2 - y1) - (x2 - x1)(y - y1) = 0.$$

For points (x, y) lying off the line, the left-hand side of equation 13-1 is either positive or negative. Thus, an endpoint (of a line segment) is on the same side of a polygon edge as one of its vertices if, when each point is substituted into equation 13-1, they have the same sign.

Function Inside_Poly returns the value of the left-hand side of equation 13-1. It is invoked twice for each edge of the polygon: once for the line segment endpoint and once for a polygon vertex not on the edge. If the product of these two function invocations is positive, the endpoint and the vertex are on the same side of that edge. In this case, this test must be performed for all other sides of the polygon. If, for some edge, the product of two invocations of Inside_Poly is negative, the endpoint cannot lie within the polygon and it is not necessary to test against the remaining edges of the polygon.

```
Function Inside_Poly (
        x1,y1,x2,y2, {edge of polygon}
        xend,yend {endpoint} : real):real;

begin
        Inside_Poly := (xend − x1)*(y2−y1) − (x2−x1)*(yend−y1)
    end; {Inside_Poly}
```

If both endpoints of the edge lie outside a polygon, there are either two or no intersection points (Figure 13-8c). Procedure Find_Intersection and function Valid_Intersection are invoked for each side of the polygon until both or no intersection points are obtained.

If we find two intersection points, (xa, ya) and (xb, yb), how do we know which line segments are outside the polygon? For example, in Figure 13-12 the outside line segments are $(x1, y1)$ to (xb, yb) and $(x2, y2)$ to (xa, ya). Fortunately, there is a simple test. The technique is best

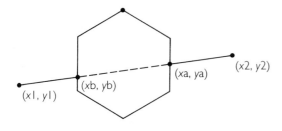

FIGURE 13–12
Line segments out-
side a polygon

expressed by the following pseudo Pascal code segment:

```
if ((x2 > x1) and (xb < xa) or
   (y2 > y1) and (yb < ya)
then
     {line segments are as above}
else
     {line segments are (x1, y1) to (xa, ya) and (x2, y2) to (xb, yb)}
```

One of the exterior line segments must be saved for further processing while the other exterior segment is tested against the remaining polygons of the closer object.

If no intersection points are found, that polygon cannot hide the edge, and the edge can continue its tests against the remaining polygons.

SUMMARY

Although the scene that we are applying the hidden-line algorithm to is very simple, the algorithm itself incorporates some of the techniques used for more complex images. These methods are designed to reduce the number of brute force computations by exploiting the geometric properties (coherence) of the objects. This savings is at the expense of increasing the complexity of the algorithm. Let us now piece together all the steps of the hidden-line algorithm.

We start out by sending both objects through the viewing transformation, the clipping algorithm, and back face removal. These resulting values are stored in a temporary data structure. The z depth of both objects is compared and the one closer to the COP (now at the origin) is assigned priority 1. The priority 1 object is projected into its x, y coordinates and placed in the side array. This closer object can now be displayed since no faces of the further object can obscure any part of it.

One at a time, each edge of the priority 2 object is now projected and tested against each polygon of the closer object. Minimax tests are used to eliminate those polygons that cannot intersect the edge. If a polygon fails the minimax test, the two endpoints of the edge are tested to determine if neither, one, or both lie within the polygon. If both lie inside, the edge is discarded and a new edge begins its test.

If one endpoint is inside the polygon, the point of intersection of the edge and the polygon is calculated. Once again, a minimax test is used to reduce the number of computations. This intersection point splits the edge into two pieces. The inside piece is discarded and the outside piece is tested against the remaining polygons of the closer object.

If both endpoints of the edge lie outside the polygon, the edge may not intersect the polygon or has two points of intersection. In the former case, the entire edge is tested against the remaining polygons. If there are two points of intersection, we first determine which two segments are outside the polygon. One of these segments is stored for future processing, while the other continues its tests. When this line segment has been compared against the remaining polygons, the stored segment is retrieved and starts its tests.

After an edge has completed its tests against the polygons of the priority 1 object, that part of the edge remaining is displayed on the screen. That's all there is to it! The reader may now have an appreciation of why the hidden-line and hidden-surface problems have been called one of the most interesting and challenging areas of computer graphics.

13–4 SURFACES OF FUNCTIONS OF TWO VARIABLES

Eliminating hidden lines is a relatively easy task if the image consists of polygons parallel to the view plane. In this case, each point on a polygon has the same z value. To correctly display the image with hidden lines removed, each polygon is projected onto the view plane in order from the closest to the farthest, making sure that the edges of the current polygon do not overlap any previously drawn polygon (Figure 13-13).

A surface defined by the equation $y = f(x,z)$ is plotted using this

FIGURE 13–13
Polygons with a constant z depth parallel to the viewer

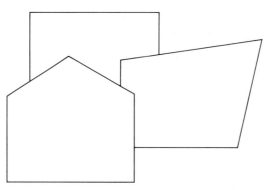

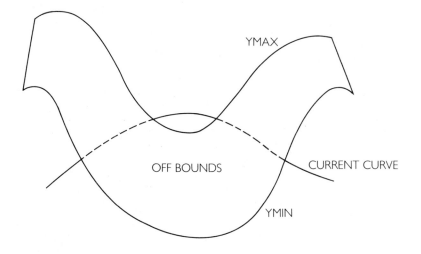

FIGURE 13–14
The region hidden
between ymax and
ymin

idea. For a given z value, we let x vary and compute the corresponding y value. These x, y points define a three-dimensional curve parallel to the display screen with constant z depth. We start with $z = 1$, draw that curve, increment the z value, draw the next curve, and so on until the maximum z value is reached.

The hidden-line effect is achieved by placing off bounds the region between the maximum and minimum y values for each x value (Figure 13-14). These maximum and minimum y values are stored and are continuously updated. A ymax and ymin array containing these extreme values has the dimension of the maximum number of x values. If a computed y value, for a given x, is greater than ymax[x], the point (x, y) is plotted and ymax[x] is assigned this y value. Similarly, if y is less than ymin[x], the point (x, y) is plotted and ymin[x] is updated.

A surface drawn this way will have all curves lying on top of each other, giving a flat appearance. In order to make it look more realistic, successive curves are shifted z units in both the x and y directions (Figure 13-15 on page 340).

Procedure Hide_Surface displays the surface $y = f(x, z)$ with hidden lines removed. Since line-drawing commands are used (instead of point plotting), we must be careful that a line is drawn between two points lying outside the blocked-off area. We do this in the following way. Assume that the point (x, y) is to be plotted. If the boolean variable valid is true, we can draw from where we left off to (x, y); otherwise, we must move to a previously plotted point in the correct extrema array and draw from there to (x, y).

Procedure Hide_Surface;

    const
        xmax = 150; {*x range*}
        zmax = 10; {*z range*}

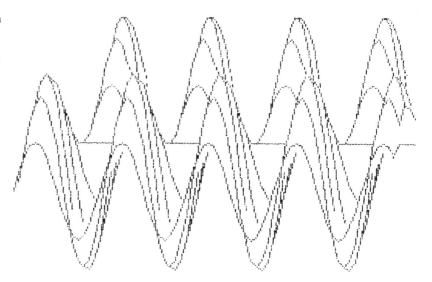

FIGURE 13–15
A hidden surface
for $y = 10 \sin (\pi/5\ x)$
$\sin (\pi/6\ z)$

```
type
    bounds = array[0..xmax] of real;

var
    y           :   real;           {y = f(x,z)}
    z,x,                            {x and z values}
    i           :   integer;        {the x loop variable}
    ymax,ymin   :   bounds;         {limits of off-bound region}
    valid       :   boolean;        {true = draw from previous point}

    begin
        {set up for function y = f(x,z)}
        window(-5,75,-20,20);
        for i := 0 to xmax do
            begin {for}
                {initialize arrays}
                ymax[i] := -20;
                ymin[i] := 20
            end; {for}
        for z := 1 to zmax do
            {main draw loop}
            begin {for}
                for i := 0 to 70 do
                    {x range}
                    begin {for}
                        {choose a function of your choice}
                        y := 10*sin(3.1416/8*i)*sin(3.1416/6*z);
                        y := y+z; {shifting the y values}
                        x := i + z; {shifting the x values}
                        if y > ymax[x] then
```

```
                begin {if}
                    ymax[x] := y; {update max}
                    if ymin[x] = 20 then
                        ymin[x] := y; {first time through}
                    if i = 0 then
                        move2(x,y) {first point of curve}
                    else
                        if valid then
                                {draw from previous point}
                                draw2(x,y)
                        else
                        {draw from previous ymax point}
                                begin {else}
                                    move2(x − 1,ymax[x − 1]);
                                    draw2(x,y)
                                end; {else}
                        valid := true {point plotted}
                end {y > ymax}
            else
                if y < ymin[x] then
                    begin {if}
                        ymin[x] := y; {update min}
                        if i = 0 then
                                move2(x,y) {first point of curve}
                        else
                                if valid then
                                    {draw from previous point}
                                    draw2(x,y)
                                else
                                    {draw from previous ymin point}
                                    begin {else}
                                        move2(x − 1,ymin[x − 1];
                                        draw2(x,y)
                                    end; {else}
                            valid := true {point plotted}
                    end {y < ymin}
                else {between ymin and ymax}
                    valid := false {point not plotted}
        end {for i}
    end {for z};
end; {Hide_Surface}
```

13–5 **CONCLUSION**

In this chapter, we have described several techniques that solve the hidden-line problem for some simple images. Objects that overlap in the z direction or, even worse, penetrate each other, require much more sophisticated algorithms. In general, as the image increases in complexity, the methods required to identify and eliminate the hidden lines become more complicated and specialized for a particular kind of image.[†]

[†]For a more comprehensive discussion of this important topic, the reader is referred to Foley/Van Dam, *Fundamentals of Interactive Computer Graphics*, 1982.

APPENDIX

THE GRAPHICAL KERNEL SYSTEM (GKS)

The Graphical Kernel System (GKS) provides a two-dimensional graphics environment that allows the application programmer to design graphics routines independent of the display system. Different programming languages (such as FORTRAN, C, Pascal) are easily interfaced with GKS since each GKS graphics command has a well-defined procedural name and associated parameter list, a concept called language binding.

GKS uses the concept of an abstraction to generate graphics output on a wide variety of different devices with different capabilities. This abstraction constructs the bridge between device-independent graphics commands and these devices. The following are eight fundamental abstractions:

1. **Workstations**

   A workstation is a single display unit with or without input devices. It might consist of a single printer, a storage tube with a light pen, or a sophisticated display with several types of input devices. The advantage of a workstation is that the programmer need not be concerned with the specifics of the graphics system on which the program will execute, thereby achieving a high level of program portability.

2. **Output Primitives**

   These are the fundamental routines that construct graphics images. Included are
   a. Polyline: generates a collection of connected lines
   b. Polymarker: generates symbols at specified positions
   c. Fill area: generates a polygon that may be hollow or filled with a uniform pattern, color, or hatch style
   d. Text: displays a character string of a specified font (type style) at a specified position.

3. **Attributes**

   Output primitives can be assigned attributes that specify color, line style (such as dash, dotted), and other image characteristics.

4. **Coordinate Systems**

There are three coordinate systems: user-defined world coordinates, device-independent normalized coordinates, and workstation-dependent device coordinates. The intermediate normalized device coordinates have x and y values ranging from 0 to 1.

5. **Windows and Viewports**

A rectangular world coordinate window is mapped to a rectangular viewport in normalized device coordinates. A final transformation is performed that selects a rectangular region of normalized-device-coordinate space and sends it to an area of the workstation display.

6. **Segments**

A collection of output primitives can be grouped together into one segment. A segment typically defines one part of an image. Once a segment is created, it can be assigned as many as five attributes: visibility, transformation matrix, priority (which segment, when overlapping another, is completely drawn?), highlighting (brightening or blinking), and detectability (enables user to select a segment with an input device).

7. **Input**

Six logical input devices are defined for interactive applications:
   a. locator: indicates an (x, y) world coordinate value (for example, paddles, digitizers)
   b. valuator: inputs a real number (for example, a keyboard, dials)
   c. stroke: inputs a series of (x, y) world coordinate values (for example, a stylus moving about a digitizer)
   d. pick: selects a primitive within a segment (such as a light pen)
   e. choice: inputs a nonnegative integer that chooses an action (for example, a keyboard entry of menu selection value)
   f. string: inputs a character string (for example, a keyboard).

8. **Metafiles**

A metafile is a graphics database of an image that can be transferred between display systems. It is typically used to save information such as segments that was created during program execution.

BIBLIOGRAPHY

Atkinson, L.V., and Harley, P.J. *An Introduction to Numerical Methods with Pascal*. Reading, Mass.: Addison-Wesley, 1983.

Bergeron, R.D., Bono, P.R., and Foley, J.D. "Graphics Programming Using the CORE System," *Computer Surveys* 10, no. 4 (December 1978): 389–443.

Foley, J.D., and Van Dam, A. *Fundamentals of Interactive Computer Graphics*. Reading, Mass.: Addison-Wesley, 1982.

International Standards Organization. Graphical Kernel System (GKS). Version 7.2, 1982.

Newman, W.M., and Sproull, R.F. *Principles of Interactive Computer Graphics*. New York: McGraw-Hill, 1973.

Rogers, D.F., and Adams, J.A. *Mathematical Elements for Computer Graphics*. New York: McGraw-Hill, 1976.

INDEX